U.S. IMMIGRATION LAW
AND THE CONTROL OF LABOR:
1820–1924

U.S. Immigration Law and the Control of Labor: 1820–1924

SECOND EDITION

Kitty Calavita

Classics of Law & Society

qp

QUID PRO BOOKS
New Orleans, Louisiana

Previously published in 1984 by Academic Press, Inc., Orlando and London.

Published in 2020 by Quid Pro Books, in the Second Edition, as part of the series *Classics of Law & Society*.

ISBN 978-1-61027-412-8 (pbk.)
ISBN 978-1-61027-416-6 (ePUB)

QUID PRO BOOKS
5860 Citrus Blvd., Suite D
New Orleans, Louisiana 70123
www.quidprobooks.com

qp

Publisher's Cataloging-in-Publication

Calavita, Kitty.
    U.S. immigration law and the control of labor: 1820–1924 / Kitty Calavita — Second Edition.
        p. cm. — (Classics of Law & Society)
    Includes bibliographical references, index, and new preface and foreword.
    New edition adapted and updated from the 1984 ed. published by Academic Press, Inc., Orlando and London.

I. Emigration and immigration law—United States—history. 2. Labor supply—United States—history. 3. United States—emigration and immigration law—history. I. Title. II. Series.
KF819 .C4 2020   2020213485

Contents

Preface • 2020

Kitty Calavita

Forty-one years have passed since I wrote the dissertation on which this book was based. The electric typewriters I clunked out drafts on are so antiquated today they are considered collectors' items. Computers and the internet have dramatically revamped the research and writing process. They have also reshaped social reality itself, contracting social space and instantly spreading information—both true and false—to all corners of the world. Related technological changes have compacted the physical world too, greatly facilitating immigration.

When this book on the history of U.S. immigration law first went to press in 1984, the U.S. Congress was debating an employer sanctions bill that became the Immigration Reform and Control Act of 1986 (IRCA). The end of the Bracero Program twenty years earlier had pushed underground the Mexican workforce that growers in the western United States had come to depend on. The undocumented migration that always supplemented legal migration now surged, and as the American economy fell into a deep recession in the early 1980s, President Reagan announced an "illegal alien" crisis. IRCA, the President infamously proclaimed as he signed it, would "regain control of the borders."

Immigration to the United States, both legal and undocumented, has predictably continued to increase despite Reagan's political fanfare, and the foreign-born now make up a larger percentage of the U.S. population than at any time since 1910. The technological changes that accelerate the movement of people and ideas are joined by an economic restructuring, as high-tech, financialization, and a service sector increasingly dominated by "gig" workers, replace industrial output as primary sources of profits.

This book describes the immigration of Europeans to a very different United States, during a century of rapid industrialization and urbanization, and offers a broadly materialist theory to explain the zigzagging policies that alternately encouraged and ostensibly were meant to control it. Drawing from government records, statutes, contemporary journals and secondary sources, I theorize immigration historically as the movement of a cheap labor force, and immigration policies as facilitating that movement but also wrestling with the fiscal and ideological dilemmas associated with that economic function, as poverty and political protest ensued.

The immigrant textile workers with which I begin this story, as well as the boot and shoe manufacturers, miners, ironworkers, railway men, and factory workers of the industrializing United States, have been supplanted by home health care workers, suburban gardeners, and cleaners and custodians for the likes of Google and Facebook. A few sectors have remained impervious to change, as first-generation immigrants continue to comprise a significant portion of the workforce in fields such as domestic services, farm work, restaurant dishwashing, and construction clean-up.

Despite the transformed economic landscape, the work these immigrants do, as with that of the ironworkers and railway men of yesteryear, is low-wage, precarious, and often stigmatized as "immigrants' work." And, that stigmatization has in turn justified the low wage. As I document in this book (p. 86), a New York City newspaper ran a classified ad for workers in 1895 that offered wages according to workers' race and immigrant origins:

- Common labor, white, $1.30–$1.50

- Common labor, colored, $1.25–$1.40

- Common labor, Italian, $1.15–$1.25

Assigning wages based on a worker's identity is of course illegal today, but the practice has merely gone underground, much as the immigrant workforce has. When IRCA was passed in 1986, some liberal Senators worried that sanctions against employers who hired workers who were unauthorized to work in the United States might cause them to discriminate against those who looked or sounded foreign. The GAO study they requisitioned found that indeed employers did discriminate ... in *favor* of hiring immigrants in those low-wage industries where vulnerable undocumented immigrants predominated.

This is not to say that skilled and highly educated immigrants are unwelcome. Much as the skilled immigrant weavers and inventors of the early 1800s found lucrative work in the emerging fields of early capitalist America, so immigrant web designers, engineers, and financiers are recruited into the high-tech and biotech hubs and financial towers that drive the twenty-first century economy. Immigrants have always brought their talents and an initiative powerful enough to propel them from their homelands.

But, it was for the almost infinite supply of cheap labor they provided that Alexander Hamilton in 1791 called for policies to encourage their entry; that Andrew Carnegie in 1886 referred to immigration as a "golden stream"; that Congress exempted Mexicans and others from contiguous countries from the Quota Laws of the 1920s; and that the otherwise conservative *Wall Street Journal* has consistently called for open borders.

But, if immigrants provide vulnerable and cheap labor, it is for this very reason that poverty, and the stigmatization and racialization associated with that poverty, have not been far behind. The Know-Nothing Nativist Party of the 1850s railed against Catholic immigrants from Ireland as an "inferior race." Twenty years later, the frenzied anti-Chinese movement depicted Chinese immigrants as a "yellow peril" of "coolie labor," who had the biological capacity to subsist on below-subsistence wages and who were therefore at an unfair advantage to the "white man." The Dillingham Commission of 1911 drew up a hierarchy of the races and declared Jews and the southern Europeans, who by then comprised the majority of immigrants, to be inferior in all respects. Members of Congress took up the theme as they debated Quota Laws in 1920, calling the new immigrants "abnormally twisted," "pernicious," and "unassimilable." During the red scare of the early 1950s, American policymakers prepared the groundwork for "Operation Wetback," warning that "illegal aliens" included untold numbers of "militant Communists, Sicilian bandits and other criminals," a "ready-made fifth column" of subversives.

Contemporary sensibilities have arguably suppressed some of the worst of the scapegoating and racist name-calling, but the racialization of immigrants has remained just below the surface. When Proposition 187 appeared on the California ballot in 1994—barring people without documents from attending public schools, or obtaining emergency health care and other such services—Republican Governor Pete Wilson aired an ad endorsing it. It featured a grainy photo of people surging across the border and a narrator ominously warning, "They keep coming. Enough is enough!" Immigrants were cast as a drain on the California economy and costing taxpayers money by overwhelming social services and relying on welfare. A Proposition 187 supporter opined, "Lots of Mexicans.... You know you're an island here and eventually that island's going to be swamped." Proposition 187—popularly known as "Save Our State" or "SOS"—won by a landslide only to be declared unconstitutional by the courts.

President Trump has revived some familiar themes and has returned to some of the explicitly racist language of the past, referring to immigrants as "rapists," "violent criminals," "enemies," and "terrorists." Central American gang members, in this playbook, "aren't people; these are animals." Ordering a wall on the U.S.-Mexico border to stop "the invasion," the President fashions his rhetoric to appeal to a swath of voters who either favor or forgive this racialization from a president who promises border control. Even some of his policies are precise echoes of the past. Once again evoking the meme of immigrants as freeloaders first inscribed into the public charge law of 1882, President Trump announced a regulation barring any immigrant who is "likely to be a public charge." He explained, "I'm tired of seeing our taxpayers paying for people to come into the country and immediately go onto welfare."

As familiar as these tropes and policies are, the specific conditions to which they are a response shift over time with the economic, political, and ideological landscape. The constant is that, even as their particularities change shape, the dilemmas and contradictions associated with capitalism and the cheap labor it thrives on and reproduces remain entrenched and are transfigured into the racialized blaming of immigrants themselves. Over the course of the century between 1820 and 1924 immigration policies were first established to encourage immigration for the cheap labor it provided; refashioned in response to the fiscal and political pressures associated with that course; used symbolically to placate labor union protests against immigrants; and ultimately closed the door to all but a fraction of immigrants from southern and eastern Europe. At each stage, policymakers struggled with the myriad contradictions of capitalism and the dilemmas they posed.

Two final points here, both relating to deliberate omissions from this book. First, during the earlier decades I examine, slavery was still in force throughout many states. While it too was extolled by its self-serving supporters for the cheap labor it provided—in that case, literally captive and free of any wage—it originated in a forced movement unlike that of even the most desperate of immigrants. For that reason, and because the further importation of slaves had been outlawed by the time this book opens, I do not focus on that other movement of labor.

Chinese immigration supplied yet another stream of labor, until the Chinese Exclusion Acts beginning in 1882 barred Chinese laborers from entry in one of the most explicitly racist immigration policies in American history. Consistent with the dialectical-materialist theory I present here, material and political-ideological conditions converged in the exclusion of the Chinese soon after they had pounded the final nail on the western railroad system.

Preface

The policies I focus on in this book pertain primarily to European immigration and the structural contradictions that in various forms dominated the economic-political landscape of early capitalist America for more than a century. Several generations later, the descendants of those contradictions continue to plague policymakers and inflame public discourse in twenty-first century America.

KITTY CALAVITA

Berkeley, California
February, 2020

Foreword • 2020

Susan Bibler Coutin

Re-reading Kitty Calavita's *U.S. Immigration Law and the Control of Labor: 1820–1924* in 2020, thirty-five years after it was first published, I am struck by the relevance of her analysis to current debates over immigration policy. On the one hand, Calavita's book details a tremendous shift from a policy of encouraging immigration to one of restricting it, yet on the other hand, there are striking resonances across time, such as efforts to pit members of one group against another, something that continues through anti-immigrant rhetoric today. It is fitting that *U.S. Immigration Law and the Control of Labor* is being published in 2020, 200 years since 1820, when the period covered by the book begins and approximately 100 years since 1924, the period when it ends. In 1984, when this book first came out, the Immigration Reform and Control Act had not yet passed, there were no employer sanctions, Employment Authorization Documents did not exist, the 1986–1987 legalization program had not yet occurred, the U.S.-Mexico border was not as heavily militarized, and immigrants had not undergone the criminalization that was wrought by 1996 reforms. Nonetheless, immigration was then, as it is today, an area of public controversy, and the words that Calavita wrote in her original preface still ring true: these laws "go to the heart of the political and economic system" (p. xi).

It may, in retrospect, seem strange to some readers to focus on immigration as an element of labor control, given that it is now often discussed in terms of law and national security. Yet, as Calavita shows, economic interests have been inextricable from immigration law. In fact, Calavita argues, immigration policy-making allows the state to promote capital accumulation (by encouraging the immigration of low-wage workers) while also providing temporary solutions to the problem of class conflict (by dividing the working class according to legal, racial, and gender categories). Therefore often, Calavita argues, immigration policy is a matter of *symbolic law*, that is, legislators may pass laws that officially restrict immigration but in practice, officials continue to allow it. By presenting a historical account of these dynamics,

Calavita is able to tease out the ways that a resolution at one moment in time gives rise to a new conflict at another, followed by a new attempted resolution, which then leads to another conflict. While the details of these dynamics have shifted, Calavita's analysis is still timely and well worth engaging. For example, current immigration policies may take a symbolic form, such as responding to calls for comprehensive immigration reform by establishing programs that provide temporary status for only a small number of potential beneficiaries, or building impressive-looking walls that do not actually prevent unauthorized entry.

A particularly valuable aspect of this social history is that it reveals alternatives to the present moment: over much of U.S. history, government officials actively recruited immigrants, even when segments of the public sought restrictions. Such recruitment occurred, not out of a sense of social justice or human rights, but rather to fuel economic expansion, depress wages, and counter unionization. Immigrants were highly exploited, but so too were other workers, a situation that fomented racism, as workers who were already in the country blamed new arrivals rather than employers and policy makers for low wages, job insecurity, and poor working conditions. These tensions exist today as well. Yet the fact that many of those who immigrated to this country were encouraged to do so by employers and officials seems to have been forgotten by those who now favor more restrictive policies.

A key example of blaming immigrants for the economic conditions to which they are subjected is the emergence of the public charge restriction, a development that Calavita discusses in some detail. In 1882, amid concerns about poverty, new legislation established that anyone who was likely to become a public charge could be barred from immigrating. Calavita attributes the public charge restriction to the contradiction between capitalism's need for a surplus workforce, and the reality that such a workforce will of necessity live in poverty. Yet the public charge provisions of U.S. immigration law, she notes, blame the poor for the economic conditions that produce poverty, treating pauperism as an individual attribute rather than as a product of circumstances. Such flawed logic helps to legitimize the economic system by characterizing its excesses as failures on the part of individual immigrants. It is especially important to know this history today, given that in 2020, the U.S. Supreme Court allowed the Trump administration to further expand grounds of inadmissibility by retroactively defining a broad range of public benefits as indications that the recipient is likely to become a public charge. On the grounds of promoting "self-sufficiency," this expansion has made immigrants' lives more difficult.

In addition to addressing immigration policymaking, the pages that follow present a detailed labor history. Readers will learn of the brutality of working conditions, the impacts of mechanization, the deskilling of the workforce, and unionization. Employers recruited and hired immigrant workers in an effort to break strikes, only to discover that these workers often became militant as well, joining the union movement. The documentary record that Calavita draws on is incredibly rich. Elite groups deliberately and unabashedly sought to foment division, playing workers of one nationality against another. For instance, Calavita quotes one employer who instructed a labor detective agency to "stir up as much bad feeling as you possibly can between the Serbians and Italians. Spread data among the Serbians that the Italians are going back to work. Call up every question you can in reference to racial hatred between these two nationalities" (p. 90). It is hard to see current denunciations of immigrant workers as anything but a continuation of this strategy

U.S. Immigration Law and the Control of Labor 1820–1924 is well worth reading. The theoretical discussion is accessible to new students as well as established scholars, and the rich documentary record sheds light on how current dynamics were set in motion. Readers will learn about the impacts of economic anxiety on racial animus; labor activists' persistence in the face of entrenched structural challenges; the contradictions woven into the U.S. political-economy; legal loopholes that enabled frontline officials to bend discretion toward desired outcomes; the double binds created by temporary solutions to structural challenges; and the solidarity that transcended national differences. What, I wondered as I read, will historical sociologists say of our time? The answer to this question is of course unknowable. But, as Calavita observes, "it is important to reexamine the historical record" (p. 186), a record that, much like the one examined in this book, will provide insight into the anxieties, contradictions, and mobilizations of our time.

SUSAN BIBLER COUTIN
Professor, Criminology, Law & Society,
and Associate Dean for Academic Programs
School of Social Ecology
University of California—Irvine

Irvine, California
February, 2020

Preface • 1984

Kitty Calavita

From the early 1830s until the Civil War in 1860, U.S. workers protested immigration, demanding laws that would limit the influx of foreign workers into the United States. These nativist protests were, according to one historian of the period, "the most violent in [U.S.] history" (Wittke, 1953, p. 4). Despite these protests and this agitation, not one piece of legislation that aimed at restricting immigration even came to a vote in Congress. On the contrary, several bills that encouraged immigration were passed without much opposition. It was almost 100 years after workers demanded restrictive immigration legislation that the first effective restriction on European immigration—the Emergency Quota Law of 1921—was passed.

This study became an attempt to put together a model of legal change that could help explain the evolution of U.S. immigration policy from the 1820s to the 1920s. Working both forward from the historical data and backward from the theory implied by those data, what emerges is both a specific explanation for the evolution of these policies and a more general model of lawmaking in an emerging capitalist democracy. It is a model that treats the relationship between law and economic structure as primary and includes as central components the political and ideological constraints that impinge on, and at times even challenge, that relationship.

Immigration laws are particularly useful for such an analysis because they go to the heart of the political and economic system. The *sine qua non* of modern nation-states and economic systems is the creation of a reliable and productive work force. Immigration policy is a major mechanism by which this work force is regulated. Too much immigration creates a surplus, too little a shortage of workers. How political decisions are rendered in this milieu is a problem second to none in importance for the sociology of law.

Acknowledgments

I would like to thank Diane Lammey Gibson and Ed Sbarbaro who collaborated with me on the initial stages of research for this project. I would especially like to thank Bill Chambliss whose work on law in western societies and whose friendship and encouragement were very important in the development of this book. As this second edition goes to press in 2020, Bill is no longer with us, but his extensive intellectual insights live on, as does the memory of his generosity, irrepressible good cheer, and love of adventure. I dedicate this book to him.

Several institutions were particularly helpful. I am grateful to the University of Delaware for providing the intellectual environment for the original conceptualization for the book; Middlebury College for granting me a year's leave to complete the project; and the Center for U.S.-Mexican Studies at the University of California, San Diego, for taking me in during that year.

K.C.

U.S. IMMIGRATION LAW
AND THE CONTROL OF LABOR:
1820–1924

1 ▪ *Theoretical Framework*

Introduction

The Statue of Liberty, given to the United States as a gesture of friendship, proclaimed to the world, "Give me your tired, your poor, your huddled masses. . . ." (Lazarus, 1886). From 1820 to 1920, over 35 million people immigrated to the United States, mostly from Europe but also from China, Mexico, and other countries. During most of this time, immigration was encouraged by government officials even to the point of actively recruiting potential immigrants and through advertising. As early as 1791, Alexander Hamilton, in his Report on Manufacturing, warned Congress that if the United States were to develop manufacturing, immigration must be encouraged so as to mitigate the "scarcity of hands" and the "dearness of labor" (Hamilton, 1791, p. 123). Immigrants were to supply the cheap labor necessary for the advance of industrial capitalism in the United States. In 1921 this policy of encouraging immigration was reversed, as Congress for the first time numerically restricted European immigration.

This is a study of that immigration and the policies that regulated it.[1] Its purpose is both to demonstrate the major role played by this massive migration in shaping the political economy of an emerging capitalist power, and to document the way in which U.S. immigration policies alternately encouraged, filtered, and controlled that migration. More generally, it is an investigation of the role of the state in creating and implementing legal solutions, in the form of immigration policies, to the problems of a developing capitalist democracy.

Fundamental to an understanding of these policies is the concept of the immigrant as worker and immigration as workforce movement. The primacy of this attribute of immigration as the relocation of a work force is underlined by an overview of migratory movements over time.

Immigration as Workforce Movement

The Great Migration, which for four centuries "took 68 million people from Europe and scattered them literally over the earth" (Scott, 1968), began in the late stages of mercantilism. When

1

plantations replaced the plunder of raw materials in colonial territories, thereby requiring large numbers of workers to realize the economic potential of these plantations, massive population movements into the plantation colonies were organized.

At first, convicts and indentured servants from Europe supplied the cheap labor required to work the tobacco and cotton plantations of Britain's southern colonies of mainland North America and her sugar plantations in the Caribbean. In response to the demand for plentiful labor in the colonies, the number of crimes for which transportation to Britian's colonies was the penalty steadily increased; as historian Eric Williams (1961, p. 12) concludes, "It is difficult to resist the conclusion that there was some connection between the law and the labor needs of the plantations, and the marvel is that so few people ended up in the colonies overseas."

It was in this setting that one of the most dramatic forced migrations in history was carried out, as "Negroes . . . were stolen in Africa to work the lands stolen from the Indians in America" (Williams, 1961, p. 9). Britain's triangular trade route paid for black slaves in Africa with British manufactured goods and took the human cargo to the plantations where they produced the cotton, tobacco, sugar, and indigo to be processed in Britain and then sold to pay for more slaves. As Williams explains it, "The profits obtained provided one of the mainstreams of that accumulation of capital in England which financed the Industrial Revolution" (1961, p. 52).

As Africans were snatched from their homeland to till the soils of British colonies overseas, another migration brought millions of immiserated Irish peasants to work in the factories of Liverpool, London, and Manchester. By virtue of their numbers and their desperation, these Irish immigrants were also essential to the vast accumulation of capital that fed the Industrial Revolution.

The Irish were followed by Germans, Poles, Italians, and Eastern European Jews, in one of the largest migrations in history. For 100 years, beginning in the early 1800s, U.S. industry was fueled with immigrants from Europe and, to a lesser extent, Asia.

Although less dramatic in scope, the African continent experienced turn-of-the-century migrations as well. There, the discovery of gold in southern mines spawned the migration of thousands of laborers from the outlying hinterland, who—heavily taxed and their land expropriated—were now "free" to sell their labor power or face starvation.

The second half of the twentieth century brought immigrant workers from North and West Africa to France; Turks, Greeks, and Yugoslavs to West Germany; Indians, Pakistanis, and West Indians to the United Kingdom; Southern Italians, Spaniards, and Yugoslavs to Switzerland; and Asians, South Americans, and Central Americans to the United States. Castles and Kosack (1973, p. 428) put this contemporary migration in historical perspective:

> Traditional colonialism took labor (in the form of slaves) as well as natural resources from the countries it dominated. Today, neocolonialism extracts capital from the underdeveloped countries in various ways.... The transfer of human resources in the form of migrant workers is an important part of this transaction.

Just as it was the migrants' embodiment of labor power that was the impetus for these migrations, it was the economic needs of the system into which they were inserted that in large part determined immigration policies. It was the advent of mercantilism that first brought the small numbers of indentured servants to the Caribbean, the expansion of the plantation economy that precipitated the movement of African slaves to the area, and the continued penetration of British capitalism that brought the substitution of the free migration of hundreds of thousands of East Indian wage laborers for the African slave trade in the Caribbean. None of these migrations was truly spontaneous but was triggered and shaped by state policies according to the labor needs of the prevailing mode of production.

If these migrations can be viewed theoretically as workforce movements filling historically specific needs related to the mode of production, then the question can be posed: What, if any, are the special advantages of immigration for an emerging capitalist economy such as that characterizing the United States in the mid-1800s?

Immigration and Capitalism

The unique qualities of capitalism as an economic system that are central to an understanding of capitalist immigration are (1) the complete separation of the work force from control of the means of production; (2) relations of production that are based on free contract and bargaining, not outright force; and (3) an insatiable drive for increasing levels of surplus labor and surplus value.

The special utility of immigration under such an economic system is that it allows for the superexploitation of immigrant workers at minimal social capital costs (such as those of maintenance and renewal), while introducing an element into the class

3

struggle that serves ideologically and materially to weaken working-class resistance to that exploitation.[2]

It is the nature of the class conflict under capitalism that imparts to immigration these special functions. As Miliband has put it,

> ... the conflict [in any period] essentially stems from the determination of the dominant classes to extract as much work as possible from the subject classes; and, conversely, from the attempts of these classes to change the terms and conditions of their subjection, or to end it altogether. In relation to capitalism, the matter is expressed by Marx in terms of the imperative necessity for the owners and controllers of capital to extract the largest possible amount of surplus value from the labor force. (1977, pp. 19–20)

The extraction of surplus labor is by no means unique to capitalism, nor is the utility of immigrant labor. However, under a system in which there is an insistent thrust toward ever-increasing levels of surplus value and in which the terms of that extraction are based on coercion, not outright force, immigrant labor takes on a special meaning as a powerful ingredient in that coercive process. Immigration, in other words, can be seen not just as an economically and ideologically useful tool to capital, but as an ideal temporary solution to dilemmas derived from the most fundamental contradiction in capitalism, the class contradiction, for immigration allows increased levels of exploitation both by providing access to a virtually unlimited supply of labor and by introducing a potentially divisive element into the working class.[3]

While immigration may enable capital and the capitalist state to minimize temporarily the effects of the class contradiction and the contradictory development of capital, it leaves untouched the contradictions themselves. The result is a dialectical maze, in which immigration and immigration policy alternately play a crucial role as countering mechanisms vis-à-vis the crisis tendencies in capitalism, and as generators of conflict.

Because immigration provides capital with an important tool with which to tamper with the contradictory development of capitalism, and because this tool is produced and reproduced by state immigration policy, the relationship between law and the economic structure potentially becomes compellingly direct and transparent. The study of immigration and immigration law under capitalism presents an opportunity to witness with unusual clarity both the conflicts associated with the construction of a surplus labor supply and the participation of the state in the resolution of those conflicts. This is particularly true of immigration to the United States in the nineteenth and early twentieth centuries, where large-scale immigration, encouraged and induced by the government, was a critical force behind a century of unprecedented capital expansion.

While immigration may provide capital with an ideological and material edge over the working class, it is also the case that a strong working class complicates this policy-making process and may be capable of periodically influencing policy itself. Unlike many other legislative issues that do not smolder so close to the surface of the class conflict and do not have such direct repercussions for the class struggle, the study of immigration has the potential to bring into focus the complexities of the class struggle as an influence on state policy setting.

Finally, because immigration usually involves distinct ethnic and cultural groups and is frequently accompanied by working-class hostility and xenophobic ideological constructs, the observer is forced to avoid simplistic or overly deterministic depictions of both the class struggle and the relationship between law and economic structure. For one thing, the contradictions inherent in the relations between resident-workers and immigrant-workers are brought dramatically to the fore, as the long-range ideals of working-class solidarity clash head on with the shorter-range pragmatics of exclusionism. As the objective tension is overlaid with xenophobic and racialist stereotypes, the capitalist-versus-worker struggle is typically buried beneath the weight of neocolonialist ideologies, which divide the working class itself.

The study of immigration law, then, presents both an opportunity and a formidable challenge to students of law, society, and economic structure. Because the relationship between law and economic interests becomes so transparent under the microscope of immigration, and because at the same time the waters are muddied by the role of the class struggle and ideology as important catalysts in the immigration law-making process, the relationship between law and economic structure becomes at once both more compelling and less tidy.

An Overview of Recent Theories of the Capitalist State

A number of neo-Marxian theories of the capitalist state have been developed in recent years, which may be of help in constructing a model of law making that can account for the evolution of U.S. immigration policies. While the theorists differ on specifics, they concur that the state in capitalist society serves the interests of the capitalist class, at least in a broad sense. Although their interpretations vary, each implicitly or explicitly refers to Marx and Engel's (1955, pp. 11–12) concept that "the modern state is but a committee for managing the common affairs of the whole bourgeoisie."

Beyond that agreement, there is fundamental disagreement. There are those (referred to here as "instrumentalists" after the classification of Gold *et al.*, 1975) who argue that the state in capitalist society is class biased because it is susceptible to the direct or indirect influence of individual capitalists. The works of Mills (1956), Domhoff (1967, 1978), and Miliband (1969)[4] are attempts to demonstrate empirically that there is a power elite or ruling class of capitalists. Probably because these works are a response to pluralists, they frequently succumb to pluralists' assumptions and methodologies. Their differences from pluralists rest primarily upon different empirical results, i.e., there is one interest group that consistently gets its way. To explain why this group is so often successful in influencing state policy, Domhoff (1967), Kolko (1963, 1965), Miliband (1969), and others focus on the economic and personal relationship between powerful capitalists and leading members of the state elite.

These analyses approach what Gold *et al.* call "a sociology of the capitalist class" (1975, p. 32). The state in this model has no apparent autonomous function but is simply an instrument for the making of policy that will promote individual capitalists' interests, because it is directly or indirectly influenced by these capitalists. If this logic is extended, the implication is that, given enough resources, any group could enjoy the same influence. For this reason, Offe (1974) argues that Miliband's book *The State in Capitalist Society* (1969) is appropriately titled since it describes a state within a capitalist society, which is in no inherent way a "capitalist state."

The most persuasive criticism of these instrumentalists has come, not from pluralists, but from other Marxist theorists. Structuralists criticize the instrumentalists on both empirical and theoretical grounds. Theoretically, Offe (1974) and Poulantzas (1969) argue that instrumentalism is not a theory at all but an empirical generalization, in the sense that nothing in their analysis implies the theoretical necessity of capitalist influence on the state.

Poulantzas (1969, p. 70) further points out that the instrumental view is voluntaristic, in that the role of the state is reduced to the "conduct and 'behavior' of the members of the state apparatus" and social action is "explained" in terms of "motivations of conduct of the individual actors." The larger context within which that behavior is shaped is ignored. Finally, instrumentalists tend to ignore the contradictions within the political economy that limit state alternatives and guarantee that capitalists' interests will often be violated in the short run (Mollenkopf, 1975; p. 254).

Related to these problems are a variety of empirical criticisms. Mollenkopf (1975) notes that capitalists' attempts to influence state policy are frequently unsuccessful. He uses as an example the New Deal, which was strenuously opposed by a variety of powerful capitalists even though it can be argued that it was in their long-term interests. Similarly, Domhoff, in *The Powers That Be* (1978, p. 119), is admittedly unable to account for the National Labor Relations Act of 1935, which was unanimously opposed by business. Conversely, many policies with consequences favoring the interests of capitalists are enacted independent of direct business influence.

Finally, Offe (1974), Poulantzas (1969), Whitt (1979), and others question the extent to which the ruling class is unified on major issues. If the state is simply and always an instrument of the ruling class, then capitalists' interests must be consistently compatible. This, however, is clearly not the case. Even Domhoff (1978, pp. 64–87), in his otherwise convincing account of the ways in which major capitalists develop and sustain class consciousness, must ultimately admit that there are important splits between ultraconservative capitalists and those who are more moderate.

In summary, structuralists point out that instrumentalists suggest too much consistency of state policy in favor of the ruling class, side by side with a lack of any theoretical reason for such consistency.

Althusser (1971), Poulantzas (1969, 1973), and O'Connor (1973) are among the most notable structuralist theorists of the capitalist state. If instrumentalist theory is primarily a response to pluralists, structuralists respond to the inadequacies of the instrumentalists. For structuralists, the state is not simply a state in a capitalist society, but a capitalist state, in that there is a structural "objective relation" (Poulantzas, 1969) between the state and capitalism that guarantees that the state, within the limits imposed by inherent contradictions and the class struggle, will operate in the long-term interests of the capitalist class, independent of the direct participation of individual capitalists.

For Poulantzas (1969, p. 70), this relationship hinges on the fact that social classes and the state are "objective structures" with an "objective system of regular connections," in that there is a "coincidence" between the function of the state in a particular social

formation and the interests of the dominant class in that formation. There is a complementarity of interests and the fact that
there is frequently direct participation of capitalists in the state is
not the cause of the state's functioning in the interests of capital,
but its effect (Poulantzas, 1969, p. 73).

What are these objective functions of the state that coincide
with the interests of capital? And why must the state fulfill these
particular functions? Structuralists agree that the state must promote the capital accumulation process while ensuring the private
appropriation of profits. This accumulation process must be protected not so much because of some individual captialist's influence, but more essentially because (1) the state's financing is
dependent on taxation of these profits, as well as on debt to private financial institutions; (2) its political stability depends on at
least a minimum of economic stability; and (3) more generally, its
survival depends on the survival of the political economy as a
whole. Since economic laws are not built into the nature of things,
and since capitalism contains a number of inherent contradictions, the state must assist in this accumulation process or risk its
own demise.

In addition to this accumulation function, the state must promote "political integration" (Friedland *et al.*, 1977), "social harmony" (O'Connor, 1973), or the "cohesion of the social formation"
(Poulantzas, 1969, 1973). If the state fails, its very survival is in
jeopardy. More indirectly, the state must pursue this stability because relative political stability is a precondition for the continued
success of the economic system upon which the state depends.
And, it must do so actively and aggressively since the very accumulation process on which the state depends tends to produce
conflicts and instability.

"These *underlying* and *systemic* reasons both make possible
and make imperative certain state actions, regardless of who attempts to instigate them" (Mollenkopf, 1975, p. 253; emphasis in
original). Furthermore, the "state acts on behalf of capitalists, but
it does not do so at their behest" (Mollenkopf, 1975, p. 249), since
"the totality of this role itself coincides with the long-term interests of the ruling class" (Poulantzas, 1969, p. 74). It is of necessity,
then, a "Capitalist State."

Structuralists further point out that not only is the state not
directly controlled by individual capitalists, but it best fulfills its
dual functions of accumulation and political integration when it is
least susceptible to direct influences, since such influences may
serve parochial capital interests rather than collective ones. It is in
this sense that the state, as a "committee for managing the com-

mon affairs of the whole bourgeoisie" (Marx and Engels, 1955, pp. 11–12) and as an "ideal collective capitalist" (Jessop, 1977, p. 362), must enjoy "relative autonomy" (Poulantzas, 1969, 1973). This autonomy is "relative" in that it is relatively free from manipulation by individual capitalists but not at all autonomous from the requirements of the political economy as a whole.

From this perspective, then, the state is not merely an instrument that subsidizes particular capitalists economically; its more essential function is the perpetuation of the whole political economy. This requires both promoting capital accumulation and engaging in conflict resolution. The theorists then demonstrate the ways law creation may reflect both of these tasks (see Cashmore, 1978; Chambliss, 1979; Friedland *et al.*, 1977; Offe, 1972; Piven and Cloward, 1977).

While this structural model of the capitalist state seems both theoretically and empirically more adequate than that of the instrumentalists, structuralists have problems of their own, though these problems do not seem inherent in the model. Among structuralists, there tends to be either an overemphasis on system stability (Althusser, 1971; Poulantzas, 1969, 1973), or too much stress on disintegration (O'Connor, 1973). In neither case is the role of class struggle sufficiently addressed, as all conscious action has been distilled out of the analysis.

Chambliss, in "Contradictions and Conflicts in Law Creation" (1979), and Whitt, in "Toward a Class-Dialectical Model of Power" (1979), avoid these weaknesses. However, neither explicitly develops a model of the capitalist state. Chambliss's concern is to put forth a model of legal development in capitalist society, and in so doing he implicitly attributes certain functions to the state. For Chambliss the moving force behind significant legal developments lies in fundamental and inherent contradictions within the political economy. Law represents the state's attempt to resolve the conflicts that derive from these contradictions.

What is particularly forceful about Chambliss's analysis is that it simultaneously emphasizes the system's crisis tendencies (contradictions and conflicts) and the short-term stability achieved by "resolutions," thereby avoiding both Poulantzas's and O'Connor's pitfalls. It furthermore makes clear that resolutions or outcomes do not always and automatically benefit capitalists but are rather the result of social conflict and struggle.

Throughout Chambliss's analysis it is implied, although never explicitly stated, that it is the state's task or function to resolve these conflicts in order to ensure the perpetuation of the political economy. This must be implied, for without such a conception of the state's function, it would make no sense to speak in terms of resolutions. One would speak instead merely of outcomes. Law, then, as one of the main tools of the state, is seen here as an attempt to resolve conflicts that threaten the political economy, within the limitations imposed by inherent contradictions and class struggle.

Whitt's (1979) class-dialectical model similarly focuses on the contradictions within social, economic, and political institutions as the force behind social change. Using the example of the conflict over the construction of BART (Bay Area Rapid Transit) in San Francisco, Whitt demonstrates how inherent contradictions within the economy lead to conflicts and attempted resolutions that produce further conflicts.

> Now something must be done to "save" the central city as a producer of profit. . . . Such systems as BART are supported by dominant business classes as a way out. That they do not really work so well and are very costly is now being realized. (Whitt, 1979, p. 97)

Although he implies that the state joins capitalists in attempting to resolve such conflicts, his is not explicitly a model of the state, but of class-conscious businessmen. As with Chambliss, Whitt's analysis is eminently dialectical, in that it recognizes the central importance of both the class struggle and the inherent contradictions that limit the effectiveness of capitalists' actions.

What is striking about all these structural analyses is that they are primarily theories about what issues are likely to emerge (as a result of contradictions and conflicts) and why the capitalist state must resolve them (because of its dual role of accumulation and integration). None deals specifically with the conditions under which one resolution is more likely than another qualitatively different one. For example, none of these theorists offers any suggestions as to when it is likely that *no* action will be taken in response to, say, worker demands; when only symbolic action will be taken; and when meaningful action is likely. As Mollenkopf (1975, p. 246) has put it, "At a methodological level, these theories cannot predict that one thing is more likely to happen than another." The instrumentalist approach is limited in the opposite way, in that it focuses exclusively on probable outcomes, ignoring the contradictions, conflicts, and the role of the state that determine that particular conflicts become issues in the first place.

The present study is an empirical analysis of law creation and requires a theoretical framework that not only suggests the ways the emergence of particular issues and conflicts is related to a particular historical context, but that also indicates the probability of one resolution or outcome rather than other very different ones. The following section is an attempt to develop such a framework.

The Accumulation Role of the State

Braverman (1974), Miliband (1969), O'Connor (1973), Offe (1972), Pearce (1976), and Wolfe (1977) concur, "State power has everywhere been used by governments to enrich the capitalist class" (Braverman, 1974, p. 294).

The provision of those conditions that maximize profit is frequently achieved through legislation, as a significant tradition within the sociology of law has demonstrated. Hall (1935) and Kolko (1963, 1965), for example, detail the ways in which powerful economic interests have influenced the creation and implementation of specific laws. Schattschneider (1935) convincingly traces the tariff legislation of 1929–1930 to the demands of important industries. Rusche and Kirchheimer (1939), correlating modes of punishment with modes of production, and Chambliss (1964), with his structural analysis of vagrancy laws, relate legal developments to historically specific requirements of the labor market [see also Marx's (1906, p. 294) account of the way Poor Law Commissioners filled gaps in the labor market in England in the early 1800s]. Cashmore (1978, p. 409) notes with regard to Canadian immigration legislation that

> systematic relationships are found between the engagement of various legislative innovations and the changing interests of powerful resource-holding groups, giving rise to a conception of immigration law as a set of strategies, designed to serve the interests of economic elites.

Since the availability of masses of laborers, free to sell their labor power and constrained to sell it at a minimum wage, is the *sine qua non* of both capitalism and a variety of precapitalist systems, the task of ensuring an abundant supply of labor frequently falls to the state, which must perpetuate those systems.

Structuralists have shown, however, that this accumulation activity is not merely the result of ruling-class influence on the law-making process as most of these theorists suggest. Rather,

> the state is an essential part of the mode of production found in any society. Its objective function is to guaran-

11

tee the reproduction of the economic system (Pearce, 1976, p. 61)

since the state itself depends on the economy's surplus-production capacity for its power and very survival.

> In short, it is impossible to conceive of a state functioning against the interests of the bourgeoisie (notwithstanding its ability to effect compromises and concessions) short of removing the basis of their power. (Bridges, 1974, p. 173)

Not only must it not function against the interests of the bourgeoisie, but it must directly subsidize capital development. At the very least, it must provide the infrastructure and raw materials of capitalist development, including such things as railroad construction, highway construction, public utilities, and most crucially for our purposes here, a work force.

The State as Resolver of Conflicts

This intervention in the capital accumulation process is not sufficient, however, to ensure the survival of the political economy even in the short run. The capitalist state, as "an essential part of the mode of production" (Pearce, 1976, p. 61), must fill a second, somewhat contradictory, role simultaneously. It must intervene to resolve the conflicts that derive from an inherent contradiction in capitalist democracies, i.e., *those very conditions that provide for and result from the maximization of profit threaten the stability upon which the political and economic system depends.* The same conditions that facilitate the maximization of profit (for example, unrestricted immigration, which provides a cheap labor supply) may promote (1) economic instability, in the form of strikes and high labor-turnover rates, as was the case by 1921 in the United States; (2) social instability, in the form of nativist uprisings and protests, as in the 1830s through the 1850s in the United States; and (3) political instability, as radical political movements from as early as the mid-nineteenth century tended to draw disproportionately from the immigrant population.

Notice, then, that these two functions of accumulation and conflict resolution are contradictory. In the first place, conflict is minimized only to the extent that this accumulation role, or the class-biased nature of the state, is concealed. Second, it is the state's perpetuation of the capitalist economy with its inherent contradictions that continually re-creates the conflicts that the state must then resolve.

This view of the dual functions of the capitalist state is similar but not identical to that of the structuralists mentioned above. O'Connor (1973), for example, argues that the state in late capitalism has two contradictory functions: that of providing conditions for capital accumulation and that of legitimation, or the maintenance of social harmony. This legitimation function, just as with Friedland, Piven, and Alford's (1977) "political integration," refers to the resolution of instabilities that have as their basis agitation and protest. The model proposed here benefits from Chambliss's (1979) and Whitt's (1979) discussions of the importance of inherent contradictions and conflicts and suggests that the maintenance of the political economy depends not only on social harmony but also on the resolution of a variety of other economic and political conflicts that derive directly from the contradictory needs of a capitalist democracy.

The objective relation (Poulantzas, 1969) between capitalism and the state is based on the fact that the capitalist state's function is, and must be, that of actively perpetuating the political economy, so that ultimately the state's interests and the long-term interests of capital are similar. In perpetuating the political economy, the state must promote capital accumulation and its private appropriation, and simultaneously respond to the conflicts that derive from perpetuating an economic system fraught with contradictions. Law creation is one of the ways by which the state attempts to resolve these conflicts. It will be argued here that *how* those conflicts are resolved—whether through legal changes, and if so, what types of changes—will depend primarily on (1) the source of the conflict, (2) the form and organization of the class struggle, (3) the level of capital development and the specific needs associated with that level, and (4) related ideological developments.

Types of Conflict Resolution

At any particular point, the conflicts that arise from the contradiction between the need for the maximization of profit and system stability (for example, the needs of U.S. industry during the 1830s, 1840s, and 1850s for an increasing and cheap labor supply versus the riots and protests that this influx of cheap, predominantly Irish-Catholic, labor provoked) present the state with the dilemma: Must it continue to promote the immediate interests of capital and jeopardize system stability? Must it respond to the disturbance by interfering with the short-term interests of capital in the interests of long-term survival? Or does it have a third, less painful, option?

This role of the state as the resolver of conflicts stemming from inherent contradictions in the political economy has been discussed by Stearns (1979) in her examination of occupational safety and health laws in Sweden. She concludes from her analysis that frequently a third option is the best temporary solution to such dilemmas. That is, disturbances and protests can often be curbed through symbolic legislation which—either through non-enforcement or minimal enforcement, or through the incorporation of loopholes into the legislation itself—does not significantly threaten even the short-term interests of the industries involved. She suggests that the ideal solution to the conflict in Sweden between the need for uninterrupted capital accumulation and the need for the social democratic state to show its concern for working-class interests was the creation of a large occupational safety and health bureaucracy, whose ostensible purpose is to ensure occupational safety and health but which, in effect, does little of the kind. Edelman (1964, 1977) similarly demonstrates the utility of this concept of symbolic action in reference to both legislation and linguistics. His discussion takes a sociopsychological twist, however, in which the focus is on our alleged psychological need for legitimation rather than on the state's need to legitimate itself.

Deliberate and self-conscious conspiring is not a necessary feature of symbolic legislation as the term is used here. To the extent that a given piece of legislation is entirely the result of potential or actual protests and this legislation is made ineffectual in action, it is symbolic legislation. It is probably often the case that some legislators are aware of the symbolic function of given legislation and consciously support it for its symbolic effect. What is important here, however, is that symbolic legislation is created as a response to specific demands and protests, yet cannot be substantially implemented because of its potential interference with powerful interests or profit making in general. Regardless of whether individual legislators are initially aware of its implications, symbolic legislation remains the ideal solution to certain kinds of conflicts. (For an example of unpremeditated symbolic law, see Calavita, 1983.)

While this conflict-resolution function of symbolic action is frequently addressed, the actual conditions that may generate symbolic action have not been clearly identified in the literature. It will be argued here that symbolic action is the likely response only when the disturbance or conflict to be resolved is the result of protest over specific conditions, the actual amelioration of which would be antagonistic to capital accumulation processes. In such cases the only solution, and a temporarily adequate one, is symbolic action.

The creation of symbolic law is not, of course, an automatic response to protest. In fact, most protest is followed by inaction and/or repression. Whether symbolic action is forthcoming depends on such things as the degree of organization and pressure that the protesting groups can exert and how crippling this pressure is perceived to be.

This is not to suggest that organized protest can never achieve substantial results. To the extent that it continues to threaten the normal workings of the political economy until demands are actually met, significant change may of course be effected. (For an excellent discussion of the characteristics of successful protest, see Piven and Cloward, 1977.)

While conflicts between capital accumulation and protest activity generally elicit inaction or symbolic action, other kinds of conflicts require a different response. Situations arise in which there is a direct conflict between two or more conditions that are otherwise beneficial to profit making. These conflicts derive from a variety of inherent contradictions within capitalism. (An example of such a conflict is the simultaneous need of capital for cheap labor and markets.)

Now, when the conflict to be resolved by the state consists primarily of protest over conditions that facilitate profit making, the solution may be symbolic action in response to that protest; but, when the disturbance is a direct outcome of conditions that serve to advance profit making, the response is more likely to have to effect some real, although perhaps minimal, change.

Let us again take the case of occupational safety and health as an example. It is expensive in the short run to improve conditions of factory safety and health. The solution to the problem of worker *health* in western industrial societies, prompted entirely by labor protest and worker demands, has been largely symbolic, in the form of unenforced legislation. However, the solution to the problem of factory *safety* in these societies has been the substantial improvement of conditions and a reduction in the accident rate. This solution was prompted not so much by labor protests, but by the fact that numerous accidents are expensive, in that they require compensation and increase the labor-turnover rate (Korman, 1967, pp. 113–127). In such cases of direct conflict between otherwise beneficial conditions, the state is likely to intervene with either limited action or substantial change. (In an ironic inversion of the public-interest model, laws that are primarily the response to public outcry are the most apt to be merely symbolic and not effect any real change.)[5]

While the direct influence of powerful capitalists, along the lines of the instrumentalist model, may often be a determining factor in this conflict-resolution process, it is not in itself of great explanatory value. It is probably more frequently the case that the desires of class-conscious capitalists and state policy coincide because their interests coincide.

The Reproduction of Conflict

It would be wrong to suggest that the state actually resolves these conflicts through its legislative attempts. To the extent that the conflicts are rooted in systemic contradictions, the resolution can provide only a temporary palliative. In the case of symbolic action, the conditions behind the protest are not themselves altered (which is, of course, what makes it such an attractive alternative), so that the action is effective only as long as its ineffectiveness goes unnoticed. As Stearns (1979) has suggested with regard to the occupational safety and health bureaucracy in Sweden, if symbolic action takes the form of the creation of a bureaucracy whose ostensible purpose is to oversee the contested conditions, the typical response to recurring protest is the further elaboration of that bureaucracy and budget increases. In the case of conflicts that are based on the mutually contradictory needs of a capitalist democracy, the solution itself inevitably creates further conflicts that in turn must be dealt with, as Whitt (1979) suggests in his discussion of the inefficiencies of the BART system.

This theoretical framework is both similar to and different from the instrumentalist and structuralist approaches reviewed above. It goes beyond the personal influence model of the instrumentalists and attempts to define the structural relationship between the economic and the political, and the importance of this relationship for law creation. This structural focus does not preclude the possibility that direct influence on the legislative process by individual capitalists may occasionally be decisive. As Gold *et al.* (1975, p. 46) put it,

> The capitalist state must be conceived both as a structure constrained by the logic of the society within which it functions and as an organization manipulated behind the scenes by the ruling class and its representatives.

By tying both the emergence of legislative issues and their probable outcome to historically specific requirements of, and contradictions in, capitalism, this framework avoids the pluralistic implications of both Chambliss's and Whitt's models in which the issue of outcomes is not treated except to say that a struggle ensues.

A Note on Methodology

This formulation as with the structuralists' relies primarily on broad social, economic, and political conditions of given historical periods as the most important explanatory factors. It eschews individualistic or behaviorist explanations of legal developments, as such voluntarist approaches cannot adequately account for any social phenomenon.

This has implications for the kind of data one regards as significant. In trying to account for a mugging incident, for example, no serious sociological explanation would rely entirely on circumstances immediately surrounding the crime nor on the mugger's account of what motivated him or her. Rather, it would examine the social context, perhaps including an analysis of the dilemmas faced by members of an underclass in an affluent capitalist society (see, for example, Hacker, 1973). The actor's comments might be used as indicators of these dilemmas, but not as explanations in and of themselves. Similarly, in examining the historical development of immigration law, it is not sufficient to analyze the congressional hearings and political events immediately surrounding the legislation. The pertinent data, if one is to avoid what Poulantzas (1969) calls the "problematic of the subject," must speak to the social, political, and economic context. Statements made during the congressional hearings and debates are thus important not as "motivations of conduct" (Poulantzas, 1969) but as confirmation of the kinds of dilemmas faced.

Related to the question of judging the adequacy of theory, Offe (1974, p. 35) warns that

> even the repeated observation of an influence relationship does not allow an analytical concept to be derived regarding power relationships but at most makes it possible to generalize empirically. No proof of their necessity is gained in this way. . . .

This is particularly a problem with regard to theories of the capitalist state, because it is part of the state's function to disguise and conceal its class nature. The methodology employed here, i.e., that of tracing the evolution of immigration policy over a long period, is useful in this regard. For if a consistent pattern emerges, it sug-

17

gests that more than a mere empirical coincidence is at work. If the whole career of the issue of immigration restriction can be traced from a legislative nonissue to an increasingly troublesome issue, and if this development, including the specific ways that its class nature is disguised, can be tied to historically specific requirements of the political economy, then a persuasive case will have been made for this dialectical—structural explanation of law making.

Organization of the Book

The book proceeds roughly according to the historical chronology of events, primarily because it must narrate a continuous sequence of conflicts, dilemmas, and resolutions, in which the resolutions of one period set the stage for the dilemmas of the next. Chapter 2 opens on the dawn of large-scale European immigration to the United States with the onset of industrialization in the early nineteenth century and traces immigration and immigration policy through the Civil War. Most notable in this period is the open encouragement of immigration by the American state, side-by-side with widespread working-class protest over capital's use of immigrants to reduce wages and break their fledgling strikes.

The birth and development of the American labor movement in the last four decades of the nineteenth century, the unprecedented expansion of American industry, and America's first federal immigration laws are treated in Chapter 3. These laws are seen as responses to specific conflicts inherent in the political economy of the period. Most important, while the power of organized labor made immigration an important weapon of American capital by the 1880s, this same strength of American labor made necessary some state response to labor's pleas for protection from that strategy.

The selective immigration policies of the turn of the century are treated in Chapter 4 as ill-fated attempts to resolve the contradictions inherent in the construction of a surplus work force with which to subordinate labor. On one hand, poverty is nurtured through the recruitment of an unlimited stream of immigrant labor; on the other, that poverty must be contended with, both materially and ideologically. Selective immigration policies were an attempt to resolve these conflicts by redefining the problem in terms of the personal attributes of the immigrants themselves.

Chapter 5 examines Progressivism in the early years of the twentieth century, the emergence of a racist xenophobia sponsored by New England elites, and the heredity-eugenics movement. Just as immigrants had been used earlier as an attempted resolution to capital's labor problems, so they were used now to solve the state's increasingly vexing problems of legitimation and stability, as these new immigrants of "racially inferior stock" were held responsible for both poverty and protest.

Chapter 6 traces the Americanization movement in the second decade of the twentieth century as a last-ditch effort to allow for the continued reproduction of the surplus work force through immigration, without thereby threatening ideological hegemony. In a period in which the whole immigrant stream had been declared defective, the Americanization movement was an attempt to reform the whole stream rather than simply filtering out a few undesirables with selective immigration policies.

Chapter 7 focuses on the congressional hearings and debates surrounding the quota restrictions of 1921 and 1924. While it is clear that the ideology of immigrant inferiority, fears of a new kind of immigrant radicalism, and rising unemployment were important elements in these restrictions, it is also clear that the changed needs of monopoly capitalism made possible these quota restrictions as the latest response to a set of dilemmas that had been plaguing U.S. law makers for decades.

Notes

1. This analysis focuses primarily on policies directed at European immigration, as the bulk of the immigration into the United States in this period was of European origin.

2. In monopoly capitalism, this use of the immigrant is paralleled by the mobility of capital itself. In terms of both the externalization of the costs of labor force reproduction and the leverage with which it provides capital in the class struggle, the flight of capital to the source of labor in less developed areas parallels and complements the movement of workers.

3. This potential for divisiveness is not an inevitable component of immigration under capitalism but reflects the lag between the internationalization of the labor market and the still national parameters of organized labor.

4. Miliband's work, *The State in Capitalist Society* (1969), presents an essentially instrumentalist view of the relationship between the capitalist class and the state; however, his later work—notably "State Power and Class Interests" (1983)—recognizes the relative autonomy

U.S. IMMIGRATION LAW AND THE CONTROL OF LABOR

of the state and focuses on the partnership between the capitalist state and the capitalist class.

5. This analysis of possible responses to conflict by the state is in some ways parallel to what Offe (1974) has called the "selective mechanisms" of the state, which guarantee its class character. *Negative selection* refers to the selective process by which anticapitalist interests are systematically excluded from state action (parallel here to *inaction* in response to anticapital demands). *Disguising selections* refers to those actions that give the appearance of class neutrality while excluding anticapital solutions (this corresponds roughly to symbolic action). *Positive selections* are those actions that attempt to address capital interests as a whole, as opposed to parochial capital interests (this is parallel to qualified action and effective change). What is unique about Offe's work is its attempt to delineate the actual mechanisms by which this avoidance of anticapital interests and the favoring of collective capital interests is guaranteed. Unfortunately, his discussion of the four *filters* (structure, ideology, process, and repression) that guarantee these selections is vague.

20

2 • *The Golden Door Opens*

Overview of U.S. Immigration, 1820–1860

U.S. immigration in the nineteenth century was consistently related to fluctuations in the business cycle. While boom years almost immediately precipitated a large influx of immigrants, in times of depression net immigration was frequently negative, as with the so-called Great Reverses of 1874. The U.S. House Industrial Commission in 1901 correlated the number of immigrants each year from 1840 to 1900 with price index numbers and concluded,

> Immigration follows business conditions . . .: In times of business expansion, when capital is seeking investment ... immigrants enter in increasing numbers ..., but in times of business depression their numbers decline. (U.S. Congress, House Industrial Commission, 1901, Vol. 15, pp. 308–309)

The push from Europe was also linked to economic factors. In England and Scandinavia, the enclosure movements forced agricultural workers off the land, as did the transition from arable to pasture land in Ireland and Germany, condemning thousands of peasants to choose between starvation and emigration.

These sporadic fluctuations in economic need were responsible for short-term immigration shifts, but it was the advent of the Industrial Revolution that was responsible for the overall movement. Europe's population doubled from 1750 to 1860 as a result of advancing medical and sanitary knowledge and the increased food supply that accompanied industrialization. The growth of the factory system in England destroyed the old system of domestic manufacture and threw thousands of artisans out of work. The reorganization of the rural economy in the form of large-scale farming added to the mass of unemployed (Bernard, 1950; Handlin, 1941; Hansen, 1930). It is hardly surprising that this surplus population preferred emigration to perpetual impoverishment.

Even so, significant numbers of Europeans did not immigrate into the United States until after 1820. This increase in immigration to the United States cannot be entirely accounted for by an intensification of push factors from Europe (a significant portion of the population had always been impoverished), nor simply by an increase in opportunities in America (land had always been available). Rather, it depended in large part on U.S. immigration policies and private-sector recruitment, both of which changed with the need for an industrial labor force (see Figure 1).

Contrary to current wisdom on the subject, preindustrial attitudes and policies with regard to immigration were far from unilaterally favorable. In spite of the fact that land and opportunity were abundant in Colonial times, most of the American colonies enacted measures to restrict and regulate immigration (Cavanaugh, 1928; Garis, 1927; pp. 13–16; Proper, 1967, p. 16). Proper (1967) introduces his investigation of colonial immigration policy: "[Among the charter governments] . . . we find very few measures expressly intended to encourage immigration, yet they took very decided ground on the question of anti-immigration." The open-door policy, which so many historians attribute to America's early years, was initiated only with the advent of industrialization and the need for an industrial work force.[1]

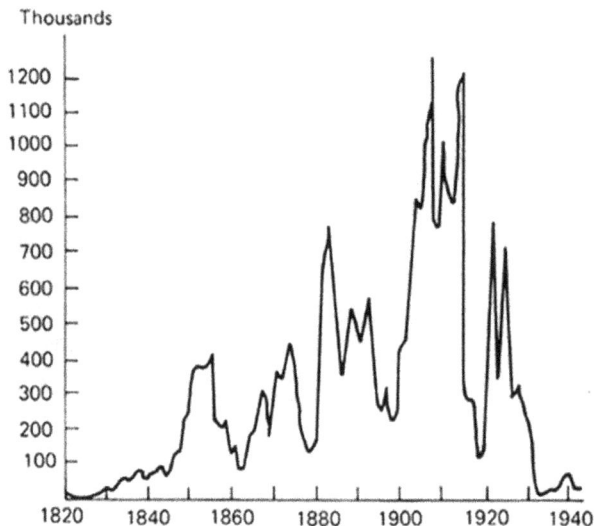

Fig. 1. Immigration to the United States, 1820–1940. (From U.S. Department of Justice Immigration and Naturalization Service.)

From Dependent Capitalist to Dependent Worker

Skilled European workers were recruited early in the nineteenth century to organize and oversee operations in America's new industries. In fact, industrialists in the United States relied on British skills in almost all those sectors in which Britain had already industrialized, and evidence suggests that a substantial part of this labor force was directly imported from England on contract (Clark, 1929; Creamer, 1941; Erickson, 1957; Jones, 1960; Ware, 1931).

The indispensability of these skilled immigrants is reflected in the favorable contracts they were able to command from their American employers. For example, the transportation expenses of imported machinists and artisans were often absorbed by their employers, and contracts frequently included profit-sharing provisions (Berthoff, 1953; Erickson, 1957). In one instance a Lowell cotton mill owner promised a salary nearly double his own in order to procure a Manchester craftsman to oversee his new printing operation (Berthoff, 1953, p. 31).

At the root of the capital-labor contradiction is the capitalist's need to

> produce a commodity whose value shall be greater than the sum of the values of the commodities used in its production, that is, of the means of production and the labour-power. (Marx, 1906, p. 207)

This extraction of surplus value from the production process and its private appropriation are the *sine qua non* of capitalist development and are possible only to the extent that labor is remunerated for only a portion of the exchange value produced. Since capitalists must continually seek to increase the amount of this surplus value, there is a perpetual attempt to reduce this remuneration proportionate to productivity.

An irony inherent in the capital-labor antagonism is that any significant part of a work force that consists of workers who are individually indispensable to capital will ultimately prove unsatisfactory to capital. It was not long before American capitalists— dependent on scarce, imported skilled labor—began to complain of its insubordination and independence. English craftsmen were allegedly always "kicking against rules, kicking against foremen, kicking against everything" (U.S. Congress, House Industrial Commission, 1901, Vol. 14, p. 415). According to textile manufacturers, the skilled workers whom they had so carefully recruited from Europe were not dependable, as they occasionally left the employ of those who had recruited them to establish factories of their own (National Association of Wool Manufacturers, 1881; Ware, 1931). Employers charged that their skilled immigrant workers refused to train others in essential techniques; some workers apparently even demanded their own buildings to work in (Lathrop, 1926, p. 94). Worse yet, English workers, because they were trained in an already industrial society—which was precisely what made them so desirable—were also experienced in trade union activities. Although English workers continued to be recognized as the most skillful, their employers regularly complained that they were "peculiarly difficult to deal with" (Earl, 1877, p. 111) and "the most beastly people I have ever seen" (textile owner, quoted in Gutman, 1976, p. 20). The superintendent of Carnegie's Braddock, Pennsylvania, steelworks warned in 1875: "We must steer clear as far as we can of the English who are great sticklers for high wages, small productivity and strikes . . ." (Bridge, 1902, p. 81). As workers from Lancashire landed at New York, one Fall River mill employer rejoiced at the new shipment of workers: "Well, we shall have a lot of greenhorns here tomorrow." His overseer was skeptical: "Yes, but you'll find that they have brought their horns with them!" (quoted in Berthoff, 1953, p. 96).

Marx discussed the disadvantages of skilled labor only a few years later:

> Since handicraft skill is the foundation of manufacturing, and since the mechanism of manufacture as a whole possesses no framework apart from the laborers themselves, capital is constantly compelled to wrestle with the insubordination of the workman. (Marx, 1906, p. 403)

The insubordination of the skilled worker was particularly troublesome to capitalists in mid-nineteenth-century America, where the necessary skills were scarce and only available among workers already versed in class struggle. A resolution soon presented itself in the form of mechanization coupled with the sudden influx of thousands of unskilled, predominantly Irish and German immigrants.

Although only 56,000 Irish emigrated to the United States in the 20 years between 1820 and 1840, 607,241 arrived in the four-year period between 1845 and 1849, and 904,859 more came between 1850 and 1854. This influx of poverty-stricken Irish immigrants, driven from their homes by the potato rot and widespread famine, provided the cutting edge of capital's efforts to subordinate the labor force. Although previously, impoverished Irish immigrants had sought refuge in the industrial centers of England, an open-door federal immigration policy in the United States combined with public and private recruitment efforts increasingly brought them across the Atlantic.

American employers were the first to admit that only with mechanization and this immigration of unskilled workers could they free themselves from the intractability of skilled immigrants, their wage demands, and their union principles (Habakkuk, 1962; Thomas, 1954). As one machinery manufacturer reported, mill owners requested "self-operating machines which can be run by a boy and will make us independent of the unreliable class of workmen we are compelled to employ" (quoted in Gibb, 1950, p. 173). The same force—the mechanization of industry—that earlier had necessitated the importation of skilled labor now allowed employers to incorporate those skills into machinery and employ the abundance of unskilled labor now available.

At the same time that unskilled immigrants and machines replaced imported skilled labor, the Irish began to replace even the unskilled American women and children who worked the textile mills, the hub of early American industry. Before the Civil War, textile manufacturers had employed "all American girls" but changed to immigrant labor after the war because "not coming from country homes, but living as the Irish do, in the town, they take no vacations, and can be relied on at the mill all year around" (mill worker, quoted in Gutman, 1976, p. 21).

As attempted production changes and wage cuts in the textile industry met the resistance of native female employees in the 1840s, immigrant labor was recruited. By 1846, labor leaders maintained that working conditions in Rhode Island, where immigrant workers were already preferred by mill owners, were worse than in Lowell and other New England mills (*Voice of Industry*, 1846). The influx of Irish labor broke down the premium on hiring women and girls, since men could now be hired at even lower wages (Handlin, 1941, p. 78). By 1865, male workers (almost 100% immigrant) outnumbered females in the woolen industry and were narrowing the gap in the cotton industry.

Irish immigrants became a central component in the expanding iron industry, on construction crews, and in the lucrative boot and shoe industry. The boot and shoe industry was second only to textiles in this period, and with the invention of the sewing machine, the industry was revolutionized. This revolution depended as much on unskilled immigrant labor to operate the machines that replaced skilled bootmakers as on the innovations themselves: "Machines alone could not create a factory system in Boston when only the 473 tailors employed in 1845 were available to man them" (Handlin, 1941, p. 81). By 1850, as Boston became the immigrant labor reservoir of the country, the number of tailors had risen to 1547, and more than 1000 of these were Irish.

Side by side with increased immigration and mechanization, America's industries expanded in an apparently boundless burst of activity. In the period between 1843 and 1860, the total value of exports and imports in the United States rose from $125,250,000 to $687,200,000. Domestic trade increased 10-fold. Railroad trackage went from just 8500 miles in 1850 to 30,000 miles in 1860. The production of steam engines and other steam machines rose 387%, the production of agricultural tools rose 101%, and boot and shoe production was up 80%. The national production of coal increased 182% in these ten years and railroad iron by 100%. Southern cotton exports went from 2,469,000 bales in 1850 to 4,387,000 bales by 1860, and Illinois's export of wheat leaped from 9 million to 24 million bushels (Dinnerstein *et al.*, 1979; North, 1966).

Wages, however, were reduced wherever immigrants were found in large numbers. In 1860, in Boston, with its concentration of Irish, tailors were paid $4.50 to $5.50 a week, while in New York they received $8.00 to $10.00, even though the average value of goods produced by the Boston tailors was $1137, while that of the New York tailors was only $788 (Handlin, 1941, p. 83). Manufacturers stabilized wages in the New England textile mills after the influx of immigrant male workers in spite of inflation and an increase in the number of spindles operated by each worker. By 1860, productivity in the mills had skyrocketed. Wages remained, in absolute numbers, what they had been in 1820 (Ware, 1931). In general, wages increased little between 1840 and 1860, many wages were reduced in absolute terms, and real wages were reduced overall (see Table I, next page). The average worker's wages in this period were insufficient to cover even the estimated minimal expenses for a family of four (U.S. Bureau of Statistics of Labor, 1872).

Wage reductions were frequently achieved through the use of newly arrived immigrants as strike breakers. Strike after strike among machinists in Pittsburgh in the 1840s was broken by imported immigrants (Abbott, 1926, p. 294). Weavers' strikes in Kensington were repeatedly defeated by the recruitment of scab labor among recent immigrants (Montgomery, 1972). In 1849, on the eve of a journeyman's strike in Boston, manufacturers explained to Mayor Bigelow that since they now had access to a steady stream of new foreign labor, no arbitration with the striking workers was necessary (Handlin, 1941, p. 82).

TABLE I
Wages of Unskilled Labor (1840–1860)[a]

Year	Average wage	Year	Average wage
1840	$0.95	1851	$0.90
1841	0.91	1852	0.91
1842	0.86	1853	0.95
1843	0.79	1854	1.02
1844	0.83	1855	1.00
1845	0.85	1856	1.02
1846	0.91	1857	1.01
1847	0.91	1858	1.01
1848	0.89	1859	1.01
1849	0.93	1860	1.03
1850	0.91		

[a] Source: Aldrich Report Data, cited in Abbott, 1905, pp. 361, 365.

American capitalists did not leave such an advantageous situation to chance alone. Dinnerstein *et al.* (1979, p. 74) describe the triangular trade whereby New England merchants went south for cotton to carry to Europe, picking up workers and manufactured goods in Europe to carry back to New England. Employers readily recognized that it would be difficult to "obtain good interest for their money, were they deprived of this constant influx of foreign labor" (Chickering, 1851, p. 50).

It was not merely a labor supply that Irish, and increasingly German, immigrants offered U.S. capitalists. As Castels (1975) argues with regard to contemporary migratory movements in Western Europe, it is not just that immigration fills abstract manpower needs related to growth. Rather, immigrant labor is one of the "motors of this growth," not only because it is an extra source of labor but because of its position in the economic structure (p. 36). Above all, "the utility of immigrant labor to capital derives primarily from the fact that it can act towards it as though the labor movement did not exist" (p. 52). Working conditions and pay scales then reflect this ability to treat labor individually rather than collectively: "Immigrant workers do not exist because there are 'arduous and badly paid' jobs to be done, but, rather, arduous and badly paid jobs exist because immigrant workers are present or can be sent for" (Castels, 1975, p. 54).

Nativist Protest

If one requirement of capitalism is a cheap and tractable labor force, another is a minimum of social stability. The very factor—the influx of unskilled Irish and German workers—that guaranteed the one, threatened to undermine the other.

The population of the United States more than tripled from about 9,600,000 in 1820 to 31,500,000 by 1860, and immigrants and their children accounted for a large part of this increase (Taeuber and Taeuber, 1958; p. 294). While the numbers to enter the United States later in the century were greater in absolute terms, immigration between 1840 and 1860 was the highest, relative to the native population, the United States has ever experienced. The 3,000,000 who entered between 1845 and 1854, remember, landed in a nation of only 20,000,000 inhabitants.

Most of these immigrants were concentrated in the largest urban areas (U.S. Congress, Senate Immigration Commission, 1911, Vol. 1, p. 140), which grew precipitously. In 1820, only 7.2% of the population were city dwellers; by 1860, 19.8% lived in urban areas (Taeuber and Taeuber, 1958, p. 118). New York quadrupled its population in this period, Philadelphia grew fivefold, and the population of Boston more than tripled. The religious composition of the population changed dramatically also. By 1860, there were 3,000,000 Catholics in the United States, compared to only about 195,000 40 years earlier (Shaughnessy, 1925).

A disproportionate number of these immigrants were unskilled. In Jersey City, where most of the adult population by 1860 was foreign-born and 37% were Irish, two-thirds of the Irish were unskilled, supplying three-quarters of the total unskilled labor force (Shaw, 1976). It is not surprising that many of these Irish were impoverished, as business slumps hit them first and hardest, and their situation even in the best of times was precarious.

This combination of circumstances—an increasing and concentrated population of impoverished Catholic immigrants, rising prices and industrial expansion, coupled with the use of foreign labor to reduce wages and break strikes—precipitated the most violent and vehement anti-immigration protest in U.S. history.

Although American nativism began as an anti-Catholic movement, it was not until the alleged Catholic plot was linked to the immigration of foreign workers that it attracted the support of the

American laborers on a large scale and attained the wider base it required to gain momentum. Samuel Morse, later inventor of the telegraph and editor of the *New York Observer*, tied the spread of Catholicism to unrestricted immigration in his widely read book *Foreign Conspiracy* (1841). Morse claimed that the Pope's plan was to flood the United States with Catholic immigrants sufficient to stage an overthrow. Thereafter, immigration restriction became the primary topic in anti-Catholic and nativist papers, and Protestant papers daily printed statistics on the numbers coming in.

Beginning with the depression of 1837–1843, violent anti-immigrant protest was aimed less at religious targets and increasingly at the immigrants themselves. The Broad Street Riot in Boston in 1837, set off by a confrontation between an Irish funeral procession and local firefighters, drew a crowd of over 15,000. Rioters marched through the Irish sections of the city, burning and sacking, and forcing the Irish from their homes. Often the violence was explicitly labor related. American and foreign workers battled repeatedly on the railroads and in the textile mills of Philadelphia in 1844 (*Native American*, 1844a). Striking weavers in Kensington in 1842 rioted in the street, setting fire to immigrant strike breakers' unfinished work (Montgomery, 1972, p. 418). The same Kensington weaving district was destroyed by rioting workers in May 1843, as they protested the immigrant competition that had allowed employers to cut wages. In the notorious Kensington Riots of 1844, nativists burned the buildings and homes of immigrant weavers. After two days of rioting, 3000 troops arrived and put Kensington under martial law (Montgomery, 1972, p. 432). By the 1850s, nearly every state was racked with armed conflict between native and immigrant workers.

Anti-immigrant protest took less violent forms also. Native American political parties were organized, the most successful of which was the so-called Know-Nothing Party of the 1850s. With its anti-immigration stance and xenophobic slogans, the Know-Nothing Party was able to attract a large percentage of the working-class vote. In Massachusetts, a Know-Nothing governor was elected in 1854 with an unprecedented majority of 33,000 votes, and all the state's senators were Know-Nothings (Haynes, 1897, pp. 21–22). Delaware, Pennsylvania, and New York were predominantly Know-Nothing by 1854, and at the national level, 75 congressmen were Know-Nothing. By 1855, Rhode Island, New Hampshire, Connecticut, Maryland, and Kentucky had become Know-Nothing states, and gains were rapidly being made all over the South (Billington, 1938, pp. 388–389). It was widely predicted, even by Catholic papers, that by 1856 the president of the United States would be from the Know-Nothing Party. Probably due to the failure of Know-Nothing politicians to effect significant change, their political power soon began to wane. Millard Fillmore, the Know-Nothing presidential candidate in 1856, did manage to receive 900,000 votes to the Republicans' 1,300,000 and the Democrats' 1,800,000, not an unimpressive tally considering that the Know-Nothings could count on very few immigrant or Catholic votes.

At first glance, it might appear that nativism was an ethnic and moral movement, unrelated to class antagonisms. But it should be remembered that it was only when immigrants became a necessary instrument of American capital that they were welcomed in large numbers. In the precapitalist colonial period, Catholics had been officially barred from most colonies, and in the immediate post-Revolution period, the Irish and Germans had emigrated elsewhere, i.e., wherever there arose a demand for cheap labor. Thus, the formal cause and necessary condition of the protests was the sudden influx of foreign workers, precipitated by capital's need for surplus labor. The nativist protest could never have achieved the momentum and popular appeal that it did without tapping the American laborer's hostility to immigrants, *because* they were instrumental to capital in cheapening labor. While it is true that the origins of the movement were related to anti-Catholicism and the official leaders and founders were recruited largely from a conservative group of aristocratic Protestant elites (Lipset and Raab, 1970; Parnet, 1966; Shaw, 1976; Soule, 1960), its mass support ultimately came from a working class embittered over its worsening position. The later riots were less anti-Catholic *per se* and less motivated by a xenophobic hatred of immigrants, than they were a response to the deteriorating position of labor through mass immigration. In the Kensington riots, for example, the homes of Catholic *and* Protestant strike breakers were burned (Montgomery, 1972, p. 433). Similarly, the Know-Nothing Party appealed to a working class whose bargaining power was being eroded.

That most of the nativist parties' support came from the working class can be gleaned from voting patterns. In both New York and Boston, where the nativist movement was most solid, the wards consistently strongest in nativist voting patterns were in the Protestant working-class districts. Similarly, in New Orleans, Baltimore, and Worchester, Massachusetts, close to three-quarters of nativist voters were manual workers (Lipset and Raab, 1970, pp. 55–59). Edward Everett, a former Massachusetts senator, wrote of

Boston, "The rank and file of the Know-Nothing order is almost wholly . . . made up of the laboring classes" (quoted in Mulkern, 1963, p. 83).

Furthermore, it was not until nativist parties launched a campaign to attract American workers, that the movement grew. The American Republican Party's papers, *Native American* and *Native Eagle*, engaged in explicit attempts to attract the workingman into the party. They adopted as their motto, "Protection to American labor, by protecting the American laborer" (*Native Eagle*, 1845). The *Native American* (1844b) argued characteristically:

> Our laboring men . . . are met at every turn . . . with recently imported workmen from the low wages countries of the world. . . . They fill our large cities, reduce the wages of labor, and increase the hardships of the old settler.

The nativist paper in Boston, *The Boston Eagle*, made foreign labor competition its central focus and claimed that the American worker not only was forced into unfair competition but was

> the victim of capitalistic legislation. . . . We can see no reason why the laborer has not the same right to protection on his capital (labor) that the rich man has on his which is money. (quoted in Lipset and Raab, 1970, p. 51)

Numerous similar papers sprang up across the country in 1844 and 1845, and many established papers increasingly embraced the nativist cause (see Billington, 1938, p. 218, for a partial list of such papers). The New York nativist paper, the *American Republican*, had a circulation surpassed only by the *New York Sun* by the fall of 1844 (Billington, 1938, p. 209).

The nativist parties also derived support from workingmen's associations. The American Laboring Confederation and the Order of the United American Mechanics argued vehemently for immigration restrictions as protection against unfair labor competition. The American Laboring Confederation had developed spontaneously out of protest meetings in New York, Poughkeepsie, and Brooklyn. An announcement of one such meeting read,

> TO MECHANICS AND WORKINGMEN. . . . All who feel the effects of the depression of labor in consequence of the number of laborers from Europe, thrown upon this city and country, and are disposed to adopt measures for self-preservation, by restricting immigration, are invited to attend. (quoted in Ernst, 1948, p. 177)

31

The *Champion of American Labor*, the United American Mechanics' newspaper, similarly had the restriction of immigration as its aim. In 1847, it sponsored a petition, demanding a tax of $250 on each immigrant for the purpose of protecting the American worker (Ernst, 1948, pp. 180–181). The paper gave a voice to embittered workers by printing letters of complaints about unfair competition with immigrant workers. Shoemakers told of losing work several times within the year to "persons just come to this country, who will work for what I can't live on" (*Champion of American Labor*, May 1, 1847, quoted in Ernst, 1948, p. 176). Tailors argued that the price they got for coats was cut in half with the immigration of masses of German tailors. Skilled workers objected that their trades had been degraded by the introduction of technological improvements and untrained immigrants (cited in Ernst, 1948, p. 175).

By the time nativism had come to maturity, its parties and its press were to a large extent focused on the hostility of the American worker. Furthermore, the violent and impassioned element of nativism was distinctly working class. From the burning of the Ursuline Convent in 1834, the riots had become exclusively working class. Not only was there a conspicuous absence of the aristocratic leaders of the movement among the rioters, but the elite leaders were horrified by such displays of mob action. The Ursuline Convent burning brought together the elite citizens of Boston to denounce "the destruction of property and danger to life caused" (Billington, 1938, p. 85). Less predictably, the religious leaders of the anti-Catholic movement condemned the violence: "Do you wish to introduce a Protestant Inquisition?" (Billington, 1938, p. 86). The Kensington riots of the 1840s precipitated a similar response among Philadelphia elites who were sympathetic to the nativist cause. As Montgomery (1972, p. 437) puts it, "They were aghast at the mob forces which nativism had unleashed." A group of these elites sent a message to the governor in which they were careful to distinguish their brand of anti-Catholicism from such mob action:

> Religion and politics have nothing whatever to do with such men as have been acting in these scenes, nor such men with them. The rioters are men cast off from all respect for law, or for our institutions. . . . (quoted in Montgomery, 1972, p. 438)

As a remedy for this threatening situation, they advised the establishment of a permanent military force in Kensington.

By the end of the 1850s, the Know-Nothings were an almost exclusively working-class party. In New Orleans, where the nativist element was strong, the Know-Nothing Party

> ... was now [1858] in the hands of the ward clubs, located in neighborhoods inhabited by workingmen.
>
> ... Increasingly, the Know-Nothings depended upon and courted this element. (Soule, 1960, pp. 126–127)

So, while it is true that alliances in this period of nativism cut across class lines and nativist aims were fragmented and, in hindsight, not necessarily enlightened, both the origins of the movement and the momentum it achieved were grounded in the capital-labor contradiction.[2] It was the immigrants' role in the class struggle that determined both the welcome accorded them by American employers and the hostility of the native worker.

State Inaction

None of this nativist agitation resulted in any change in the prevailing open-door policy. State response to the violence of the 1830s and 1840s focused on the more effective repression of such episodes rather than any serious reconsideration of immigration law. The Ursuline Convent burning of 1834 produced a "Bill More Effectively to Suppress Riots" (Commonwealth of Massachusetts, 1835, pp. 1–5). The Kensington riots precipitated a meeting of local and national elites who urged that there must be "paid police on a basis which would always be in action—like Sir Robert Peel's men in England" (quoted in Montgomery, 1972, p. 437). In Boston and Kensington, the elites got some of the first professionally trained police in the United States. Working-class protesters got continued immigration.

No bills related to the restriction or regulation of immigration were even brought to a vote in Congress. As a result of insistent petitions from various northeastern states (*Congressional Globe*, 1836, p. 373; U.S. Congress, House Executive Documents, 1836; U.S. Congress, Senate Documents, 1836a), the Senate in 1836 agreed to a resolution directing the State Department to collect information on the immigration of paupers and criminals. After a reply that no such information was available (U.S. Congress, Senate Documents, 1836a), the Senate sent the task to the treasury department (*Congressional Globe*, 1836, pp. 414, 614). The Treasury Department Report (U.S. Congress, Senate Documents, 1836b) confirmed that several European governments were assisting paupers and criminals to emigrate, yet no further action was taken until 1836. This time, a house resolution directed the Committee on the Judiciary to consider a revision of naturalization laws as well as the advisability of prohibiting the immigration of paupers deported from abroad. Again, the conclusion of this committee was that

> The fact is unquestionable that large numbers of foreigners are annually brought to our country by the authority, and at the expense of, foreign governments, and landed upon our shores in a state of absolute destitution and dependency. (U.S. Congress, House Report, 1838, p. 9)

Legislation to restrict the immigration of paupers, as well as the immigration of lunatics, idiots, the diseased, and convicts, was recommended (U.S. Congress, House Report, 1838). Again, Congress did not consider the bill. No vote was taken, nor was the bill revived in the next Congress, despite renewed demands by petitioners.

Not until 1844, the year of the worst Kensington riots, did Congress again address nativist demands. By then, the period required for the naturalization of immigrants was a major issue among nativists, not only because of a fear of the immigrants' economic and political influence, but because a short naturalization period was thought to encourage immigration (*Native Eagle*, 1846a,b). Petitions from western states requesting investigations into a 21-year naturalization period were read in the House of Representatives in May 1844, but the matter was tabled without being sent to committee (*Congressional Globe*, 1844a, p. 674). Later petitions were referred to the judiciary committee where they piled up month after month.

By December 1844, a resolution was finally submitted requiring the judiciary committee of the Senate to inquire into the

> expediency of modifying the naturalization laws of the U.S., so as to extend the time allowed to enable foreigners to become citizens, to prevent, as far as is practicable, frauds and violence at elections, . . . and to prohibit the introduction of foreign convicts into the U.S. (*Congressional Globe*, 1844b, pp. 19, 32)

The committee, however, did not concern itself with the extension of the length of the naturalization period, nor with the immigration of convicts (i.e., those issues of most concern to nativists); even its narrow recommendations designed to prevent voting fraud were ignored (U.S. Congress, Senate Documents, 1845).

The House Committee on the Judiciary in December 1845 was similarly asked to review the issue of naturalization laws. The committee's report concluded that "no alteration of the naturalization laws is necessary" (*Congressional Globe*, 1846, p. 353).

The rapid growth of the Know-Nothing Party in the 1850s precipitated another brief and ineffective flurry of congressional debates over naturalization laws and the barring of certain types of immigrants. Petitions from New England states in 1854 requested that consideration be given again to a naturalization period of 21 years (U.S. Congress, Senate Miscellaneous Documents, 1855; U.S. Congress, House Miscellaneous Documents, 1855). The wording of these petitions and Senator Stephen Adams's introduction of the bill embodying the naturalization proposal suggest that the demand for a 21-year naturalization period emanated from a desire to discourage immigration. Adams argued,

> . . . believing as I do, that the facility with which they become citizens serves as a great stimulant to immigration, I desire to see it changed. (*Congressional Globe*, 1854, p. 26)

The bill was sent as usual to the judiciary committee, where it remained. Although Adams reintroduced the bill in the Senate in the next Congress, it died without a whimper (*Congressional Globe*, 1856, pp. 350, 616).

Finally, a bill was introduced in the House in January 1855 which would have made illegal the importation of foreign "paupers, criminals, lunatics, and the blind" (*Congressional Globe*, 1855, pp. 166–167). This too died without a vote, as it was considered unconstitutional and "an infringement on states' rights." Congress, it was argued, did not have the right to bar any class of immigrants (U.S. Congress, Reports of Congressional Committees, 1856).

While bills to regulate immigration were consistently disregarded, bills to facilitate immigration were passed without difficulty. In 1847 and 1848, despite vehement opposition by nativists, the Passenger Law of 1819 was amended to improve steerage conditions on immigrant ships. In 1854, while Know-Nothings were unsuccessfully introducing bills to extend the naturalization period, the act that organized the territories of Nebraska and Kansas provided that suffrage be extended immediately there to all those who declared the intention of becoming citizens, in an explicit effort to encourage immigration (U.S. Congress, Senate

Immigration Commission, 1911, Vol. 1; p. 564). Finally, the Supreme Court, in the so-called Passenger Cases beginning in 1849, began to question the constitutionality of individual state laws regulating immigration. In 1849, Massachusetts's and New York's policy of imposing a head tax on landing immigrants was declared unconstitutional, and by 1876, all state laws that regulated immigration were declared void (U.S. Congress, Senate Immigration Commission, 1911, Vol. 1, p. 568).

President Tyler's message to Congress on June 1, 1841, provides a good summary of immigration policy in this period:

> We hold out to the people of other countries an invitation to come and settle among us as members of our rapidly growing family. (quoted in U.S. Congress, Senate Immigration Commission, 1911, Vol. 1, p. 562)

Billington (1938, p. 417) notes that Know-Nothing leaders, once in power, failed to effect any change. He accounts for this legislative inaction in response to widespread nativist demands on the grounds that "its principles were inimical to those on which the American nation had been founded; its demands were of a sort that could never be realized in a country constituted as was the United States." His explanation is misleading on both counts: (1) "the American nation had been founded" on colonies that had stringent immigration laws much like those that nativists demanded in the 1850s, and (2) such changes in immigration as the nativists demanded *could* "be realized in a country constituted like the United States" and indeed *were* realized in later immigration legislation. It is more likely that the legislative inaction in response to the conflict between capital's need for a cheap and tractable labor force versus the nativist protest that immigration evoked is tied to the fact that (1) the source of the conflict was protest over underlying conditions and not the conditions themselves; (2) the nativist struggle was fragmented and without the benefit of an organized labor movement; and (3) capital's rapid expansion was critically linked to just those conditions being protested, i.e., an ever-increasing stream of immigrant labor.

The Civil War Period: State Encouragement of Immigration

A comparison of legislative action on immigration in the Civil War period lends further support to this interpretation. The Civil War, not coincidentally, both hushed the voice of nativist protest and depleted the surplus labor supply. Just as the war increased the need for immigration as industry expanded for war production, the war reduced the flow of immigration sharply. Making things worse for the American industrialist, as immigration was cut in half, an estimated one and one-quarter million laborers left the labor force for the army.

What trade union movement had existed prior to 1857 had almost dissolved under the combined impetus of the 1857–1862 depression and the disbanding of whole union locals as their members joined the army. By the end of 1862, it was clear that despite rising prices and unprecedented industrial profits, wages would remain below subsistence level in the absence of an organized labor effort. The following year brought just such an effort. Strike after successful strike in 1863 achieved wage increases and a restrengthening of the trade union movement. The *Springfield Republican* on March 26, 1863, noted that

> . . . the workingmen of almost every branch of trade have had their strikes within the last few months. . . . In almost every instance the demands of the employed have been acceded to. The strikes, which have all been conducted very quickly . . . have led to the formation of numerous leagues or unions. (quoted in Boyer and Morais, 1980, p. 25)

The *San Francisco Evening Bulletin* on November 5, 1863, wrote, ". . . striking for higher wages is now the rage among the working people of San Francisco" (quoted in Boyer and Morais, 1980, p. 25). With immigration reduced by the war, labor's efforts paid off well. Not only did wages improve, but union membership went from just a few thousand in 1861 to over 200,000 in 1864 (Boyer and Morais, 1980, p. 26).

Just as workers in the 1840s and 1850s recognized that it was the constant influx of immigrants that defeated their efforts then, capitalists in the 1860s were quick to pinpoint the source of their powerlessness now. By late 1863 and 1864, mine operators, iron manufacturers, and railroad officials launched regular complaints relating to the decrease in immigration, the loss of a surplus labor force, and consequent wage increases (Pittsburgh and Boston Mining Company, *Annual Report* [1864]: 8; Belmont Coal Mining Company, *Report* [1863]: 12; Mount Pleasant Coal Company, *Report* [April 1864]: 4; Lehigh Valley Coal Company, *Annual Report* [1864]: 16; Bear Valley Coal Company, *First Report of Directors* [October 1864]: 23; Harewood Iron and Mining Company, *Report of Directors* [Boston, 1864]; Atlantic and Great Western, *Annual Report* [1864]: 5–6; Cleveland and Pittsburgh Railroad, *Annual*

Report [1863]: 10; *Hardware Reporter*, October 1863: 3, all cited in Erickson, 1957, p. 200).

Many of the same tactics used earlier were readopted by capital in an attempt to solve its current problem. More reliance was placed on machinery, and the number of innovations surpassed that of any previous period. Fite (1910, p. 197) notes the "remarkable increase" in the number of patents issued in this period. Resistant workmen were increasingly replaced by women and blacks, just as unskilled immigrants had been used to replace skilled labor in the earlier period. Striking printers, dissatisfied clerks, and operatives in light industries were superseded by women (Fite, 1910, p. 188). While blacks had previously been excluded from most industries, they were now used to break strikes. Striking longshoremen, most of whom were Irish, were often replaced by blacks. Just as the earlier conflict between capital's need to maximize surplus value versus the power of relatively scarce labor now repeated itself, the attempted solution was similar, i.e., the use of an industrial reserve and mechanization to defeat worker resistance. So too was the reaction of labor similar to that of the earlier period, as the Irish, who had been part of capital's earlier solution, clashed now with black strike breakers.

The draft riots in 1863 in New York, in which thousands of Irish rioted against military service on behalf of their black rivals, were a culmination of antipathies created by the class struggle much as the earlier nativist riots had been (Jones, 1960, pp. 173–174). The Irish similarly struck in protest over being replaced by machinery. In 1862, 2000 Irish launched an unsuccessful strike in New York against the use of floating grain elevators. The following year, just as their colleagues across the East River were protesting the draft, Irish workers in Brooklyn burned down two large elevators (Fite, 1910).

The state reaction to the reduction in immigration, strikes, and rising wages was quick. The Tariff Acts of 1862 and 1864 were one response, as they were aimed at protecting American capital from the effects of rising wages. Congress passed duties on almost all imported goods (except, of course, imported workers). By 1862 duties averaged 37%, and in 1864, after only 5 days of debate, Congress raised duties to at least 47% on every imported good, with some items taxed as much as 80% (Weisberger, 1969, p. 26). Although these tariffs were supposed to be war measures, they remained in force for decades after the war had ended, freeing U.S. industry to raise prices almost indefinitely.

The state also engaged in direct attempts to increase immigration. In 1861 Henry Carey, a prominent American economist who advocated the combination of protective tariffs and immigration as the way to speed up industrialization, had convinced Secretary of the Treasury Salmon Chase of the merits of direct government inducement of immigration. In 1862 Secretary of State William Seward saturated U.S. officials in Europe with pamphlets for distribution, advertising high wages in the United States and publicizing the advantages of the Homestead Act, in an effort to induce immigration. To this end, the U.S. Consul in London in 1863 employed a full-time agent to stir up emigration to the United States (Erickson, 1957, p. 8).

That same year President Abraham Lincoln, in his annual address to Congress, called attention to the need for laborers and pressed for more effective government action to stimulate immigration. On July 4, 1864, the Act to Encourage Immigration was passed (13 U.S. Statutes at Large). The Homestead Act had attracted many immigrants to the United States, but it had the effect of enticing many away from industry. Furthermore, the Union army attracted thousands of recently recruited immigrants with bounties far greater than an unskilled laborer's earnings. The 1864 law, in an effort to curb the numbers of immigrants who left industry for homesteading and army enlistment, made pre-emigration contracts binding. It was believed that making such contracts binding before the courts would also encourage employers to increase their importations by making imported labor more reliable. In anticipation of possible objections, Congress announced self-consciously that "no such contract would in any way be considered as creating a condition of slavery" (U.S. Congress, Senate Immigration Commission, 1911, Vol. 1, p. 565). In addition to making contracts binding, the law provided that no immigrant could be involuntarily drafted, thereby allaying any fears of a potential immigrant that he might be drafted upon arrival.

An equally important provision of the law established the first Federal Bureau of Immigration. The Senate Committee on Agriculture, in recommending this provision, declared that "The advantages which have accrued heretofore from immigration can scarcely be computed." It was particularly important to facilitate immigration now, the report went on, as "the demand for labor ... never [was] greater," and, after the war, the South would require cheap immigrant labor as well (U.S. Congress, Senate Report, 1864, pp. 1–8). A commissioner of immigration was appointed by the president to enforce the bill's provisions, and an immigration office was established in New York for the purpose of arranging for the transportation of immigrants to their destinations. In addition, the bill ordered the commissioner to encourage U.S. consuls abroad to advertise the advantageous terms of the act.

The discussions surrounding the creation of the Federal Bureau of Immigration and the New York immigration office make it clear that the intent was the redevelopment of a surplus labor force. Senator John Sherman reminisced in 1884 that the only argument put forth for the law was the high price of labor (*Congressional Record*, 1884, p. 1785). While Congress had not intervened to limit or even regulate immigration in the face of 30 years of nativist outcry, a momentary lapse in immigration and a reduction of surplus labor sent state actors scurrying to restore the surplus.

Although the Act to Encourage Immigration was repealed in 1868, it was largely responsible for the emergence of a variety of private agencies of labor recruitment that continued for many years to be an important force behind the immigrant stream.

Two labor recruitment agencies were the direct outcome of the state's efforts to promote immigration: the Foreign Emigrant Aid Society and the American Emigrant Company. By 1863, Secretary of State Seward's propaganda on American wage rates and working conditions was having a profound effect, and thousands of aspiring immigrants were applying at American consulates in Europe for help in emigrating. In response Seward advised the Boston Board of Trade that manufacturers might collectively raise the money for transportation costs.

Some industrialists were already beginning to unite to recruit immigrant labor. Mining companies in the Lake Superior region were pooling resources to import labor, and the Philadelphia iron industry was initiating a similar move (Erickson, 1957, p. 7). Late in 1863, in reaction to the information communicated by Seward and as a culmination of tentative steps to import labor collectively, a meeting of some of the most important manufacturers of textiles, machinery, and iron was held at the Boston Board of Trade, out of which the Foreign Emigrant Aid Society was formed. The society comprised the prominent manufacturers and capitalists of New England and began with a sum of $200,000 for loans to immigrants "to induce them to join us" (quoted in Erickson, 1952, p. 68).

At the same time the American Emigrant Company was formed with an operating budget of $1,000,000 (Fite, 1910, p. 191). From the beginning it was connected to the newly created Federal Bureau of Immigration, even sharing offices with the immigration superintendent in New York. This company specialized in spreading propaganda throughout Europe on the benefits of emigration to the United States and educating U.S. capitalists on the merits of contract labor from Europe. The American Emigrant

Company was indeed, as it referred to itself, the "handmaid of the new Immigration Bureau" (quoted in Erickson, 1957, p. 13). After the war E. Pershine Smith, a Carey enthusiast instrumental in persuading Secretary of State Seward on the merits of government-induced immigration, was appointed commissioner of immigration. Pointing to the "continued success of strikes by workmen of almost all kinds," Smith saw his primary duty to be the encouragement of immigration (Smith, quoted in Erickson, 1957, p. 13).

The combined effect of legislative efforts to encourage immigration and industry's related efforts quickly achieved results. Although immigration in the two-year period 1861–1862 reached only 89,000, it averaged 200,000 *per year* in 1863, 1864, and 1865 (Fite, 1910, p. 196). By 1865, wages were again reduced, as strike after strike was defeated with the use of blacks and immigrants (Foner, 1955). Overall, real wages for the war period were cut in half (Fite, 1910, p. 184).

Notes

1. The idealist interpretation of this change to an open-door immigration policy in the nineteenth century is quite common and is laid out succinctly by Hansen (1940a, p. 4): ". . . nineteenth century liberalism did not relish restrictions upon the individual; and as its doctrines became embodied in official policies, the regulations [of the pre-industrial era] were modified, and then repealed or allowed to fall into disuse." That this is an inadequate explanation for laissez-faire immigration policies is clear from even a cursory look at tariff acts in this same period. While labor was not protected from competition by foreign immigrant labor, tariff acts throughout the century guaranteed American capital a significant level of protection. From 1816 until the Civil War, tariffs on manufactured goods averaged about 20–24%, were raised during the war to an average of 47%, and remained essentially steady throughout the rest of the century (Weisberger, 1969). This glaring inconsistency between the protection accorded labor and that accorded capital in this period puts to rest any interpretation of the open-door immigration policy that is based entirely on the concept of liberalism.

2. Montgomery (1972) traces this fragmentation of aims and lack of class solidarity in "The Shuttle and the Cross: Weavers and Artisans in the Kensington Riots of 1844." According to Montgomery, an initial awakening of class solidarity, which he calls "as significant as any in American history" (p. 419), disintegrated in the depression of

1839–1843, to be replaced by an anticollectivist self-improvement theme. He relates the development of the self-improvement ideology to the "bible-reading issue" and the temperance movement of the anti-Catholic elite. Educators such as Dewey in Massachusetts saw "moral education" as the solution to "combinations of the employed to secure higher wages" and "political workingmen's parties" (quoted in Montgomery, 1972, p. 424). According to Dewey, the study of the Protestant Bible in schools would increase literacy and morality simultaneously. The Bible-reading issue had the effect Dewey had hoped for, but in an ironic way. Catholic immigrants, objecting to the use of the Protestant Bible in their schools, were singled out as an immoral element in society. The temperance movement was focusing at the same time on the immigrant's drinking habits, so that the immigrant's personal attributes were increasingly at issue. Not only did this fragment the aims of the nativists, but it tended to displace hostilities aroused by the economic system onto the supposed personal attributes of the immigrant. Working-class anger was further displaced onto the person of the immigrant by the rapid rise in poverty concomitant with increased immigration.

3 ▪ Symbolic Law and the Emergence of New Conflicts, 1865–1900

Industrial Expansion and Immigration in the Late 1800s

The last four decades of the nineteenth century were unique in American history in terms of industrial and capital expansion. Between the end of the Civil War and the turn of the century, the number of manufacturing establishments in the United States more than doubled and production increased fourfold (Clark, 1929). The value of manufactured products rose from $1,885,862,000 in 1860 to $11,406,927,000 in 1900 (Bimba, 1927). To put this growth in relative terms, the United States went from fourth place, behind England, France, and Germany, in the production of industrial goods in 1860 to an unrivaled first place by 1894. By the turn of the century, it produced one-third of the world's total industrial output, an amount almost equal to that of England, France, and Germany combined.

Again, mechanization was a central component of this expansion. "Horsepower," increasing 18-fold between 1860 and 1900, replaced "manpower" in all industries as new energy sources became available and innovations continued to proliferate. By the 1870s, patents were granted on an average of 13,000 annually, and by the 1880s, 21,000 was the annual average. It was widely recognized by both American capitalists and their European competitors that a major element of America's industrial lead was her unrivaled mechanization of production.

It was not just increased productivity per worker that mechanization contributed in this period of strong unionism. Rather, mechanization allowed manufacturers to displace unionized labor with the thousands of unskilled, nonunionized immigrants that entered the country each month. As one labor representative put it, so-called "labor-saving machines" were more accurately "wage-saving and labor-displacing machines" (quoted in Foner, 1955, p. 14).

In the textile industry, mechanization was a conscious strategy to circumvent workers' demands. The National Association of Wool

Manufacturers (NAWM) advised in 1878 that the use of machinery to replace skilled workmen was an especially effective policy in times of strikes (National Association of Wool Manufacturers, 1878). By the late 1870s, wool manufacturers were regularly replacing skilled handjack spinners with machinery and unskilled laborers, because, as one manufacturer put it, "of the disorderly habits of English skilled workmen" (Hayes, 1879, pp. 31–32). In the cotton mills of the 1890s, ring frames for spinning, the Northrup loom, and other new automatic machinery enabled manufacturers to dispense with the skilled and unionized craftsman. The overseer of the spinning department in a large cotton mill in Maine in the 1890s reported that more than 60,000 mule spindles had already been thrown out of the mill, partly because the mule spinners were "always out to strike" (Young, 1903, p. 45). When mule spinners at one Fall River mill in the 1890s demanded higher pay, they were easily replaced. "On Saturday afternoon after they had gone home," the superintendent chuckled to a British reporter (Young, 1903, p. 4),

> we started right in and smashed up a room full of mules with sledge hammers.... On Monday morning they were astonished to find that there was no work for them. That room is now full of ring frames run by girls.

In an aside, Young (1903; p. 34) notes,

> The association of machine smashing with the introduction of labor-saving appliances is nothing new; but whereas formerly laborers smashed the new machines to protect the old, now capital smashes the old machines to protect the new.

By 1889, unskilled French-Canadian, Mediterranean, and Slavic ring spinners, operating at $6 to $8 a week, had been substituted for skilled English, Scottish, and Irish mule spinners at $12 to $14 a week (*Massachusetts Labor Bulletin*, 1905; U.S. Congress, Senate Immigration Commission, 1911, Vol. I, pp. 34–37).

Mechanization, particularly the introduction of the Bessemer process, similarly revolutionized the iron and steel industry (Berthoff, 1953; Brody, 1960; Fitch, 1911). It not only reduced the number of puddlers, the most skilled and unionized of iron workers, but it made possible the introduction of unskilled, unorganized immigrants as strike breakers.

Just as crucial as mechanization to American industrial expansion was the continued increase in immigration. Twenty-five million immigrants entered the United States in this period, most of them remaining in the cities and joining the industrial work force. By 1880, more than 70% of the populations in each of America's largest cities were immigrants or children of immigrants, and the proportion was not much lower in the small industrial towns of the East. The foreign-born increasingly made up the bulk of the industrial labor force. Samuel Lane Loomis (quoted in Gutman, 1976, p. 40) noted in 1887 that "Not every foreigner is a working man, but in the cities, at least, it may almost be said that every workingman is a foreigner."

This immigrant influx can be attributed in part to the continued recruitment efforts of a wide variety of interested parties. In 1868, the same year that the Contract Labor Law of the Civil War period was repealed, all American consuls in Northern Europe were urged to encourage people to emigrate to the United States (U.S. Congress, House Committee on Foreign Affairs, 1868). Southern and midwestern states had state immigration commissions whose sole purpose was the recruitment of immigrants to their states. Railroad agents interested both in inducing immigrants to purchase land and in acquiring construction workers advertised that they would "employ all the labor that may be offered," that there was "abundant employment," and that "willing hands do not wait long for employment" (quoted in Erickson, 1957, p. 75). Steamship agents interested in recruiting passengers

> cover[ed] Italy as the locusts covered Egypt.... They paint the charms of big wages in the U.S.... There is a good deal of emigration that is assisted by rhetoric as well as by logic. (an agent of the U.S. State Department, quoted in Stephenson, 1926, p. 71)

A Senate immigration commission in 1911 (U.S. Congress, Senate Immigration Commission, 1911, Vol. I, p. 190) reported that in these years, two steamship companies employed 5000 agents in Galicia alone "in a great hunt for emigration."

The Mobilization of Labor: 1865–1885

As Boyer and Morais (1980, pp. 21–22) describe this era, in the midst of the unparalleled expansion of industry and the concentration of more and more capital in fewer and fewer hands, "Everything would have been perfect in a perfect world had it not been for certain unfortunate aspects of the rising industrial system." Paramount was the fact that this industrial system was producing class struggle and a militant labor movement as systematically as it produced commodities and profits.

By 1885, a national labor movement had developed in the United States unlike any that had been seen before. John Swinton (1894, preface), the prolific labor journalist of the period, warned, "The times are revolutionary. There is a new spirit abroad."

This epoch in labor history, which culminated in the unprecedented power of the Knights of Labor by 1885, began in the last years of the Civil War and can best be described as a period of the tightening of ranks of capital and labor, as troops mobilizing for battle.

As the war came to a close, it was clear that capital could no longer be fought by a few local craft unions, because, while the country itself was divided by the Civil War, its capital was being concentrated and power centralized. Without wider labor organizations, one labor leader urged in 1863, "capital and capitalists will have the industrial classes *completely* within their grasp" (Andrews, quoted in Foner, 1962, p. 339; emphasis in the original). When the National Labor Union united local unions into one national organization in 1866, a new era in the capital-labor struggle was initiated. It was now, and would continue to be, a struggle organized at the national level; by the end of one civil war, the battle lines had been drawn for another, much longer one.

Labor's newly acquired ability to wage crippling strikes energized, and was made possible by, the powerful postwar labor movement. Striking workers in the anthracite mines of Pennsylvania, organized by John Siney in the Workingman's Benevolent Association, achieved a 10% wage increase for these mostly Welsh- and Irish-born miners. By 1870, wages in the anthracite industry were higher than ever, and more than 85% of the anthracite miners were union members (Boyer and Morais, 1980; Commons, 1918; Erickson, 1957; Foner, 1962; Ware, 1929).

Many of the locals backed by the National Labor Union were successful in their strikes for the eight-hour day. In 1872, the eight-hour strike movement began with a three-month strike of 100,000 New York City workers in the well-organized building trades (Adamic, 1963, p. 25; Boyer and Morais, 1980; Commons, 1918; Foner, 1962). The building trade unions in New York won their fight for an eight-hour day, and similar victories followed in city after city (Foner, 1962).

Although the depression of 1873–1878 wiped out most of these labor victories (by 1877, less than one-fifth of the work force was regularly employed and wages had been cut in most industries by 40–60%), capital had been challenged as never before and not even the devastation of the depression completely halted labor's progress. While strikes were less frequent in this period of desperation, that desperation precipitated massive demonstrations, the advance of socialist ideologies, and the formation of socialist political parties. Furthermore, capitalists were not free from the spontaneous resistance of workers pushed to their limits. In the Baltimore and Ohio Railroad strikes, federal troops had to be called in, as local militias frequently joined the strikers. Although the strikers ultimately lost this battle, "the underdog had given capitalism in America its first big scare" (Adamic, 1963, p. 36).

This was the period of the maturation of the first major national labor union in the United States. The Noble and Holy Order of the Knights of Labor had been formed in 1869 with regional groupings of laborers from various occupations. Unlike other unions of the period, this secret organization continued to grow and expand throughout the depression of 1873–1878. From 1881, when Terence Powderly became "Grand Master Workman" of the organization and the secrecy principle was formally revoked, until 1886 when the Knights of Labor went into decline, the Knights attained a position of power previously unknown in the labor movement. Membership rose from about 20,000 in 1881 to triple that by 1884, and membership in 1886 has been estimated at between 700,000 and 1,000,000 (Bimba, 1927; Boyer and Morais, 1980, p. 89; Foner, 1955, p. 54; Hillquit, 1965). Even more important than its numerical strength was its promotion of labor solidarity by providing the arena in which the various craft unions could unify their strength nationally and by successfully bringing together for the first time the skilled and the unskilled, the native and the foreign-born, into one national organization.

With nearly a million members and financial stability, the Knights of Labor backed skirmish after skirmish on the industrial battlefield and came through it with a significant record of success. Foner (1955, p. 47) emphasizes their unique importance: "The meteoric career of this organization has had few if any parallels in the history of the labor movement of the world. . . . All previous labor movements in the United States seem insignificant in contrast." The successful Gould Strike of 1885 is perhaps most indicative of the Knights of Labor strength, as labor took on Jay Gould, one of the most powerful of the robber barons, and won.

Although many of these successful strikes were followed by counterattacks from capital and many of their gains ultimately diminished, labor's vehement and persistent struggle did win labor some concessions. According to a report by the Pennsylvania

Bureau of Labor Statistics, real wages increased in the period 1865–1873, largely as a result of labor union activity (Pennsylvania Bureau of Labor Statistics, 1873). Furthermore, the wage increases in industries in which workers were organized were 40% higher than in industries with unorganized workers. The New Jersey Bureau of Labor Statistics (1887) reported that of 890 labor disputes in New Jersey in the period 1881–1887, 6% ended in compromise, 40% ended in the employer making gains, and 54% ended in worker victories. In 80% of the industrial battles in New Jersey involving hours and wages, the workers won.

It was not by coincidence that the decades following the Civil War posed problems for American capital somewhat reminiscent of those of 50 years earlier. While the immigration of hundreds of thousands of Irish, German, and other Northern European immigrants had temporarily resolved the problem of "belligerent" and independent skilled labor, the capital-labor antagonism had remained untouched. The degradation of labor through mechanization and the expansion of the work force through immigration had in one sense weakened the position of labor, yet the potential power of labor was advanced as the ever-increasing proletariat responded to capital's declaration of war by a tightening of ranks. This new-found power of labor via unions and strikes was in some ways more threatening than their earlier belligerence based on a relative labor scarcity. As Engels (1950, pp. 218–219) put it,

> What gives unions and the strikes arising from them their real importance is ... that they are the first attempt of the workers to abolish competition. They imply the recognition of the fact that the supremacy of the bourgeoisie is based wholly upon the competition of the workers among themselves; i.e., upon their want of cohesion. And precisely because the unions direct themselves against the vital nerve of the present social order, however one-sidedly, in however narrow a way, are they so dangerous to this social order. The workingmen cannot attack the bourgeoisie, and with it the whole existing order of society, at any more sour point than this.

Not surprisingly, the Irish and German immigrants, who had initially supplied capital with a cheap and tractable work force, acquired the tactics and attitudes of industrial class struggle as inevitably as they acquired other industrial skills. If the conflict now —that of the power of labor versus the maximization of profit— was similar to that of 50 years earlier, so was its temporary solution. Once again, the continued influx of hundreds of thousands of

European immigrants each year provided capital with some alleviation.

Foreign Contract Labor and the Private Labor Exchange

During and immediately after the Civil War, employers resorted to importing immigrant workers for the purpose of breaking strikes and generally undermining unions. The *Workingman's Advocate* (1869b, p. 2), a Chicago labor paper, noted the trend:

> Ever since the completion of the Atlantic telegraph, it has been the threat of unprincipled employers, in every state where unpleasantness has occurred, to threaten the importation of foreign workmen, and in many instances they have been enabled to put their threats into execution.

Bricklayers, carpenters, printers, and stonemasons saw strike after strike defeated in the 1860s as employers advertised in British papers or sent agents to Britain to hire strike breakers (*Workingman's Advocate*, 1867, 1869a). Workers in the iron industry, mining, and railroads were particularly plagued by the practice. In 1865–1866, emigration agencies supplied British workers as strike breakers in the coal mines of Pennsylvania, West Virginia, and Illinois where workers were resisting wage reductions (Erickson, 1957, p. 50). Ironworkers in Pittsburgh recalled that in 1866, when they protested their employers' attempts to reduce wages, they were "triumphantly told by [their] employers that 800 puddlers from England were hourly expected at New York, and were coming on here to take [their] places at reduced wages" (quoted in Erickson, 1957, p. 53).

Despite employers' occasional successes in breaking strikes with imported workers, the system had one major drawback. The very union strength that made such importations necessary also made it likely that the union might succeed in persuading immigrants to break their contracts and join the struggle, or leave the area. Frequently, for example, imported British miners, when it had become clear that they were to be used to break a strike, either joined the American union or returned to England, declaring that contracts made under "false pretenses" were not morally or legally binding (*Workingman's Advocate*, 1873). Similarly, 800 "puddlers from England" who were "hourly expected" proved unsatisfactory. As soon as the first fifteen arrived, the Sons of Vulcan persuaded them to join their strike.

The Iron Molders Union, led by William Sylvis, was particularly adept at communicating with potential strike breakers. An 1864 strike of stove and machine foundry workers in St. Louis had prompted employers to import 25 German molders to replace the strikers. Their contract stipulated that the Germans would work for $2 a day (while other molders earned $3) and would "not . . . join any clubs or associations, of which in any way harm or disadvantage could arise to Mr. Filley [sic]," the employer (contract quoted in Grossman, 1945, pp. 281–282). Union members, having learned of the importation scheme, met the German molders as they changed trains in Indianapolis. Upon arrival in St. Louis, the immigrants broke their contracts and joined the triumphant Iron Molders Union.

Because of this potential loss of new immigrants to the unions, it was necessary to import more workers than were actually needed. The payment of passage money for more immigrants than were ultimately used was, of course, financially burdensome. The uncertainties of the economy made formal contracts with European workers even more problematic, as economic collapse every six or seven years made it quite likely that contract workers would have to be carried over periods of unemployment by the employer. Furthermore, American capitalists had to secure European strike breakers as quickly as possible when they were needed, and while large American port cities increasingly served as reservoirs of immigrant labor, their transportation to the strike location remained problematic.

The private labor exchange fit well into this set of circumstances, and it remained the primary mechanism by which immigrant labor was distributed for several decades. Most of these private labor bureaus were concentrated in New York. Located on Greenwich and Mulberry Streets directly opposite the Castle Garden depot where most immigrants landed, by 1906 there were at least 61 such labor exchanges. Nor were these agencies small concerns. One agency's circulars advertised that 20,000 workers could be supplied (*John Swinton's Paper*, February 1, 1885, cited in Erickson, 1957, p. 100). An order was filled for 5000 workers in 1885; in 1883, 11,000 immigrant workers were supplied to the New York and West Shore Railroad; one batch of 3000 was sold to an employer in Pennsylvania (Erickson, 1957, pp. 100–101). All were apparently provided "at a moment's notice" (*Congressional Record*, 1885, p. 1633) and none at superfluous expense or risk to the employer. The usual fee of $1 per worker was minimal, particularly because many labor exchanges supplied labor at below the usual pay scale.

Immigrant workers supplied by the exchanges worked in Pennsylvania mines for as little as $.80 a day, about one-half the going rate (*John Swinton's Paper*, 1884a,b). Workers from the New York City Italian Labor Bureau worked for $.50 to $.60 a day and the Bureau guaranteed "that the laborers will serve from one to five years without demanding an increase" (U.S. Congress, Senate Committee on Education and Labor, 1885, Vol. I, pp. 810–811). The higher fee of $2 per immigrant worker for strikebreakers was a small price to pay for the freedom to ignore workers' demands.

By the 1880s, the private labor exchange was the established system of distributing immigrant labor.[1] The direct contract system was resorted to only when highly skilled labor was required. Traveling to Italy to investigate the extent of the contract labor system, Powderly (by then, immigration commissioner) requested contract labor from an Italian agent. The agent was shocked that he had traveled all the way to Italy "when it could have been done just as well by the agents in Mulberry Street, New York" (quoted in U.S. Secretary of the Treasury Report, 1892, p. 300). In fact it could be done better by the agents in Mulberry Street, as the labor exchange system reduced the uncertainties and financial obligations involved in direct contracts with immigrants in their native lands.

The Labor Exchange as Strike-Breaking Agency

The use of immigrants from these labor exchanges as strike breakers became a regular weapon in capital's arsenal against striking workers. In the three-year period between 1872 and 1875, when the Miners National Association under the leadership of Siney backed strike after strike, fourteen strikes were broken by introducing Swedish, Italian, and German strike breakers (Erickson, 1957, p. 110). Coming directly from the New York exchanges, the immigrants arrived under guard, both to protect themselves and to isolate them from the strikers. Swedish strike breakers who arrived in the Blossburg district of Pennsylvania in 1873 were housed in buildings "surrounded by special constables sworn in by the coal companies" (Roy, 1970, p. 104). Italians came from New York to the western Pennsylvania mines during a general strike in 1874 "armed as a regiment of soldiers" (*Iron Molders Journal*, 1874).

As the depression of 1873–1877 came to a close and the Knights of Labor gained momentum, Slavic, Hungarian, and Italian strike breakers from the labor exchanges were introduced in almost every strike in the bituminous coal region of Pennslyvania and Ohio (Erickson, 1957, p. 112; Jones, 1960, p. 222). One of the most extensive mining strikes in this period and one of the most determined efforts by employers to crush the union with immigrant strike breakers occurred near Cumberland, Maryland, in 1882. In March 1882, twelve companies in the region issued orders for wage reductions coupled with the lengthening of the workday to twelve hours, precipitating the walkout of 8000 miners. In August, the companies began construction on special housing for the 1000 immigrants they had ordered from a New York exchange. Three barracks were created (one to house a special police force), the barracks and mines were fenced off, and the strikers evicted from their company housing. The mines reopened within days after the immigrants' arrival. Months later, destitute and starving, the striking miners returned to work, the strike was crushed, and 234 strikers were blacklisted (Erickson, 1957, pp. 112–115).

Not only miners were plagued by strike breakers from the labor exchanges. In New York City in the 1870s, when 400 freight workers from the Erie Railroad went out on strike, the company easily replaced them with Italians and Germans from the nearby labor bureaus (Gutman, 1976, p. 313). In 1882, when 300 freight handlers from the New York Central Railroad, the Pennsylvania Railroad, the Lake Erie and Western Railroad, and the Lehigh Valley Railroad demanded wage increases, Italian immigrants were brought over from Castle Garden, the immigrant depot in New York City, to take their places. Because the piers were so close to Castle Garden, the immigrants were not only easy to obtain, but were sent back to Castle Garden to sleep at night, thus ensuring their isolation from the strikers. Additional immigrants arrived each morning from Castle Garden and by August the companies had a nearly complete work force of new immigrant freight handlers. As the vice-president of the Jersey City local put it at the strike's defeat, "It's that ... Castle Garden that's killing us" (New Jersey Bureau of Industry and Labor, 1884).

Of course, the older systems of recruitment were not entirely replaced by the labor exchange. Some employers still advertised for strike breakers in newspapers abroad (Berthoff, 1953, p. 80). The New England textile industry counted on immigrant workers recruited directly from Canada, but not on contract. In 1878, in one of the most extensive strikes in textile history, Fall River textile barons attempted to institute a 45% wage reduction, and as 1000 spinners and 100 children walked out on strike, scabs brought from Canada and armed with revolvers (which they were told to use if any striker approached them) effectively crushed the 16-week strike (McNeill, 1888, pp. 221–233). What is important to note is that in these cases, too, no pre-immigration contract was signed between employer and immigrant.

This use of immigrant strike breakers was not always an effort simply to circumvent strikers' demands, but was often used for union smashing in general. For example, in a Shenango Valley strike in 1875, the mine operators actually paid immigrant strike breakers $.05 to $.35 a ton *more* than was being demanded by the strikers themselves (*National Labor Tribune*, 1875). *Iron Age* (1881a,b) applauded capital's achievements in defeating union efforts and congratulated firms that had succeeded in abolishing unions by using immigrant strike breakers.

The influx of immigrant labor served more generally to build up labor surpluses. This building-up of a surplus work force via immigration was not always left to chance. In the early 1870s, the Lehigh Coal Company and the Philadelphia and Reading Railroads brought to their region hundreds of Irish immigrants from the New York and Philadelphia exchanges, housed them in company barracks at $4 a month, and kept them there, unemployed, until such time as wage reductions were to be implemented (Erickson, 1957, p. 109).

The advantages of this massive influx of European workers did not go unrecognized. The *Commercial and Financial Chronicle* (1882) heralded the immigration: "In the present immigration movement we are laying the foundations for great activity in the immediate future and paving the way for business expansion on a greater scale than ever before." Andrew Carnegie (1886, pp. 34–35), in a passage that is worth repeating in full, expressed similar appreciation and even placed a price tag on each immigrant:

> The value to the country of the annual foreign influx is very great indeed. . . . During the ten years between 1870–1880, the number of immigrants averaged 280,000 per annum. In one year, 1882, nearly three times this number arrived.

> Sixty percent of this mass were adults between 15–40 years of age. These adults were surely worth $1500 each—for in former days an efficient slave sold for that sum.

Later in the passage Carnegie referred to immigration as "a golden stream which flows into the country each year." Young (1872, p. ix), a statistician at the U.S. Treasury Department, calculated that each immigrant was worth, on the average, $800 (see also *Bank-*

er's *Magazine*, 1875; *The American*, 1882; *Manhattan Magazine* 1883). The *New York Journal of Commerce* (1892) was even more blunt: "Men, like cows, are expensive to raise and a gift of either should be gladly received. And a man can be put to more valuable use than a cow."

The U.S. Industrial Commission (U.S. Congress, House Industrial Commission, 1901, Vol. 14, pp. 313–314) pointed out with regard to the combined effect of mechanization and immigrant labor: "The fact that machinery and the division of labor opens a place for the unskilled immigrants makes it possible not only to get the advantages of machinery, but also to get the advantages of cheap labor." The editor of the *Engineering and Mining Journal* (1880, p. 335) noted approvingly that "Castle Garden, with its hosts of immigrants, appears to be solving the labor question."

In the immediate sense this was partially true. However, the capital-labor contradiction underlying the labor question was not solved; its symptoms were merely changed and conflict re-created, as organized labor protested capital's use of immigrants to undermine union efforts.

The double irony of this sequence of contradictions, conflicts, and resolutions is that not only do previous resolutions precipitate later conflicts, but the same immigrant groups, the Irish and Germans, who had provided capitalists with a cheap and compliant work force, now are the very ones who, like a Trojan horse welcomed into their midst, comprise the backbone of the class struggle via strikes and union activity. This necessitates the continued immigration of cheap labor, a condition that contributes to the class-conflict nature of the situation as this tactic is protested. This irony, that the same national groups that now advance the class struggle had once been elements of its resolution, is not only intuitively appealing, as it paints human faces into the abstract dialectic, but it underlines the fact that the dialectical process is not propelled by personal attributes of individuals or individual ethnic groups, but is structurally driven.

Labor Makes Legal Demands That Cannot Be Ignored

Much of organized labor's agitation for protection from immigrant competition and strike breakers was formulated in broad, general terms. During the elections of 1880, labor newspapers across the country made an issue of the harmful effects on unions of unrestricted immigration. At a major labor rally in Pittsburgh in 1882, workers protested being forced to compete with "the pauper labor of Europe" (*Philadelphia Times*, 1882).

An independent Labor Party in New York City submitted a petition to Congress in 1883 requesting a head tax of $100 on each
landing immigrant in the hopes of reducing the stream and protecting American labor (*Congressional Record*, 1882, p. 5574). In
Philadelphia, the National Home Labor League was formed in the
attempt "to preserve the American labor market for American
workingmen" (quoted in Higham, 1955, p. 46).

The bill that came to be seen, both by politicians and capitalists of the period and by later historians, as the culmination of organized labor's demands for protection from immigrant labor—the
Anti-Contract Labor Law of 1885—was initially the formulation of
a relatively small group of skilled laborers. In 1881, the Federation
of Organized Trades and Labor Unions (FOTLU) included as a
goal in its Declaration of Principles, the abolition of the contract
labor system by which immigrants were directly recruited from
abroad. Later the same year, the FOTLU sent newsletters to other
unions urging their support for the prohibition of foreign contract
labor. In 1883, representatives of FOTLU informed the Senate
Committee on Education and Labor that the abolition of contract
labor from abroad was a top priority of American trade unions
(U.S. Congress, Senate Committee on Education and Labor, 1885,
Vol I, pp. 334–336, 583, 791–792; Vol. II, pp. 5–6). It is important
to note that, unlike the Knights of Labor, the FOTLU was comprised entirely of skilled craftsmen, including among others,
printers, carpenters, cigar makers, iron molders, and most importantly, the Window-Glass Workers of America.

It has already been pointed out that for most sectors of American industry it was no longer feasible to import workers from Europe on contract, nor was it necessary. The immigrant strike
breakers that were the Achilles' heel of labor unions in this period
were obtained at the urban labor exchanges and were *not on contract from abroad*. The one exception was in the case of workers
trained in scarce skills. In particular, highly skilled window-glass
workers were regularly imported. Because of the specialized nature of window-glass work and the relative scarcity of workers
trained in these skills, employers had for years imported many of
their glass workers on contract from Europe (Erickson, 1957, p.
140).

By the late 1870s and early 1880s, American glass workers
had achieved almost complete unionization (Ware, 1929, p. 191).
In an attempt to undercut these unions and stabilize wages, window-glass manufacturers came together in New Jersey in July
1883, and established "that the Treasurer be authorized to pay
a sum not exceeding $30 per man for each blower or gatherer

brought over from Europe after August 11, 1883 . . ." (*Congressional Record*, 1884, p. 5350).

It is not surprising, then, that the real impetus for a law prohibiting foreign contracts came from the Window-Glass Workers of America, Local 300 of the Knights of Labor. In March 1883, Local 300 drafted and sent to Washington a bill that would make it illegal to import foreign labor on contract. It was only afterwards that the Knights of Labor agreed to support the bill (Erickson, 1957, p. 154).

For the next three years, until the Anti-Contract Labor Law was passed, labor's discussion of the restriction of immigration focused on the issue of contract labor. The protection of American labor via some kind of immigration regulation became synonymous with the prohibition of contract labor. It is not difficult to understand why the Knights of Labor, although they had not themselves formulated the issue in these terms, supported the Anti-Contract Labor Bill and came to see it as their salvation. In the first place the Slavic, Hungarian, Italian, and other unskilled immigrants who were repeatedly brought from the New York exchanges and used by employers to break strikes were almost invariably brought en masse to the strike location under guard, surrounded by employers' men and police contingents hired for the occasion. It understandably appeared (and in one sense, but not the crucial one, the appearance was real) that these immigrants were of a captive status—owned, transported, and guarded by capital.

As Erickson (1957, p. 153) points out, the Window-Glass Workers of Local 300 "were able to capitalize upon the growing opposition to immigration in the balance of the labor movement whose proposals for dealing with the question were less clearly formulated."

By 1884 labor unions, and particularly the Knights of Labor, had assumed unprecedented proportions, and the class-conflict nature of the issue of foreign labor had become vividly apparent. Once the Anti-Contract Labor Bill (also known as the Foran Act after its sponsor in the House of Representatives) had been introduced in Congress in 1884, the concern was frequently voiced that "if such action as this is not had, I believe there will be great labor troubles in this country" (*Congressional Record*, 1885, p. 1778). While capital required foreign labor to circumvent the strikes and union activity of now powerful labor, the very fact that organized labor was now so potentially threatening made necessary some state response to their demands for protection. It is precisely in such situations that symbolic action by the state is most likely. Labor's focus on foreign *contract* labor influenced the form the symbolic action would take, facilitated its passage, and affected later court interpretations of the law.

The Anti-Contract Labor Law: Symbolic Action

The state can resolve conflict symbolically—i.e., temporarily placate protesting groups by legislation without substantially interfering with the conditions being protested—in any of four ways. It can incorporate loopholes into the legislation so that the legislation can easily be circumvented; it can address only a narrow and relatively insignificant aspect of the issue involved; it can designate no enforcement procedures or fail to appropriate sufficient funds for its enforcement; or, the court's interpretation of the legislation can be such as to virtually eliminate any potential effect. The Foran Act of 1885 did of these things.

First introduced by Ohio Republican Martin Foran in the House of Representatives in January, 1884, the Foran Act was passed a year later on February 18, 1885. It stipulated that

> Sec. 1. . . . it shall be unlawful for any person, company, partnership, or corporation, in any manner whatsoever, to repay the transportation or in any way assist, . . . any foreigner or foreigners, into the United States . . . under contract or agreement, parol or special, express or implied, made previous to the importation or migration of such alien or aliens . . . to perform labor or service of any kind in the United States. . . .

> Sec. 3. . . . That for every violation . . . of this act, the person, partnership, company, or corporation violating the same . . . shall forfeit and pay for every such offense the sum of $1000. . . .

> Sec. 5 . . . That nothing in this act shall be construed to prevent any person, or persons, partnership, or corporation from engaging, under contract or agreement, skilled workmen in foreign countries to perform labor in the United States in or upon any new industry not at present established in the United States: *Provided*, that skilled labor for that purpose cannot be otherwise obtained. (*Congressional Record*, 1885, p. 1622; emphasis in original)

The debates surrounding this act are worth examining in some detail, for these discussions make it clear that the bill was above all an attempt to placate organized labor without exacting sacrifices from capital, i.e., without significantly altering the protested conditions.

The first requirement of symbolic legislation is that it must seem to respond to the demands being made by the protesting group. There is no doubt that the participants in the debates surrounding the Foran Act in the House in June 1884, and in the Senate in February 1885, were concerned with demonstrating to American labor that this bill was to serve them. Without exception, those who spoke in favor of the bill rhetorically pronounced that the bill was to be the salvation of the American laborer, against both immigrant labor and the "greedy capitalists" who imported it. Foran introduced the bill:

> Mr. Speaker, . . . its object is to prevent and prohibit men whose love of self is above their love of country and humanity from importing into this country large bodies of foreign labor to take the places of and crowd out American labor. . . . No greater evil could be inflicted upon American workingmen than to bring them into competition with this species of slave labor. (*Congressional Record*, 1884, p. 5349)

Similarly, in the Senate, John Sherman—the father of the 1864 Contract Labor Law, which had made foreign contract labor legally binding[2]—applauded the Foran Bill:

> I believe that the Senate of the U.S. is as ready to recognize the rights of laboring men as the rights of the rich to employ labor. Now what is this bill? It is a bill which proposes to declare, as I understand, two things . . .: first, that the policy of this government is to protect its laboring men, its workers, to protect them to the extent that they shall be elevated rather than degraded. . . . I look, Sir, for relief to the labor of this country. . . . (*Congressional Record*, 1885, pp. 1785–1786)

Representative Thomas Ferrell, in the House, outshone all others in his six pages of "American labor" rhetoric:

> . . . I rejoice that I am enabled from this exalted position to raise my voice and to aid by my vote the toiling millions of my countrymen who are made to suffer unjustly the bitter discrimination of this system, and assisting them to procure relief by the enactment of wholesome and just laws. . . . I sincerely hope the time has come when the great labor associations and the poor toilers who know how this system affects their social condition

in this beautiful land of perpetual harvest are to soon proclaim, from the mines in the bowels of the earth to the workshop in every valley and on every hilltop, that Congress here assembled has passed a bill to prevent pauper-wage prices for their labor, and that the dismal period has passed from the land forever. (*Congressional Record*, 1884, pp. 5352, 5364)

So repetitive were such pronouncements that the bill's few opponents complained,

Representatives have unloaded their choicest rhetoric, heavily freighted with glittering generalities, upon the laborer until he must be akin to Atlas, or blessed with sinews of iron and legs of brass to bear the burden. (*Congressional Record*, 1884, p. 5364)

And, "We have heard so much froth . . . about the protection of American labor that it is absolutely getting to be nauseating to me" (*Congressional Record*, 1885, p. 1835).

That it was pressure from an organized and potentially challenging labor movement that made some legislative response necessary was well recognized. Again, it is the few opponents of the bill whose words are most revealing:

In our eager desire to gratify public demands . . . I should regret very much—it makes no difference what might be the clamor in this country, it makes no difference if the labor-union societies were 10 to where there is one—I would regret very much as a Senator to feel that I was compelled to yield to a demand made on me from that direction. . . . I could very conveniently allow this matter to go along and yield to the pressure that is brought to bear . . . by these hundreds and hundreds of labor unions if I chose to do so. . . . (*Congressional Record*, 1885, pp. 1631–1632)

If the congressional discussions make it clear that the bill was a response to organized labor's demands for protection, close attention to the debates makes it equally clear that no such protection was to be forthcoming. In the first place, two amendments were added immediately that provided effective loopholes for industry. One amendment stipulated that relatives could be assisted to immigrate by those already here without violating the "assist or encourage" clause, thus leaving untouched by the law an avenue that supplied many more workers to industry than did the direct contract system. The second amendment specified that new industries that required skilled labor that could not be otherwise obtained were exempt from the provisions of the act.

That this second amendment was particularly important to the bill's congressional supporters is clear from the response to a suggestion that the clause be struck out. It was declared an affront to labor even to consider striking out a clause of a bill that labor had helped frame.

> The bill was not framed by children and babes, but by the men whose interests it undertakes to guard and conserve. . . . The provision which the Senator from Nebraska moves to strike out is one which they [unionists] were particularly careful to have included in the bill; and to strike it out would, in the general estimate of all those who take any affirmative interest in the enactment of the bill into a law, entirely emasculate it. *They very likely would then prefer its defeat, or* at all events would become indifferent to its enactment. (*Congressional Record*, 1885, p. 1622; emphasis added)

This, despite the fact that the provision with regard to new industries had been added, not by organized labor, but by the Committee on Labor in the House. Labor's only comment on the provision came from a glassworker during testimony taken by the committee and was hardly enthusiastic: "I would not object to men being brought to start a new industry" (*Congressional Record*, 1884, Summary of Testimony, p. 6066). Once the move to strike this clause had been defeated, a motion was introduced to strike that part of the clause that stipulated, "provided that skilled labor for that purpose cannot be otherwise obtained." While Senator Henry Blair had earlier refused to touch the section on the grounds that labor had framed it, he was now less protective: "I have no objection to the Senator's moving to strike that out" (*Congressional Record*, 1885, p. 1628), even though this deletion would have affected labor adversely, while the provision as a whole had been an essentially pro-industry loophole.

More important than these amendments in limiting the bill's impact, however, the bill itself referred only to the narrow issue of foreign labor on contract from abroad. As its spokesman in the House put it, "This bill in no way seeks to restrict or prohibit voluntary or free immigration . . ." (*Congressional Record*, 1884, p. 5349). Since most of the immigrant labor used to break strikes and reduce wages was obtained at urban labor exchanges, the law had no potential effect on the real scourge of American workers.

An amendment introduced in the House on the first day of debate stipulated that only those contracts made before emigration were covered in the act (*Congressional Record*, 1884, pp. 5370–5371), thus exempting contracts made between the immigrant upon arrival and the labor exchanges, and excluding from the law's provisions that very segment of immigrant labor that was most detrimental to organized labor. The only potential beneficiaries of the law were that small minority of highly skilled workers not yet replaceable with machinery and unskilled immigrant labor.

If the bill was to placate organized labor beyond that small number of craft workers, however, it must seem to apply to them. This it did admirably. Speaker after speaker denounced the "pauper labor of Europe," the unskilled Hungarians, Poles, Slavs, and Italians who broke strikes and reduced wages, *who were not, however, on pre-emigration contract.* "Large numbers of degraded, ignorant, brutal Italian and Hungarian laborers. . . . This is the class of persons, this is the species of immigration with which this bill seeks to deal . . ." (*Congressional Record*, 1884, p. 5349).

The emphasis throughout the debates was on these so-called new immigrants—the Italians, Poles, Hungarians; and Slavs—and the issue was diverted to their allegedly inferior living standards. These new immigrants were denounced as "slaves," "paupers," "serfs," "lowest beings," and as receiving "30 percent to 50 percent less wages than American laborers" (*Congressional Record*, 1884, p. 5350). Foran warned that "that large numbers of inferior, unskilled, degraded laborers are annually imported under contract is known to everybody" (p. 5351). Others declared that "[this] servile contract . . . is worse than the African slavery of the South, an ignoble and degrading competition" (*Congressional Record*, 1885, p. 1625).

This diversion to the living standards of the new immigrants not only made the bill seem to apply to the kind of labor that most threatened American workers but it reconfirmed to the American worker Congress's contempt for such a slave labor system.

The state's spokesmen were able to accomplish this appearance of protecting American labor, while fashioning the bill so as not to exact any substantial changes, by utilizing vague and ambiguous terminology throughout the discussions. *Contract labor* was never explicitly defined in the debates, nor was there consensus on what the bill actually prohibited. Its many supporters apparently found it irksome that there were a few uncooperative naysayers who preferred to understand the bill's terms and how it would affect labor. While Foran and others referred to the slave labor obtained at Castle Garden and other labor exchanges, under questioning, they had to admit that their only data on contracts made abroad referred to 200 glass workers (*Congressional Record*, 1884, p. 5350).

Neither its spokesmen nor its few opponents were unaware that the bill was "crude and imperfect." Regarding its ambiguities, one of the bill's few opponents commented,

> ... whoever it was that proposed this bill ... he was a very poor lawyer.... How can it be that the law can imply a contract out of the relations of two people and then denounce as a crime that contract thus implied ...? What more monstrous absurdity ever yet characterized a bill than that? I submit it to the judgment of every lawyer in the Senate if there was ever anything more monstrous as an absurdity than that. (*Congressional Record*, 1885, p. 1631)

And later:

> ... almost everyone who has risen to advocate the bill ... has got up and explained that the bill was crude and imperfect.... The whole door of mischief that is intended to be closed out by this bill is left wide open ... and yet this is a bill about which so much is said and about which every Senator's judgment is challenged when he presumes to make a criticism upon it. (p. 1796)

Another stated briefly in the House:

> After what I have heard spoken on the floor of this House ... my faith in the infallibility of language to convey its true meaning, or at least the intended meaning ... has been badly shaken. (*Congressional Record*, 1884, p. 5364)

Even those who rose in favor of the bill complained of its loose terminology: "I expect to vote for this bill. I think the bill is immature and crude, but I shall vote for it on account of the salient principle which it announces" (*Congressional Record*, 1885, p. 1780).

Without exception, those who supported the bill, yet admitted to its ambiguities and imprecisions, rejected amendments whose purpose was to clarify its terms. When Senator John Morgan of Alabama urged, for example, "If we have got to amend it so that it has to go back to the House ... why not make the bill so that it shall be clearly intelligible?" Senator James George of Mississippi responded impatiently, *"That is a very immaterial difficulty"* (*Congressional Record*, 1885, p. 1794; emphasis added).

Amendments to clarify the intent of the bill were repeatedly rejected by overwhelming margins, and criticisms that the bill was "an absurdity" were conspicuously ignored. Increasingly, the attention focused on more comfortable subjects:

> I should like to have a verbal transposition made of the words "service or labor" in the 6th line of the second section, so as to read "labor or service." That would be altogether more poetic, while the other phrase savors rather of blank verse. (*Congressional Record*, 1885, p. 1839)

This amendment was agreed to.

More important for our purposes, the bill was recognized as unenforceable, particularly by its proponents.

> From a careful examination of it, there is no part of it which seems to me to be at all effective. . . . The penalties imposed in this bill I do not think can ever be enforced. . . . I expect to vote for the bill, but I want to put on my record my understanding of it. (*Congressional Record*, 1885, pp. 1628–1629)

Similarly, Senator Wilkinson Call of Florida declared, "I shall support the bill. . . . And I do so with the conviction that the bill will be of no benefit to them [the laborers]" (*Congressional Record*, 1885, p. 1785). Senator William Frye of Maine concurred, "Under the provisions here—I agree with the Senator from Connecticut that it is not drawn for an indictment by any manner of means—I do not believe any man on earth would ever be punished" (*Congressional Record*, 1885, p. 1628).

Not infrequently, it was even stated that this very unenforceability was an asset.

> I do not myself believe that there is any efficacy whatever in this idea or that it will afford anything of the protection to the American laborer that is anticipated. . . . *Still I cannot see that there is any harm in gratifying this desire* . . . . (*Congressional Record*, 1885, p. 1628; emphasis added)

In response to a comment that the bill would be difficult to enforce, Blair (*Congressional Record*, 1885, p. 1629) patiently explained, "If it cannot be enforced will it do any hurt?" Finally, and perhaps most revealingly,

> I do not believe that any of the provisions of the bill will work hardship or do any substantial harm, *but I do believe that we shall do infinite harm if we fail now, this subject having come to the consideration of the Senate, to put on record our adherence to the principles which I believe are contained in this bill.* . . . (*Congressional Record*, 1885, p. 1782; emphasis added)

The bill's opponents were even more explicit in their recognition of the purely symbolic nature of the bill. After three days of debates, Senator Matthew Butler (*Congressional Record*, 1885, p. 1835; emphasis added) concluded,

> Taking the assertion of the advocates of this bill that they are really anxious to prevent what is said to be an evil, it has occurred to me that this bill offered a premium upon its very face for its own violation. . . . This bill as it stands reaches nobody. It is and will be found to be whenever the attempt is made to enforce it, absolutely inoperative . . . and in its operations *a sham and a pretense;* . . . it has no penalty whatever which can reach anybody and which may not be evaded at any moment. It will be evaded, because a premium is offered in the bill itself for doing so. . . . When American labor clamors for recognition by Congress we provide them a bureau of labor, as we did last year. . . . *The laborers literally ask for bread and we have given them a stone, and we propose to give them another in this bill* if it passes. . . . My objection to this bill . . . is that *it pretends to do something and really and practically does nothing except to throw a sop to Cerberus, to pat the American laborer on the head by giving him a bill which amounts to nothing.* . . . We throw him this taffy to satisfy the clamor of the American laborer, *giving him a sham* when he wants something real. . . . I do not intend . . . to vote for a measure that will be as inoperative as a blank piece of paper.

Another Senator remarked simply, "There is a scorpion in it" (*Congressional Record*, p. 1835).

The political maneuverings within the debates make it clear that both the bill's proponents and its opponents were vividly aware that the bill's success was based on this inoperability. Butler, one of the most vehement opponents of the bill, introduced

a simple amendment that would make it illegal for contract laborers to land. It was introduced under the pretense that it would improve the bill, because it might thereby be made effective: "There
is no ambiguity about it. It is distinct. It has its penalties. Its penalties can be enforced" (*Congressional Record*, p. 1835). It soon
became clear that the attempt was to add to the bill an amendment that might supply an enforcement mechanism and thereby
cause the bill to be defeated.

Blair (*Congressional Record*, 1885, p. 1836), the major
spokesman for the bill in the Senate, was duly suspicious:

> ... I feel reminded of the proverb that it is well to be-
> ware of the Greeks when they come bearing gifts. I have
> examined his amendment with a suspicion that he might
> not be from the very bottom of his soul the most anxious
> to conserve the purpose of this bill.

The amendment was soundly defeated.

In spite of the fact that the bill had been declared "inopera-
tive," "crude," "ambiguous," and "a sham," the Senate motion that
it be referred to the Committee on the Judiciary to be reworded so
as to "more effectively reach the ends aimed at," was rejected, 41
to 15 (*Congressional Record*, 1885, p. 1839).

Representative Charles O'Neill (*Congressional Record*, 1884,
p. 5357) aptly summarized the proceedings in the House: "...
there are often circumstances arising in connection with debate
which cause us to pause to understand motives. ... Friends of La
bor! Heaven save workmen from such friends ...!" The bill passed
in the House by a voice vote almost unanimously. In the Senate it
passed 49 to 9, being favored by both Republicans and Democrats,
Northerners and Southerners (see Table II).

Industry, when not conspicuously silent on the issue of the
Foran Act, displayed a telling indifference, grounded in the
knowledge that the bill's terms would leave it unaffected. Articles
in the *Anglo-American Times* (1887a,b; 1889a,b, 1890) revealed
industry's indifference to the act. Neither the *Railroad Gazette*
nor the *Engineering and Mining Journal* even mentioned the Act,
even though the congressional discussions of the Foran Act had
emphasized the alleged role of mines and railroads as importers of
contract labor, and trade journals frequently reported on factors
that would affect the supply of labor.

The act passed overwhelmingly.

TABLE II
Senate Vote on Foran Act,
February 18, 1885[a]

YEAS

Nelson W. Aldrich—Rhode Island (R)[b]

William B. Allison—Iowa (R)

Henry W. Blair—New Hampshire (R)

Thomas M. Bowen—Colorado (R)

Joseph E. Brown—Georgia (D)

Wilkinson Call—Florida (D)

Johnson N. Camden—West Virginia (D)

Angus Cameron—Wisconsin (R)

Jonathan Chace—Rhode Island (R)

Omar D. Conger—Michigan (R)

Shelby M. Cullom—Illinois (R)

Henry L. Dawes—Massachusetts (R)

Joseph N. Dolph—Oregon (R)

James G. Fair—Nevada (D)

William P. Frye—Maine (R)

James Z. George—Mississippi (D)

Randall L. Gibson—Louisiana (D)

Arthur Pue Gorman—Maryland (D)

Eugene Hale—Maine (R)

Isham G. Harris—Tennessee (D)

Benjamin Harrison—Indiana (R)

John J. Ingalls—Kansas (R)

Howell E. Jackson—Tennessee (D)

John P. Jones—Nevada (R)

John E. Kenna—West Virginia (D)

Lucius Lamar—Mississippi (D)

Elbridge G. Lapham—New York (R)

Samuel J. R. McMillan—Minnesota (R)

John R. McPherson—New Jersey (D)

William Mahone—Virginia (D)

John F. Miller—California (R)

Warner Miller—New York (R)

John I. Mitchell—Pennsylvania (R)

Justin S. Morrill—Vermont (R)

Thomas W. Palmer—Michigan (R)

Austin F. Pike—New Hampshire (R)

Orville H. Platt—Connecticut (R)

Preston B. Plumb—Kansas (R)

James L. Pugh—Alabama (D)

Matt W. Ransom—North Carolina (D)

Dwight M. Sabin—Minnesota (R)

Philetus Sawyer—Wisconsin (R)

William J. Sewell—New Jersey (D)

John Sherman—Ohio (R)

Charles H. Van Wyck—Nebraska (R)

George G. Vest—Missouri (D)

Daniel W. Voorhees—Indiana (D)

James D. Walker—Arkansas (D)

James F. Wilson—Iowa (R)

NAYS

Matthew L. Butler—South Carolina (D)

James B. Groome—Maryland (D)

Wade Hampton—South Carolina (D)

Joseph R. Hawley—Connecticut (R)

Samuel B. Maxey—Texas (D)

John T. Morgan—Alabama (D)

Eli Saulsbury—Delaware (D)

Zebulon Vance—North Carolina (D)

John S. Williams—Kentucky (D)

[a] Source: *Congressional Record*, 1885, p. 1839.
[b] R, Republican; D, Democrat.

Symbolic Law in Action

Industry had calculated correctly; the Anti-Contract Labor Law exacted few sacrifices from capital. In the fourteen years between 1887 and 1901, out of an immigration flow of about 6,000,000, at the most 8000 immigrants were barred as contract laborers, and it was estimated that only one employer of contract labor in 1000 was convicted (testimony of Ullo, U.S. Congress, House Industrial Commission, 1901, Vol. 15, p. 110). After several hundred pages had been devoted to the Anti-Contract Labor Law, the Industrial Commission (U.S. Congress, House Industrial Commission, 1901, Vol. 15, p. LVIII) concluded in 1901:

> [This law is] practically a nullity, as affected by the decisions of the court, and by the practices of the inspectors, and the administrative authorities.

The lawyer who had for six years been in charge of preparing for court the contract labor cases at the port of New York, put it simply: "If it is advisable to restrict contract labor, the law as it stands does not restrict it" (testimony of Ullo, U.S. Congress, House Industrial Commission, 1901, Vol. 15, p. 143).

It had not been written with enforcement in mind, nor were subsequent amendments much help. As the Ford Committee, a House select committee formed in 1888 to investigate the enforcement of federal immigration laws, reported (*Congressional Record*, 1889, p. 999),

> The enforcement of this act is not easily accomplished. Evasions of the law are much more numerous than convictions. . . . [This] is not so much due to a want of diligence on the part of the officials having their administration in charge as it is to a lack of proper machinery to carry them into effect.

Congress had in fact appropriated no funds for the enforcement of the Anti-Contract Labor Law, nor was any machinery established for its operationalization. For three years after the passage of the law, no immigrants nor employers were ever even questioned with regard to contract labor.

In response to demands from the craft unions of the FOTLU, Congress amended the Foran Act in 1887, 1888, 1891, 1893, 1894, and 1903 but never significantly altered its fundamental weaknesses (or strengths, as it were). Symbolic law, it will be remembered, responds to a conflict comprising, on the one hand, protest by potentially threatening groups over particular conditions, and on the other, profit-making activity that is sustained by those very conditions. The resolution, in the form of symbolic law that temporarily appeases the protest without disturbing the profitable conditions, leaves untouched the underlying contradiction. Thus, while symbolic law is an ideal temporary solution in these situations, it remains effective only until its actual inefficiency is recognized, and conflict is re-created. Subsequent protests are likely to call forth further symbolic response in the form of a series of ineffective amendments, budgetary increases, and the like.

In 1887, following pressure from the FOTLU, Congress passed an amendment stipulating that the secretary of the treasury was responsible for the enforcement of the Foran Act and was to contract with state immigration officials for the inspection of arriving immigrants. Still, no appropriations were made for the law's enforcement.

The law as originally written applied only to the importer of contract labor and nowhere barred the contracted laborer from landing. An amendment of 1888 provided that contract laborers must be returned to their country of emigration. The same year, Congress for the first time appropriated a small budget for the enforcement of the law that had been enacted almost unanimously three years earlier. Subsequent changes in 1894 included day laborers, or "birds of passage," in the provisions of the law, although importers of day labor still could not be fined.

Pari passu with these amendments that might have had a tightening effect on the already small traffic of contract labor, court interpretations and the administration of the law by immigration inspectors became increasingly liberal.

Immigrants upon arrival filed in groups past a registry clerk who questioned them as to their health and other aspects of their eligibility for landing. No questions were put to the immigrants regarding their contract labor status. Rather, a contract labor inspector stood by the registry clerk, listening to the questions and answers; if they became suspicious, they took the alien aside and questioned him individually. Quinlan (U.S. Congress, House Industrial Commission, 1901, Vol. 15, p. 125; emphasis added), the supervising inspector of the Contract Labor Bureau of the port of New York in 1899, described this process in his testimony to the Industrial Commission:

Q: Does the registry clerk ask questions that bear on the contract labor subject?

A. Not as a rule; sometimes they do and call our attention

TABLE III
Number of Contract Laborers Debarred for Every
10,000 Immigrants Admitted[a]

Year	Number debarred	Year	Number debarred
1892	16	1901	7
1893	12	1902	4
1894	19	1903	13
1895	27	1904	18
1896	23	1905	11
1897	14	1906	21
1898	18	1907	11
1899	24	1908	25
1900	19	1909	16
		1910	17

[a] Source: Jenks, 1913, p. 624.

to it; *it is where the man volunteers*, or they discover something suspicious, and they invite our attention to the fact.

In other words, the question of contract labor was not brought up at all unless the immigrant himself happened to bring it up. Given the ease with which immigrants brought over on contract could be advised ahead of time as to the appropriate responses, detection was rare (see Table III).

Strict enforcement of the law would have been logistically impossible, given staff size. In 1899, 800 immigrants a day filed past the New York registry clerks. Until 1909, there were only two full-time contract labor inspectors in the country—one in Boston and one in New York! (U.S. Commissioner General of Immigration, 1910). The Boards of Special Inquiry, to whom the immigrants were sent if they were suspected of being contract laborers, were similarly understaffed. The report of one member of the New York Board (U.S. Congress, House Industrial Commission, 1901, Vol. 15, p. 134) speaks for itself: "We try to be very thorough in our examination. We handle on an average during the busy season 100 cases a day."

Ultimately, enforcement depended on the discretion of these inspectors and Boards of Special Inquiry. Their attitudes regarding the law were therefore crucial. Although there is little direct documentation on the subject, the U.S. Commissioner General of Immigration (1904) remarked that enforcement was lax because inspectors were of the general opinion that labor had forced the law on Congress. American Federation of Labor (AFL) President Samuel Gompers, referring to the negative attitudes of the port inspectors with regard to the Foran Act, testified before the Ford Committee in 1888 (U.S. Congress, House Miscellaneous Documents, 1888, p. 401), ". . . officers of the government seem to make it their purpose to bring odium and ridicule upon the law by its non-enforcement."

While the port inspectors determined whether an alien should be deported, federal courts were responsible for prosecuting the importers, and court convictions of importers were far rarer even than the deportation of contract laborers. Ullo (U.S. Congress, House Industrial Commission, 1901, p. 139), the New York lawyer who had been in charge of prosecuting contract labor cases, reported that "not one case in a thousand can be brought to a satisfactory result or conviction." He added that in his six years of experience, he knew of only one case of an employer being convicted. The crux of this low conviction rate lay in the court's narrow interpretation of what constituted a contract, side by side with its very liberal interpretation of which kinds of laborers were legally exempt from the provisions of the law. This was no accident, nor was it a purely legally inspired formula. Rather, a New York district attorney, in 1898, expressed what he called the "contempt the U.S. judges have for the contract-labor law" (U.S. Congress, House Industrial Commission, 1901, Vol. 15, p. 125).

The courts held that, in order to convict an importer, (1) the contract must be written (the law said the contract could be "expressed or implied") and must designate the time period over which the employment was to continue as well as the rate of wages to be paid;[3] (2) the contract had to be drawn up previous to the alien's emigration; and (3) the immigrant had to have already landed in the United States.

Ullo (U.S. Congress, House Industrial Commission, 1901, Vol. 15, p. 140) remarked, "It is very rare that anyone makes such a contract, and it is rare too that the Government can find the proofs of such a contract." Evidence for such a contract could be secured in only three ways: (1) through third parties present at the time the contract was made, but the contract had to have been drawn up abroad; (2) by the confession of the alien himself, but this was unlikely, as Ullo (U.S. Congress, House Industrial Commission, 1901, Vol. 15, p. 140; emphasis added) explained,

> Importation is an essential element of the prohibition; if we deport a man who is imported, the courts have released the importer from the fine on the ground that the man has not been imported. If we find he is a contract laborer, *he is sent back*. . . . Therefore, they are required to send back their only witness to the contract!

(3) Evidence could be obtained from the importer himself; but of course, this was unlikely.

In those few instances when a written contract of the kind required by the courts was proven, the case was frequently dropped anyway. Weihe, New York Immigration Inspector (U.S. Congress, House Industrial Commission, 1901, Vol. 15, pp. 152–153), explained,

> I will state one particular case; the La Lanc Gros Jean Company, through its manager, wrote for a roll turner and an annealer, promising the roller $30 a week and the annealer $25. We had the letters written by the manager on the letterhead of the company. . . . These men came here and worked. . . . We were told we could not prosecute the company on account of the acts of the manager, who was a hired man, and the case was dropped. Everything was proven—that the money was sent, and even that the passage money was returned out of their salaries; but we could not prove that the president of the company directly authorized it. . . .

If the court worked with a very narrow definition of what constituted a contract, they interpreted liberally the provisions for certain exemptions. The Industrial Commission (p. 59) reported that

> . . . the importer is given every benefit of the doubt . . . the courts hold strictly to the letter of the law in defining a contract, but hold to the so-called spirit of the law in exempting from its penalties all those laborers who could not be shown to be specifically and unquestioningly excluded by its terms from the country. In other words, if the contract reveals any flaw whatever, the importer is released, and if an imported laborer can possibly be admitted, the importer is also released.

Because the wording of the law referred to "alien immigrants," the courts excluded from the law all immigrant residents (in practice if the immigrant had ever previously been in the United States, he was excluded from the law's terms) and those who were not technically immigrants (i.e., day laborers commuting across the border were exempt). In addition the courts interpreted liberally the "new industries" clause:

> In the Keck diamond case they imported all the diamond cutters. It took over a week's trial to find out whether it was a "new industry" in this country to cut diamonds. [It was] proven that cutting of diamonds was done in this country since 1830, but whether it was really an *established* industry was a question. (Ullo, U.S. Congress, House Industrial Commission, 1901, Vol. 15, p. 140; emphasis in original)

The diamond cutters were exempt from the law.

Worse yet from the point of view of the American worker, an amendment of 1903 substituted for the original "new industries" clause, a clause that stipulated vaguely that labor could be imported "if labor of like kind" could not otherwise be obtained (32 U.S. Statutes at Large). The courts frequently interpreted this to mean "if labor of like kind could not be obtained" without increasing wages. Thus in 1907 the New York Board of Inquiry, following the lead of the courts, validated the importation of two German lithographers even though hundreds of Americans with identical skills had been unemployed for almost a year due to a company lockout (Erickson, 1957, p. 175).

A series of court decisions dealt the final blow to the Anti-Contract Labor Law. The Supreme Court in 1888 had maintained the right of the courts to examine congressional debates in order to ascertain the true intent of the law makers. In 1889 the courts inferred from an inspection of the debates that "Congress intended to exclude only those whose labor or service is manual in character, and that all other classes could be admitted even under contract" (quoted in U.S. Congress, House Industrial Commission, 1901, Vol. 15, p. 60). In a circuit court of appeals in 1899 it was determined that not only were professional classes exempt from the prohibition of the law, but all skilled labor. It was held in this decision that "the law does not exclude such classes as engineer, bookkeeper, stenographer, typewriter, clerk, saleswoman, draper, or window dresser." In fact, "*Congress never intended to include in the act skilled labor of any kind*" (U.S. Congress, House Industrial Commission, 1901, Vol. 15, p. 60; emphasis added). The only intention, the court concluded, was "to shut out the cheaper, grosser sort of unskilled and unhoused labor." This, despite the fact that even a cursory examination of the debates reveals repeated reference to both unskilled and skilled labor, and the only actual documentation of contract labor was among the highly skilled glassworkers. The U.S. Congress, House Industrial Commission (1901, Vol. 15, pp. 60–61; emphasis added) summarizes the effect of this interpretation by the court:

> This decision of the appellate court, accepted as it has been by other courts and by the administrative authorities, has reduced the law to such a point that it is no longer a practical means of restricting immigration. . . . *The cheap labor from East and South Europe does not come under contract, and so evades the law, while skilled laborers, who naturally would be more likely to enter into contracts, are by this decision exempt.*

The courts had capitalized on the diversion of the issue in the congressional debates from the issue of contract labor to the living standards of the new unskilled immigrants—a diversion that had been part of the attempt to present the bill as the salvation of American labor. Thus, ironically, the concentration on the unskilled in the debates served not only to promote the law as labor's salvation, but was subsequently used by the courts to guarantee that labor was in fact unaffected.[4]

The Emergence of New Conflicts

As Congress was scurrying to put on record its endorsement of the protection of American labor, the seeds of conflicts that could not be so painlessly resolved had already been sown. The conflicts and dilemmas that would culminate in the 1921 and 1924 quota laws were already discernible and increasingly plagued the capitalist state and class-conscious employers.

Perhaps the best way to conceptualize the source of these conflicts is in terms of the various needs or requirements of any modern nation-state—needs that in capitalism are fraught with contradictions. O'Donnell (1977, p. 98) in "Industrial Capitalism and the Rise in Modern American Cities," draws attention to the deceptively simple fact that all social systems must reproduce their work forces. This reproduction must be sustained at three levels: the biological-demographic, the material, and the socio-cultural. By *biological-demographic reproduction*, O'Donnell intends simply the physical reproduction of the work force; *material reproduction* of the work force refers to the need to provide for the material sustenance of that population in some way (for example, through work opportunities, self-help networks, state welfare, etc.); *sociocultural reproduction* refers to the fact that some minimal level of political legitimation and cultural hegemony must be achieved.

In a capitalist democracy these three requisites tend to be mutually contradictory. Specifically, the need to reproduce a surplus labor supply (biological reproduction) with which to feed the voracious appetite of capital places an increasing burden on the capitalist state for the material sustenance (material reproduction) of that industrial reserve army. This contradiction is compounded by the need for system legitimation (sociocultural reproduction). The choice, then, is between fiscal crisis and legitimation crisis.

By the last decades of the nineteenth century, the symptoms of these contradictions were beginning to emerge. Much of the immigration legislation in the United States in the late nineteenth and early twentieth centuries can be seen as attempts to resolve the conflicts and dilemmas derived from these antagonistic needs of biological, material, and political reproduction. The remainder of this chapter focuses on the contradictions between the need in capitalism to biologically reproduce a surplus work force versus the task of materially sustaining the masses that are thereby thrust into poverty. To put this contradiction in another way: on one hand, poverty is nurtured; on the other, it must be contended with. The ways in which the situation was further complicated by the need for the political and cultural reproduction of that work force will be dealt with later.

If all economic systems depend on the biological reproduction of the work force, in capitalism this entails the production and reproduction of a surplus labor supply. In the United States, this was accomplished by (1) the proletarianization of the population through the substitution of wage labor for self-employment; (2) mechanization; and (3) immigration.

The burden of materially sustaining this surplus work force falls on the state. This task is all the more problematic since the logic of capitalism is such that periodic economic crises are inevitably produced. Just as automatically as these crises occur, "the power of the sudden expansion of capital grows also" (Braverman, 1974, p. 254). Both to minimize social disorder during depressions and to sustain the unemployed until their labor power is required for such expansion, the state is called on to extend some form of relief. The level at which the unemployed are thus sustained is of course historically specific and depends on such things as political legitimation requirements and the stage of the class struggle.

The contradiction between the need for a surplus labor force and the poverty that results is essentially unresolvable. By the end of the nineteenth century in the United States, however, the attempt was made to grapple with the fiscal dilemma that sprang from this contradiction. Congress's first attempt to resolve the dilemma involved defining the problem of immigrant pauperism in terms of immigrants' personal attributes.

The dilemma, in other words, was to be resolved not by curtailing the immigrant stream but by picking out the "defective" elements. The first comprehensive federal immigration law passed in 1882 was designed to do just that (22 U.S. Statutes at Large). Establishing a head tax of $.50 on each arriving immigrant for the purpose of financing immigration regulation and barring convicts, lunatics, idiots, and "any other person unable to care for himself or herself without becoming a public charge,"[5] the bill explicitly aimed at alleviating the fiscal burden on the states attending immigration (*Congressional Record*, 1882, p. 5106) without cutting down on what Carnegie called "that golden stream." It was pointed out in the congressional discussions of this law that New York State alone spent $4,000,000 annually on its poorhouses, $6,000,000 on other caretaker institutions, and that a disproportionate number of those sustained in this way were foreign-born (*Congressional Record*, 1882, p. 5108). Given the economic function of immigrants, it was inevitable that they should be the first victims of the contradiction between the need for a surplus labor supply versus the poverty thereby produced. And, since poor immigrants were the most visible component of this contradiction, they were held individually responsible for the failures of the very system that crushed them.

The bill produced very little debate and passed both houses by overwhelming majorities. Thus began the era, sometimes referred to as the selective period, in which immigration problems were defined in terms of the individual qualities of immigrants themselves. It is not surprising that time after time policies based on this definition of the problem were found to be unsatisfactory. What is perhaps less obvious is that, given the dilemma, no more satisfactory resolution was possible.

In 1882, capital was still enjoying a period of overall expansion, despite periodic crises, and the labor movement was increasingly a force to be contended with. In both cases, the unlimited immigrant stream was an indispensable asset. The qualified action that Congress endorsed in the 1882 immigration law was an attempt to resolve the structural conflict confronting them by leaving unrestricted this immigrant stream and selecting out what they saw as its undesirable elements, i.e., "those unable to care for themselves without becoming public charges." This blame-the-victim response was facilitated by the fact that the source of immigration was beginning to shift from Northern and Western Europe to Southern and Eastern Europe. Although the Irish and Germans who had immigrated 30 years earlier were also impoverished, unskilled, and scapegoated at the time of their entry, these groups were now held up as the ideal, to be contrasted to the poverty stricken Italians, Poles, and Jews.

The end of the nineteenth century brought a flurry of congressional investigations into immigration and immigration policy. In 1888, the Ford Committee was formed to investigate the efficacy of the 1882 and 1885 laws. In 1889, the Committee on Immigration in the Senate and the Select Committee on Immigration and Naturalization in the House were established, and the following year they were authorized to make investigations relative to immigration. In 1892, a joint committee was charged with examining the workings of the immigration laws. In 1901 the Industrial Commission reported on the effect of immigration and the efficiency of U.S. immigration laws. The conclusions of these reports were remarkably similar. First, no "radical change in the laws" was advisable (U.S. Congress, House Report, 1891, p. 8). Rather,

> It cannot be gainsaid that immigration in the past has been an important factor in the development and growth of this Republic. . . .
>
> [But] the time has now come to draw the line, to select the good from the bad, and to sift the wheat from the chaff. (*Congressional Record*, 1889, p. 999)

Similarly, "the intent of our immigration laws is not to restrict immigration, but to sift it, to separate the desirable from the undesirable immigrants" (U.S. Congress, House Report, 1891, p. 1).

The purpose of the 1882 law, then, was to "sift the wheat from the chaff"—the chaff being those with a predisposition to become public charges. The law aimed in part at guaranteeing the employability of arriving immigrants as a way to reduce the fiscal burden on the state without reducing the labor supply. The broader assumption upon which it was based was that, even among the able-bodied, there are those with recognizable personal traits that predispose them to pauperism.

The second conclusion of these investigations was that the 1882 law was not working well: "The result of the investigation into the enforcement of the law of 1882 demonstrates beyond a doubt that it has been and is being repeatedly violated" (*Congressional Record*, 1889, p. 978). It *could* not work well, given its contradictory purpose. For one thing, the law called for the individual inspection of each landing inunigrant without, however, affecting the overall flow of immigration. Eighteen eighty-two was a peak year for immigration, as close to 800,000 immigrants entered the country; 9000 immigrants came through the gates of Castle Garden each day. As New York inspectors reported to the Ford Committee (*Congressional Record*, 1889, p. 998; emphasis added), *"in order that there may be no undue delay in landing them* ... it was almost impossible to properly inspect the large number of persons who arrive daily." After an extensive study of exclusion procedures, one legal scholar summarized the attitude of the inspectors: "Better to run the risk of the occasional admission of an alien inadmissible under the law than to slow up the process. In the exclusion process, the fundamental necessity is swift, summary action" (quoted in Van Vleck, 1932, p. 28).

Even had it been possible to inspect each immigrant without slowing down the flow, the law would have remained hopelessly ineffective, given the faulty logic of blame upon which it was based. Since pauperism is not an innate characteristic but the effect of an economic system that requires and nurtures a surplus labor supply, how were officials to recognize "public-charge types"? The problem was not simply one of personnel shortages but involved the law's inherent inability to accomplish its task, i.e., the reduction of the fiscal strain on the state produced by the very poverty upon which the economic system thrived.[6]

Such *qualified action* as a state response to conflict is characteristically unsatisfactory even in the short run. This is so because it is an attempt to resolve conflicts based on inherent contradictions at a time when capital's needs are still rigid and inflexible with regard to the conditions involved. The legislative result is likely to be a series of amendments or legal attempts to fortify the hapless resolution. A series of acts in 1891, 1893, 1894, and 1903, involving rewordings and administrative changes, were directed at some of the most apparent deficiencies of the 1882 law. Their content reconfirms the contradictory purpose of this law and the faulty logic of blaming the victim for poverty and pauperism. The law of 1891 (26 U.S. Statutes at Large; emphasis added), in addition to excluding those "suffering from a loathesome or dangerous contagious disease," polygamists, and "those convicted of crime involving moral turpitude," changed the wording of "those unable to care for themselves without becoming public charges" to "those *likely to become* public charges." The emphasis was thus shifted away from the inspector's perception of a present condition within the immigrant. The inspector was now asked to predict whether given immigrants would, for whatever reasons, become public charges. In addition, the new law stipulated that those who became public charges within one year could be deported. There was in both these changes the implicit recognition that pauperism was at least in part the result of industrial conditions; in fact, inspectors were instructed to consider industrial conditions in the region to which the immigrant was destined.

The Act of 1893 was an administrative attempt to rationalize the inherently irrational process of selection (27 U.S. Statutes at Large). Vessel masters were required to compile lists of detailed information about each alien on board and to deliver the lists to the local immigration officials upon landing; in addition, commissioners of immigration were named for each large port of entry. In 1894, the head tax on arriving immigrants was raised to $1 (28 U.S. Statutes at Large). In 1903, it was stipulated that immigrants who became public charges within two years after entry were deemed to have entered in violation of the law and were subject to deportation (32 U.S. Statutes at Large).

Partly because it was not the state's purpose to restrict the quantity of immigration, and partly because there was in fact no such thing as a "potential public charge," the effects of this law and its subsequent changes were minimal. Only 0.5–1% were debarred each year through 1900 (U.S. Congress, House Industrial Commission, 1901, Vol. 15, p. 16). Furthermore, the law had no significant effect on the number of state-supported paupers. At the time of the Ford Committee Report in 1889, every charitable institution—public and private—was "not only filled with occupants, but overflowing." The cost to the state of New York alone was $20,000,000 a year—twice the reported figure for 1882. Furthermore, the number of state-supported foreign-born had little to do, statistically speaking, with the number of "public charge types" debarred but varied with economic booms and crises (*Congressional Record*, 1889, p. 998). In the meantime, the golden stream continued and in 1905 passed the 1,000,000 mark for the first time.

Notes

1. Other methods used at this time were the padrone system, Italian "banks," and the "immigrant letter" (U.S. Congress, House Industrial Commission, 1901, Vol. 15; U.S. Congress, Senate Immigration Commission, 1911, Vol. I). Italian banks imported immigrants, prepaid their passage, boarded them, and then were repaid with a 6% interest on the immigrant's wages. The owner of the New York Banca Italiana claimed to have imported 14,000 Italians in this way (U.S. Congress, House Industrial Commission, Vol. 15, p. 9). The padrone system was similar, except that the padrone contracted directly with the immigrant, then profited by hiring him out at a higher rate. The immigrant letter was frequently used by American industry as a way to secure additional workers without resorting to contracts, as employers encouraged their workers to write home to relatives and friends telling them of work opportunities.

2. Sherman was challenged during the Senate debates as to the apparent contradiction between his instrumental role in developing the 1864 Contract Labor Law and his wholehearted endorsement of the Foran Act, condemning contract labor as "slave labor" of the worst kind. His response to this challenge is quite revealing: "If the Senator from Missouri will hold me responsible for legislation that he disapproves, I hope he will look at the date of that legislation ... and whether we were not just, under the circumstances, in passing that law and laws much more severe in their character for that purpose, and when the objective has been accomplished, to repeal the law. . . . *There were many things that we deemed to be constitutional then which I would not regard to be constitutional* . . ." (*Congressional Record*, 1885, p. 1785; emphasis added).

3. Case after case is documented in the Industrial Commission reports, in which no conviction was forthcoming despite the written proof of a contract, because either the duration or the rate of wages had not been clearly specified.

4. It is interesting to note the striking similarities between this Anti-Contract Labor Law of 1885 and Canada's Alien Labor Act of 1897. As in the United States, previous years had witnessed in Canada a variety of promotional activities to encourage immigration. Cashmore (1978, p. 416) describes the Canadian government's reaction to possible labor protest as a result of this recruitment by the state and by industry:

"In 1897, the government must have anticipated some indigenous hostility to the wholesale import of labor and so passed the Alien Labor Act which was designed to prevent Canadian employers from importing contract laborers from certain countries, especially railroad workers from the United States. The significance of the particular piece of legislation is in its dormancy for it was never implemented! If it had been enforced then, it would almost certainly have worked to the detriment of certain powerful groups, especially the railway companies. However, it seems that the law in this case was conceived of as a panacea for potential unrest, thus establishing a climate for restoration of order, without seriously affecting employers' opportunities for recruiting inexpensive labor."

5. On one hand, the law of 1882 told immigration officials that those who were unable to care for themselves or anyone who was not plainly and beyond a doubt entitled to admission must be barred; on the other hand, the Anti-Contract Labor Law of 1885 stipulated that anyone with prearranged employment must also be barred. In other words, there must be no doubt as to the immigrant's immediately securing employment, but those who already have such employment must be deported. Such a contradiction speaks less to congressional incompetence or logical failings, as some have implied (see, for example, Erickson, 1957; Higham, 1955), than to the fact that these laws were not designed as a uniform policy but were responses to two different conflicts. Even though a literal interpretation of these two laws would have barred almost everyone, only 0.5% were barred each year.

6. That pauperism was not a condition inflicted on the industrial system by the immigrant but rather was inflicted on the immigrant by the industrial system is borne out by statistics. In 1890, 92% of the foreign-born almshouse paupers had been in this country ten years or more; Italians who asked for some form of relief in New York in 1904 had been in the country on an average eight and a half years before their first request for relief, and three-quarters had been here at least five years (Claghorn, 1904, p. 190; Hourwich, 1912, pp. 353ff.). As Claghorn (1904, p. 187) concludes from her extensive analysis of immigration and pauperism, "While it is plain enough that foreign immigration has some connection with the problem of pauperism since common observation and all the statistics available unite in showing that the majority of the recipients of our "charity"—private and public—are of foreign birth, it is equally certain that pauperism is not something that the immigrant brings with him."

4 · Selective Immigration as Qualified Action: "We Cannot Have Too Much Immigration of the Right Sort"

(Message from President Roosevelt,
Congressional Record, 1905.
59th Congress, 1st session, p. 101)

Introduction

The selective immigration legislation of the late nineteenth and early twentieth centuries represented an attempt to deal with ideological as well as fiscal dilemmas. Unrestricted immigration, on one hand, placed a financial burden on the local and state governments that were called on to warehouse unemployed and discarded workers in their jails, hospitals, asylums and other miscellaneous poorhouses. The reproduction of a surplus work force living at or beneath the subsistence level also threatened to undermine political stability and ideological control at precisely the moment that advancing monopoly capitalism increasingly depended on long-term predictability.

Before turning to an examination of these structural dilemmas and resulting modifications in immigration policies, the political and economic background must be filled in—in particular, the progress of the class struggle, the continued role of the immigrant in industry and in the labor movement, and the expansion and concentration of U.S. capital.

Class War and the Radicalization of Immigrants

The year after the Anti-Contract Labor Law was passed, 1886, was an eventful year in the class struggle in industrializing America. One historian called it a "revolutionary year" (Ware, 1929, p. 302). Engels wrote, "A revolution has been accomplished in American society such as, in any other country, would have taken at least ten years" (Engels, 1950, Preface).

On May 1, 1886, 350,000 workers went out on strike across the country demanding an eight-hour workday. Two days later, 1400 locked-out, unarmed workers at the McCormick Harvester Plant in Chicago were fired on by police, killing four and wounding hundreds. The following day, a meeting was called in Haymarket Square to protest the police brutality. As the last speaker was concluding his remarks before the small crowd that had withstood the rainstorm, a large body of police approached the platform and ordered the crowd to disperse. Without warning, a dynamite bomb was hurled through the air. The police opened fire, and in a matter of seconds one policeman and one spectator were killed and hundreds more were wounded (David, 1958).

The autumn of 1886 saw what Philip Foner (1955, p. 115) called "one of the most significant events in American history," the politicization of an embittered working class. In New York the Independent Labor Party was formed by the New York Central Labor Union and received 68,000 votes, or 31% of the total, encouraging workers all over the country to independent political action. In Chicago the labor party elected a state senator; the people's party in Milwaukee elected a mayor, state senator, assemblyman, and a congressman; in Colorado a state senator was elected; other victories were won in New Jersey, Virginia, Texas, Ohio, Massachusetts, Connecticut, and Florida. One journalist reported of the United Labor Party success in Chicago, "No party ever polled so large a vote nor made itself so generally felt at so young an age" (quoted in Foner, 1955, p. 131).

The capitalists' counteroffensive to these events, together with conflicts within the labor movement itself, temporarily stifled labor's voice, but the violence and organized struggle resumed in full force by the 1890s. By 1890, the AFL, organized on a strict craft union basis and regarding the interests of the skilled mechanic as of paramount importance, had replaced the less exclusive Knights of Labor. Despite the AFL's resistance to organizing the unskilled, the 1890s witnessed strikes, boycotts, and spontaneous resistance of unprecedented proportions.

The movement for the eight-hour workday intensified in 1890, bringing together thousands of the skilled and unskilled, native and foreign-born and winning for workers substantial gains (Boyer and Morais, 1980; Brecher, 1972; Foner, 1955). The Homestead Strike of 1892 was the most violent battle yet in the class war, as 3800 iron and steel workers at the Carnegie Steel Company in Homestead were locked out before they could strike against a 22%

wage reduction. For five months, 8000 soldiers occupied the small Pennsylvania town of 12,000, until—desperate and starving, and with an empty union treasury—the workers were defeated. The Amalgamated Association of Iron and Steel Workers was silenced for years.[1]

The following year began the most devastating economic breakdown American capitalism had known. Wage reductions and worker layoffs were daily occurrences, and by the end of 1893, three million out of a total work force of five million were unemployed. The Pullman Strike of 1894, or the "Debs Rebellion," was the response of men who had had wages cut as much as 50% and thousands laid off. More than 150,000 workers went out on strike, paralyzing the entire central and western railway system. If this strike was reminiscent of the 1877 Baltimore and Ohio strikes, capital's counterattack was predictably similar also, as 10,000 federal soldiers, infantry, cavalry, and field artillery marched into Chicago. Capital had added another weapon to their arsenal, in the court injunction. With both federal troops and the weight of legal sanction supporting them, capital's victory was secured.

As the century closed, the United Mine Workers (UMW) won one of the most resounding victories yet in the class struggle. In 1897 as the economic crisis dragged on, 200,000 miners went out on strike, shutting down 70% of the U.S. soft coal production. Their victory, winning a 33% wage increase and an eight-hour day, marked the first time any major industry in the United States signed a national agreement with its workers. In 1897 the UMW had 10,000 members; by 1900 117,000 miners were dues-paying members of this organization, which united "regardless of creed, color or nationality, all workmen employed in and around coal mines" (Warne, 1905, p. 35).

To contemporary observers, Senator John Ingalls's speech to the Senate in 1892 must not have seemed an overreaction. He spoke ominously of the period: "We cannot disguise the truth that we are on the verge of a revolution . . ." (quoted in Adamic, 1963, p. 109).

European immigrants and blacks continued to be used by capital to break strikes and reduce wages. Newspaper advertisements for workers of specific nationalities were still common, as were labor exchange offers to employers. This advertisement was printed in a Pittsburgh paper as late as 1915:

> Men wanted—Tinners, catchers, and helpers to work in open shops; Syrians, Poles, and Roumanians preferred. Steady employment and good wages to men willing to

work. Fare paid and no fees charged. (quoted in *Congressional Record*, 1915, p. 3049)

The following letter was sent to a variety of industries around the country in 1913:

Gentlemen: Foreign laborers are now available in this city for less wages than you can secure men for in your State. Are you in need of any? If so, we can offer for immediate shipment any number of them of any desired nationality. Trusting to hear from you, we are,

> Very truly yours,
> M. Engel, Manager
> Edward H. Labor Agency
> New York, New York
> Oct. 4, 1913

(quoted in *Congressional Record*, 1915, p. 3040)

Wage scales were dependent on the race and national origin of the worker. This ad for workers appeared in a New York City newspaper in 1895:

- Common labor, white, $1.30–$1.50
- Common labor, colored, $1.25–$1.40
- Common labor, Italian, $1.15–$1.25

(cited in Gambino, 1975, p. 77)

The conclusions of many historians, however, that the ethnic groups immigrating in this period were tractable and docile, are not borne out by the data. Immigrants were initially tractable, partly because of their desperation and inexperience in industrial relations. Many immigrant strike breakers no doubt had no conception of what a strike was and were at first unaware of their place in it. It was not long, however, before the immigrants themselves had become "the labor problem." With the immigrant solution, capital's labor problems were rebounded back on them with ever greater intensity, as the same immigrant stream that initially supplied them with strike breakers contributed to an increasingly class-conscious proletariat.

In an effort to combat the development of class consciousness, employers isolated immigrant workers. Senator Foran (*Congressional Record*, 1884, p. 5350) reported as early as 1884 that 400 Italians who replaced striking Buffalo longshoremen at $40 a month were "fenced in" and "kept by themselves." The president of the Knights of Labor, Powderly, testified that in the Frostburg region of Maryland, immigrants lived in barracks which were "fenced in to prevent them from being communicated with by the people whose places they had taken" (*Congressional Record*, 1884, p. 5360). The isolation was continued after the strike, according to Powderly, as returning strikers were housed and worked in different buildings from the recruited immigrants. He explained: "the men were not permitted to associate with American workmen lest they might find out the true state of affairs" (*Congressional Record*, 1884, p. 6065).

One immigrant described to Congress his arrival in the United States:

> When we arrived, a friend of one of us was met by a man whom he knew in Europe. As soon as they commenced to talk, the manager ordered the arrest of the party. When we arrived in Mainsfield, Ohio, a member of the firm came into the car and inquired if any of us could speak English. I answered that my father and I could. He then warned us not to talk to the men. (*Congressional Record*, 1884, p. 6065)

The mixing of nationalities as a technique of isolation lasted well into the twentieth century (Fitch, 1911, p. 147; Jones, 1960; Leiserson, 1971, p. 175). A manager of a Pittsburgh mill explained that a tractable force is best obtained by a "judiciously mixed" combination of foreigners and "young American country boys" (Bridge, 1902, p. 81). Similarly, Roberts (1912, p. 75) reports that "while talking to the superintendent of a large ore dock on Lake Erie, I asked him 'How do you get along with a half dozen people of different tongues; do you keep them separate?' 'No sir' was his reply, 'I mix them up. I get better results.'"

Roberts (1912, p. 75) goes on to tell of the ways in which national differences were used not only to isolate workers, but to increase productivity. "A foreman on the B&O pitted a gang of Italians against an equal number of Austrians, then played upon their racial prejudices and hatred, and got more work from each." Samuel Gompers (1925, p. 155), president of the AFL, explained that steel manufacturers employed "foreigners of different nationalities in order that there may not be free-speaking intercourse between them," in an effort "to keep wages down and workmen tractable."

Despite capital's efforts to isolate foreign workers and minimize their assimilation into the labor movement; despite the difficulties of unionizing them due to their transience and the unskilled and unstable nature of their employment; and, despite the AFL's reluctance to include them in their organizing efforts, the immigrants quickly learned both the meaning of industrial strife and the techniques of class struggle.

It is not difficult to understand the increased prominence of immigrants at the vanguard of the labor movement. By 1909, new immigrants constituted the majority of the industrial working class, as 60% of the men and 47% of the women wage workers in the 20 largest mining and manufacturing industries in the United States were recent immigrants (U.S. Congress, Senate Immigration Commission, 1911, Vol. 1, p. 322). By 1924, a majority of workers in each of the major manufacturing industries in the United States were foreign-born (see Table IV). Furthermore, wage reductions and layoffs hit these recent immigrants first and hardest, as they almost invariably occupied the least desirable and most unstable positions in each industry. Not surprisingly, these desperate newcomers began to fight back.

Higham (1955, p. 51) describes one of the incidents that triggered the end of the American businessman's unequivocal appreciation of the immigrant, as Hungarian coke miners took on Henry Clay Frick in 1886 and won. "Several thousand Hungarian coke miners displayed a belligerence and solidarity that confounded the anticipations of unions and operators alike."

TABLE IV

Proportion of Foreign-Born Workers to
Native Workers in Basic Manufacturing
Industries, 1924[a]

Industry	%
Iron and steel	58
Bituminous coal	62
Slaughtering and packing houses	61
Woolen and worsted	62
Cotton goods	62
Clothing	69
Leather	67
Furniture	59
Oil refining	67

[a] Source: Bimba (1927, p. 224).

The general bituminous coal strike in 1897 similarly drew its strength from the support of the industry's immigrants. While the UMW at the outbreak of the strike had only 10,000 members, 100,000—many unorganized Slavs and Italians—responded to the strike call. A similar strike was organized in the anthracite fields in 1902, again with the full support of the immigrant work force.

With the support of the Industrial Workers of the World (IWW) and a variety of small, independent unions by 1906, many spontaneous uprisings led by immigrant workers stunned both their American employers and, increasingly, their native-born co-workers. Foreign workers on streetcars, in the clothing trades, in textiles, in packing houses, and in steel mills launched some of the most crippling strikes of the period.

> In the summer of 1909 there was a demonstration of the spirit of immigrant workmen that opened the eyes of the public to qualities heretofore unknown. For many weeks . . . they persisted in their strike against the Pressed Steel Car Company. It had been thought that the Slavs were too sluggish to resist their employers, and unable to organize along industrial lines. It was proved in this conflict that neither theory was correct. (Fitch, 1911, pp. 237–238)

The Lawrence Textile Strike in 1912 and the Great Steel Strike of 1919 are good examples of the new role of the Southern and Eastern European immigrant in the militant labor movement. In January, 1912, a Massachusetts state law reduced the permissible labor hours of women and children from 56 to 54, Lawrence mill wages were reduced, and machines speeded up. On January 12, in the predominantly Italian-worked Everett textile mill in Lawrence, a shout of desperation went out, "Goddamn it to hell! Let's strike! Strike!" (Adamic, 1963, p. 166). Instantly the cry went out, "Strike! Strike!", and within minutes 1000 Italian workers crowded the streets. The strike spread to other mills in the city, and in less than an hour, thousands of immigrant mill workers filled the streets of Lawrence. An observer warned that "the capacity of this great host of recent immigrants representing a number of supposedly alienated nationalities, for continuous, effective solidarity is one of the revelations of the present strike" (quoted in Hourwich, 1912, p. 392).

Another Lawrence textile strike, spearheaded by unskilled immigrant workers, occurred in 1919 and spread through all the textile towns of New England and New Jersey, as 120,000 textile workers walked out (Brecher, 1972, pp. 114–115).

The role of recent immigrants in the steel strikes of 1919 was also critical. The Pittsburgh region, including dozens of small steel towns throughout western Pennsylvania, was the heart of the U.S. steel industry. It was here that the great steel strike found its major battlefield. Many of the 350,000 workers who struck the steel plants were unskilled Southern European immigrants. Despite repeated attempts by the AFL to moderate their demands and postpone the strike, the embittered rank and file stood firm, crippling steel production. The repression of civil liberties, arrests, beatings, and red raids, initiated by employers, private strike-breaking agencies, and the federal government, followed quickly. Employers did not hesitate to play upon the fact that immigrants formed the core of the strike effort, as indicated by these instructions from an employer to a labor detective agency operating in the South Chicago steel mills:

> We want you to stir up as much bad feeling as you possibly can between the Serbians and Italians. Spread data among the Serbians that the Italians are going back to work. Call up every question you can in reference to racial hatred between these two nationalities. . . . Urge them to go back to work or the Italians will get their jobs. (quoted in the Commission of Inquiry, 1920, p. 230)

Ultimately the censorship of the labor press during the strike, the rigid surveillance of strikers, the arrests, the beatings, and the steel companies' control over communications resulted in the strikers' defeat. Nonetheless, the effect of the steel strike and the hundreds of other revolts of 1919 was profound: the immigrant workers had demonstrated that despite obstacles to their organization, they were at least as capable of labor solidarity as skilled, unionized American-born workers.

Not only did immigrants form the vanguard of many strikes in this period, but many of these spontaneous immigrant uprisings were defeated with the use of AFL members and other native workers. Leiserson (1971, p. 175) notes that in the Southern cotton mills, it was the native workers who prevented organization. Numerous railway strikes by immigrants after World War I were broken by American workers, and in clothing, textiles, and packing houses, labor leaders had less difficulty organizing foreigners than natives (Hourwich, 1912; Leiserson, 1971, p. 175; Montgomery, 1974). In the Lawrence Textile Strike of 1919, of which the conservative United Textile Workers (UTW) disapproved, the English-speaking employees continued to work as the non-English-speaking workers walked out (Leiserson, 1971, p. 204).

Immigrants strengthened the labor movement not only with their solidarity and readiness to strike, but by increasingly joining those labor unions from which they were not excluded. When the UMW was organized in 1890, most of its members were from Southern and Eastern Europe (Erickson, 1957, p. 117). In 1910 according to the Dillingham Commission's statistics (U.S. Congress, Senate Immigration Commission, 1911, Vol. 1, p. 418), 11.4% of the old immigrants of their sample were unionized as compared to 16.6% of the new immigrants. The trades in which Jewish immigrants predominated were unionized one after the other: the Cap Makers in 1901, the Fur Workers in 1904, the Amalgamated Clothing Workers in 1914. By 1918 more than 250,000 Jewish workers were affiliated with the United Hebrew Trades (Meltzer, 1976, p. 227). The International Ladies Garment Workers and the Amalgamated Clothing Workers of America, claiming 175,000 members apiece and made up overwhelmingly of Jews, Italians, and Poles, were "two of the strongest labor unions in America" (Leiserson, 1971, p. 207).

In those industries dominated by the narrow craft unionism that excluded the unskilled, recent immigrants formed alternative organizations based on industrial unionism. While over two-thirds of textile operatives were recent immigrants by 1920, only 10% of the members of the exclusive UTW were immigrants. After the Lawrence textile strike in which the immigrant strikers secured a 15% wage increase and a 48-hour week, immigrants formed the Amalgamated Textile Workers as a satellite of the Amalgamated Clothing Workers, both based on an alliance between Italian and Jewish workers (Montgomery, 1974, p. 522).

Before World War I, the bulk of organized labor was composed of skilled workers (Wolman, 1915, p. 516), but after the war it was clear to some organizations that the unskilled, predominantly immigrant elements, could make a major contribution. By enlisting unskilled immigrants, the International Association of Machinists reached 250,000 members by 1920, and the Maintenance of Way Employees grew from 50,000 to 200,000. When, in 1918, the AFL reluctantly began enlisting all steelworkers regardless of skill, Poles, Italians, Croats, and Serbs joined rapidly, and by 1920 about 320,000 unskilled iron- and steelworkers had been organized (Leiserson, 1971).

Almost as bothersome to capital as the immigrants' militant labor activity was their visibility in a variety of socialist and anarchist organizations. German-Americans had dominated organizations of anarchists and socialists in the 1880s, as the International Working Peoples Association, the Socialist Labor Party, and social revolutionary clubs were formed in cities across the country. Jewish immigrants in the 1880s founded socialist organizations, initiating a tradition of socialism among Jewish workers. By the turn of the century, Southern and Eastern Europeans were increasingly represented in socialist and anarchist parties and organizations.

The organization that more than any other alarmed the capitalist class for more than two decades emerged out of discussions in the Western Federation of Miners in 1903. Formed as an industrial union, the IWW had as its aim "to put the working class in possession of the economic power, the means of life, in control of the machinery of production and distribution, without regard to capitalist masters" (Bill Haywood, quoted in Adamic, 1963, p. 157). Although its major aim was to revolutionize society as a whole, and the leadership scorned the more narrow goals of most unions, it backed hundreds of strikes by unorganized immigrants and often carried them to victory (Brissenden, 1920). While precise statistics are not available, Brissenden (1920, pp. 158–159) estimates that "a large proportion" of the IWW membership were recent Southern and Eastern European immigrants.

Finally, the foreign-born membership of the American Socialist Party, in spite of a pronounced anti-immigrant bias largely derived from its affiliation with the AFL, grew from about 29% in 1908 to at least 68% in 1919; furthermore, the bulk of this growth was due to the membership of recent immigrants from Southern and Eastern Europe (Montgomery, 1974, pp. 1, 22; Jones, 1960, pp. 229–230). The foreign-language federations of the party grew steadily from 15,340 members in 1912 to 56,680 by 1919 (Montgomery, 1974, p. 522).

Of course, not all immigrant workers in this period were militant labor activists or members of socialist or anarchist organizations, nor did they necessarily form the bulk of the labor movement. But capital could no longer count on immigrant docility. Just as with the Irish and Germans before them, the Southern and Eastern European immigrants—recruited to resolve capital's problems in the class struggle—now refurbished that struggle.

In the meantime, the continued expansion and concentration of capital was changing the face of the U.S. industrial and financial landscape.

Industrial Expansion, Capital Concentration, and Economic Breakdown

Despite increasingly frequent and long-lasting recessions, the value of the U.S. manufactured product grew fivefold in the 20 years between 1899 and 1919, as the United States achieved the undisputed position of industrial and financial center of the world. By 1900, industry had assumed the leading role in the U.S. economy, as the value of all manufactured products exceeded $13 billion; by 1919, that value reached $63 billion. The number of immigrant workers doubled in this period, and capital investments grew fivefold (Faulkner, 1962).

This growth of the U.S. industrial product was not accompanied by a parallel growth in the number of manufacturing establishments. Instead, mechanization by the twentieth century minimized competition through a dramatic reduction in the number of manufacturers who could afford the capital investment required and an equally dramatic increase in the size of the average industrial enterprise. As Weisberger (1969, p. 17) puts it, "In the game of business, it was necessary each year for a player to put in higher and higher stakes to stay at the table."

The concentration of American industry at the turn of the century rested on two factors: the need for massive sums of capital for the establishment and operation of a modern industry, and the need for market and price stability that the investment of such sums necessitates. According to Brody (1960, p. 16), the minimum initial investment required for a steel-making plant in 1900, for example, was approximately $20 million. In response the corporation emerged, raising huge amounts of capital by the selling of stock. By 1919, 86% of all manufacturing employees worked in corporation-owned establishments, and corporations manufactured 88% of all U.S. products. While the corporation, by virtue of the increased availability of capital and its invulnerability to deaths, arguments, and individual failings, had clear advantages over the individual capitalist-dominated firm of the past, it did not altogether eliminate competition and market and price instability.

It was this need to achieve stability in an unstable environment that precipitated monopolization, trusts, pooling, and ultimately the control over much U.S. industry by a few finance capitalists. Pools had been established as early as the 1870s among railroads in order to reduce competition in a business that required massive capital outlays over extended periods of time (Foner, 1955, p. 12; Weisberger, 1969, p. 19). Pools, with no benefit of any legal standing, were replaced by trusts and holding companies by 1900. In 1897, the 82 largest corporations in the United States together capitalized at $1 billion. Four years later, U.S. Steel alone, having merged 158 companies, capitalized at over $1 billion. By 1915, names such as U.S. Steel, Standard Oil, General

Electric, AT&T and American Tobacco had become symbols of a dramatically altered economic structure in the United States.

As industrial expansion went beyond the resources of individual entrepreneurs and bankers, and as these combinations became so large as to require the orchestration of a central investment house, control over U.S. manufacturing began to shift from the industrial to the finance capitalist. By the turn of the century, giant banking houses like J. P. Morgan emerged, and with their access to the large capital resources required by modern industry, held the strings that moved the bulk of the U.S. economy (Faulkner, 1962; Weisberger, 1969).

The shift to capital-intensive, mechanized industry was central in this expansion and concentration process. Not only did mechanization increase productivity, but as earlier in the nineteenth century, it effected the degradation of skills and the weakening of the position of the skilled laborer, both of which cut total labor costs. As Fitch (1911, p. 141) wrote of the steel industry in 1911: "Fifteen or twenty years ago a large proportion of the employees in any steel plant were skilled men. The percentage of the highly skilled has steadily grown less; and the percentage of the unskilled has as steadily increased." With the decreased need for the highly skilled, their bargaining power was eroded, and the steel makers were able to implement an "equalizing of pay differentials." By 1900, skilled steelworkers had suffered an absolute decline in their wages (Brody, 1960, p. 45).

Two effects of the capital-labor relationship that stemmed from this mechanization and the monopolization that made it possible are of most concern to us here. In the first place the homogenization of the labor force, which began with the development of the factory system, quickened with the rapid mechanization of production. As skilled craftsmen became increasingly superfluous and the percentage of the work force that was unskilled increased, the homogenization of the work force in industrial America was complete. Bimba describes the result of this simultaneous monopolization of capital and the homogenization of the work force:

> Gigantic factories have been established where hundreds and sometimes thousands of workers are employed under such conditions, and the class structure naturally becomes sharper. The differences between the capitalist class and the working class become more clearly defined. (Bimba, 1927, p. 222)

Secondly, as the number of self-employed and small entrepreneurs steadily decreased with advancing monopolization, and as the wages of skilled labor continued to decline, the vast wealth that was daily re-created was increasingly polarized. By 1890, seven-eighths of American families held only one-eighth of the wealth, and 1% of the families held more wealth than the other 99% (Faulkner, 1962, p. 21). Studies done ten years later indicate that while 20% of the population enjoyed the harvest of industrialization, 80% lived on the very margins of existence (King, 1915, pp. 217–237). This polarization can also be viewed in terms of the percentages of annual income earned by the two groups. In 1910, the top three-tenths of the population earned 56% of the annual income reported, while the bottom three-tenths earned only 13%. In 1921, the difference had increased to 61% and 10%, respectively (Kolko, 1962, p. 14). While these income figures undoubtedly understate the actual gap in wealth between the two groups, they are useful as indicators of the increased polarization over time.

Exacerbating the polarized distribution of wealth, the rapid increase of productive capacity that accompanied increased mechanization and monopolization made for a chronically unstable economy. As Baran and Sweezy (1966, p. 218) describe it, "The growth of monopoly generates a strong tendency for surplus to rise without at the same time providing adequate mechanisms of surplus absorption." In the short run, this implies more frequent and longer lasting periods of economic collapse as production outstrips consumption; in the longer run, it implies chronic stagnation, since

> surplus that is not absorbed is also surplus that is not produced: It is merely potential surplus, and it leaves its statistical trace not in the figures of profits and investment but rather in the figures of unemployment and unutilized productive capacity. (Baran and Sweezy, 1966, p. 218)

Baran and Sweezy are careful to emphasize that this tendency toward economic stagnation in advanced capitalism is in fact a *tendency* that may be offset by counterforces. They argue that the major counterforces that have temporarily negated the depressive effects of monopolization are "epoch-making innovations," such as the railroad, the automobile, and wars. They argue that these forces, by opening huge investment outlets and creating vast new markets, have been responsible for the full survival of capitalism since the end of the last century.

In the last two decades of the nineteenth century, when monopolization was beginning to take hold, and when therefore, surplus absorption difficulties would have become evident, close to 50% of all private capital formation was invested in the railroads (Baran and Sweezy, 1966, p. 221). With the crisis of 1907, however, railroad investment took a nose dive and never returned to its central place in the economy.

> In other words, the big shake-up, which began even before the Civil War, was largely over. If we are right about this, it was in 1907 that the greatest external stimulus in capitalist history lost its tremendous force. (Baran and Sweezy, 1966, p. 227)

With the disappearance from the economic scene of this epoch-making force, clear signs of chronic stagnation set in, to be relieved in 1915 by another major investment outlet, World War I and its aftermath. The major statistical traces were a rather dramatic change in the pattern of business cycles, with business contractions now more extended than business expansions, and unemployment figures that—with the exception of the war period—did not dip far below pre-1907 figures even in expansion periods (see Table V).

The continued advance of the class war, the new role played by immigrants in strike activity and the class struggle in general, the expansion and concentration of industry, and the increasingly unstable economic environment—these are the crucial components of the socioeconomic setting of the last years of the nineteenth and the first years of the twentieth century. It was in this context that the first serious efforts to regulate immigration were formulated.

The Public Charge Provision Expanded

Remember that the public charge restriction was an attempt to grapple with the conflict between the advantages of reproducing a surplus work force versus the need to provide it with a minimum level of subsistence. As mechanization and monopolization swelled the ranks of the surplus supply of labor, immigration policy began to show an even more urgent concern to exclude potential paupers and public charges.

The Act of 1903 (32 U.S. Statutes at Large), developed on the basis of recommendations by the Industrial Commission, excluded

TABLE V

Percentage of the Civilian Work Force Unemployed[a]

Year	% of work force unemployed	Year	% of work force unemployed
1900	5	1911	6.2
1901	2.4	1912	5.2
1902	2.7	1913	4.4
1903	2.6	1914	8.0
1904	4.8	1915	9.7
1905	3.1	1916	4.8
1906	.8	1917	4.8
1907	1.8	1918	1.4
1908	8.5	1919	2.3
1909	5.2	1920	4.0
1910	5.9	1921	11.9

[a] Source: U.S. Bureau of the Census (1960, p. 73).

epileptics, the insane, and professional beggars. In addition, the period within which public charges could be deported was extended to two years.[2] The bill elicited little discussion in Congress, was passed unanimously by both congressional committees, and passed by overwhelming margins in both houses. The bill's major spokesman in the House of Representatives declared,

> The statistics of the various states present some startling revelations concerning the great burden placed by immigrants upon the penal and charity institutions of this country, the larger percent of the inmates of jails, insane asylums, and charity institutions, having been furnished by immigrants. . . .

But:

> It is evident . . . *that legislation must be carefully considered and be along conservative lines. . . . [We] must avoid measures so drastic as to cripple American industry, agriculture, and the great shipping and transportation interests.* (*Congressional Record*, 1902, pp. 5763–5764, emphasis added)

Representative Underwood (*Congressional Record*, 1902, p. 5769;

emphasis added) expressed the problem this way:

> The object of bringing this immense number of immigrants to this country now is to supply the demands for labor. But, even today, *when the demand for labor is at its height, the field for employment is overcrowded.... There is no place for the surplus to go.*

If this sounds like the Mad Hatter lecturing the March Hare, Underwood was not nearly as confused as he might seem. He was merely verbalizing as well as he could the state's essentially irresolvable dilemma.

The next significant immigration law, passed on February 20, 1907 (34 U.S. Statutes at Large), raised the head tax to $4, added to the excluded classes "imbeciles," the "feebleminded," those with tuberculosis, unaccompanied children under 16, and others

> who are found to be mentally or physically defective, such ... defect being of a nature which may affect the ability of the alien to earn a living.

The emphasis was on the further clarification of those undesirable classes who might contribute to the strain on the state through poverty. The act further extended the period within which paupers could be deported to three years. The act clearly followed the earlier logic in attempting to sift out those with inherent attributes that predisposed them to poverty. However, at the same time—in allowing for the deportation of those who became public charges within three years—it was implicitly recognized that poverty was frequently imposed by the industrial system itself.

The Immigration Act of 1917 (39 U.S. Statutes at Large) continued this concern with public charges. Persons of "psychopathic constitutional inferiority" (the definition of which remained obscure) and persons with chronic alcoholism were added to the list of undesirables. The act also included a change in the wording of the 1907 law as it related to public charges. In the Act of 1907, "persons likely to become public charges" had appeared in Section 2, between "paupers" and "professional beggars." The implication of this wording was that "likelihood to become a public charge" was an attribute of the immigrant himself. Nonetheless, immigration inspectors, recognizing the overriding importance of economic considerations, regularly weighed regional and national industrial conditions in determining the likelihood of an immigrant becoming a public charge.

In 1915, the U.S. Supreme Court determined that the exclusion of a group of Russians headed for Portland, due to Portland's poor industrial conditions, could not be upheld. Aliens, they said, could be excluded only "on the ground of *permanent personal characteristics*" (emphasis added), since public charges were listed among beggars, paupers, idiots, and others with "defective personal attributes."

The Supreme Court had thus highlighted one of the major dilemmas with which Congress had to deal and which had no logical solution. Congress, in an effort to allow immigration inspectors to continue to consider economic conditions in their decisions, in 1917 shifted the position of "persons likely to become public charges" away from Section 2, which dealt with personal characteristics, to Section 3, following a clause dealing with contract labor.

The provision for the deportation of immigrants who became public charges was extended to five years after entry, and the burden of proof that a propensity for pauperism had not existed at the time of entry was shifted to the alien. Of course, it was rare that an alien could convince officials that present pauperism had not evolved from an inherent condition five years earlier, since the dominant explanation at the time with regard to almost all undesirable behavior was that it was hereditary.

Throughout these first years of the twentieth century, organized labor continued to object to unrestricted immigration. While Congress sporadically enacted amendments to the 1885 Anti-Contract Labor Law, and while sympathy was regularly expressed in Congress for the plight of the American laborer, immigration laws overwhelmingly focused on the exclusion of this minority of "physical and mental defectives." As one congressman put it:

> From the beginning of this controversy, down to this hour, the demand of the workers of this country has been that the stalwart 6-foot laborer, capable of competing in the labor market with those already toiling for a living here—not the organ-grinder or the beggar—shall be excluded. No effort has been made to meet this demand. This bill [Act of 1903] does not even squint at it. (*Congressional Record*, 1902, p. 5817)

None of the immigration bills of this period took seriously workers' demands for restrictions. Instead, these bills were directed at a completely different type of dilemma—one that could not be resolved with symbolic concessions to American workers. This dilemma derived from one of the most fundamental contradictions in capitalism: the system nurtures poverty at the same time that it must cope with poverty's effects.

The personalization of the problem of poverty as a response was no doubt not only an effort to deal with this irksome dilemma, but was also an attempt to legitimate the system that regularly reproduced such poverty, by defining it as a personal failing. As Axinn and Levin (1975, p. 90) note, "The situation was one in which the more obvious the social causes of poverty, the more insistence there was upon the personal aberrations and immorality of paupers." As we will see, those who were not successfully entrapped in capital's hegemonic net were similarly defined as personally defective.

Sociopolitical Reproduction of the Work Force

The increases in pauperism, unemployment, and poor working conditions that accompanied the construction of a surplus labor supply not only placed a fiscal burden on the state, but also had potentially devastating sociopolitical consequences. As Edelman (1977) and others have pointed out, while capitalism depends on and propagates severe economic inequalities, the consent of the governed must nonetheless be achieved. This consent became increasingly problematic as the surplus labor supply and mechanization, fed by immigration and monopolization, respectively, swelled the ranks of the unemployed and "deskilled" the work force.

Compounding an already critical situation, the advance of monopoly capitalism—based as it was on massive, long-range investments—required more than ever a climate of economic and political stability. At precisely the moment that legitimation and political stability were increasingly precarious, the economic structure of monopoly capitalism depended on long-term predictability. Crippling strikes and mass political action, the outward symbols of withdrawal of consent, accelerated just as their effects were most disruptive.

Just as the fiscal problem associated with immigrant poverty was traced to individual deficiencies and dealt with by sifting immigrants, so the problem of hegemony and legitimation was rhetorically linked to the character of individual immigrants. While the immigrant stream that supplied the biological reproduction of the work force was not to be interrupted, those who were "predisposed" to unacceptable political activity could be barred. Again, the systemic contradiction was redefined as a problem of individual deficiencies. The predictable inadequacy of this selective, individualistic approach is less indicative of congressional incompetence than of the narrow parameters within which these policy makers had to act.

The first step toward barring those thought to be predisposed to troublemaking was the Act of 1903 (32 U.S. Statutes at Large). A central element of this act was the exclusion or deportation, up to three years after entry, of

> anarchists, or persons who believe in or advocate the overthrow by force or violence of the government of the U.S., or of all government, or of all forms of law, or the assassination of public officials.

The bill was sent from the House and Senate committees with unanimous support and passed in the full House 194 to 11 (*Congressional Record*, 1903, p. 3011) and in the Senate without a record vote (*Congressional Record*, 1903, p. 2895). With this act, exclusion or deportation for proscribed opinions was provided for the first time since the Alien and Sedition Acts of 1798 and continued to be a primary focus of early twentieth century immigration laws. (For a summary of previous, unsuccessful efforts to exclude anarchists, see Burrows, 1901.)

Selective Immigration, Administrative Discretion, and the Literacy Test Proposal

The strategy behind selective immigration laws was to deal individualistically with the conflicts to which massive immigration contributed, while not numerically limiting the golden stream. As President Roosevelt said in his annual message to Congress in 1905 (*Congressional Record*, 1905, p. 101), "We cannot have too much immigration of the right sort," but

> there should be an increase in the stringency of the laws to keep out insane, idiotic, epileptic, and pauper immigrants. . . . Not merely the anarchist, but every man of anarchistic tendencies, all violent and disorderly people, all people of bad character, the incompetent, the lazy, the vicious, the physically unfit, defective, or degenerate, should be kept out.

As Cashmore (1978, p. 417) notes with regard to Canadian immigration policy in the same period, "the ideal immigrant would be: healthy, industrious, and politically conservative!"

If these selective policies were an attempt to resolve unresolvable dilemmas, two imperatives follow logically: (1) administrative discretion had to be maximized, and (2) this solution of barring undesirables would only be acceptable as long as those undesirables constituted only a small part of the immigrant flow.

Administrative discretion had to be maximized, because any legislative resolution to structural dilemmas must seesaw as dexterously as possible between the incompatible components. In such cases, it is particularly useful if, as sporadic fluctuations in conditions take place, the seesaw may tip slightly in one or another direction to suit temporary needs. For example, while these selective measures were generally adapted to the continued need for a surplus laboring population, the effectiveness of the laws could be increased if their interpretation and enforcement varied with economic spurts and breakdowns and other fluctuations in industrial conditions.

To this end, the first general immigration law in 1882 had included the provision that the secretary of the treasury was empowered to make any rule or regulation "as he shall deem best calculated for carrying out the provisions of this act and the immigration law of the U.S." (22 U.S. Statutes at Large, p. 214). Thus, the power of administrative officers to effectively create immigration law was established.

The wide discretion accorded immigration inspectors has already been discussed in interpreting the Anti-Contract Labor Law. This discretion operated almost unchecked in the application of the public charge clause. At least two-thirds of those who were excluded each year were excluded under the public charge clause (Jenks, 1913, p. 509). While other exclusionary measures were relatively easy to evade, the public charge clause was used increasingly to limit immigration in sections of the country and at times when industrial conditions diminished the demand for labor. The law explicitly required inspectors to use their discretion as to whether a particular alien was likely to become a public charge. Not only were national and local economic conditions considered, but every aspect of the immigrant's background entered into the inspector's judgment. Van Vleck (1932, p. 54) describes it this way in *The Administrative Control of Aliens:*

> "Likely to become a public charge" is used as a kind of miscellaneous file into which are placed cases where the officers think the alien ought not to enter, but the facts do not come within any specific requirements of the statutes.

Exclusions and deportations increased in 1900 and again in 1903 and 1904 (Jenks, 1913, p. 509), as high unemployment and a trough in the business cycle reduced the need for labor. In 1904, when unemployment almost doubled, the number of immigrants barred doubled with it. With the economic stagnation of 1907, capital investment plummeted, unemployment reached unprecedented peaks, and exclusions shot up. In the fiscal year ending June, 1907, just before the panic, those barred numbered only 1% of the total immigrant flow; in 1908, the barred reached 1.5% for the first time; by 1911, 6.1% of the total were excluded.

This increasing stringency at a time of depressed industrial conditions was not left to chance. A letter issued by Commissioner General of Immigration William Williams, dated June 21, 1910, and sent to all major ports of entry emphasized that for aliens to be admissible, they must "be clearly and beyond a doubt entitled to land" (quoted in Kohler, 1936, p. 5). Furthermore, he went on, the "inspector must not leniently *conjecture* that the alien will be able to get along, but such fact *must appear clearly and beyond a doubt*" (Kohler, 1936, p. 6; emphasis in original). The 1909 Annual Report of the U.S. Commissioner General of Immigration advised,

> In the absence of a statutory provision, no hard and fast rule can be laid down as to the amount of money an alien must have with him, but in most cases it will be unsafe for immigrants to arrive with less than $25 and a railroad ticket, and sometimes more.

Prior to the depression of 1907, a bill had been submitted to Congress to require all incoming aliens to have in their possession at least $25, but the bill had been rejected as too harsh (Kohler, 1936, p. 53). Now, in the midst of economic disaster, the immigration commissioner was asking inspectors to establish the requirement in practice.

This ability to expand and contract the provisions of the law is crucial in the face of dilemmas that are unresolvable in any real sense, but that must be dealt with in the most effective way possible.

Secondly, this solution of barring undesirables will only be acceptable if the undesirables constitute a minority, since the purpose of selective policies is to filter out undesirables without substantially reducing the amount of immigration. The 20-year debate on a literacy test for aspiring immigrants provides a good example.

The debate over a literacy test requirement emerged at the same time as the concern over the alleged anarchism of immigrants and their disruptive potential. The nature of the debate reflects the law makers' dilemma that the capitalist system at the turn of the century continued to demand an expanding and surplus labor-ing population, while the state had to contend with the class struggle and delegitimation that this exploitation precipitated.

When the literacy test bill was first introduced by Senator Henry Cabot Lodge in 1896, the issue was approached in racial terms. Its proponents argued that the new immigrant of "inferior stock" must be excluded by means of a literacy test, or they would menace U.S. institutions and civilization (*Congressional Record*, 1896, pp. 2818, 5477). By the turn of the century, proponents of a literacy test contended that the illiterate laborer was likely to have anarchistic tendencies. In their view, illiterates were among the undesirables, with paupers, criminals, anarchists, and others. Thus Roosevelt, in his first annual message to Congress following McKinley's assassination in 1901, warned,

> ... [one] object of a proper immigration law ought to be to secure by a careful and not merely perfunctory educa-tional test some intelligent capacity to appreciate Ameri-can institutions.... [This would] tend to decrease the sum of ignorance so potent in producing the envy, suspi-cion, malignant passion, and hatred of order, out of which anarchistic sentiment inevitably springs.... (*Con-gressional Record*, 1902, p. 84)

In support of a literacy test to bar the entry of undesirables from Southern and Eastern Europe, this editorial from a major urban newspaper was quoted in Congress in 1913:

> ... thinking men all over the country have fully realized the menace to our free institutions involved in the arri-val of people without training in self-government.... (*Congressional Record*, 1913a, p. 2296)

The issue of industrial unrest was just as important as strictly political considerations in the later period. As Albert Johnson, Chair of the House Committee on Immigration and Naturaliza-tion, put it in 1915:

> These teachings [of "industrial sabotage"] are coming right along with the influx of more than a million aliens a year. The more illiterate of the aliens, once here, quick-ly absorb the teachings. Some of the worst of our recent strikes can be attributed, in part, to these things.... Personally, I went over to Paterson, New Jersey, during the IWW strike in the silk mills and heard such stuff preached to the foreign workers.... They were told to

drop threads and let dyes run, and that the time would soon come when they would themselves run the mills and factories. And they believed it. (*Congressional Record*, 1915, p. 3028)

Those opposed to the literacy test noted two problems: (1) such a qualification would severely curtail immigration and cut off an essential source of labor, and (2) it was not clear that barring illiterates would effectively exclude political and industrial troublemakers. There was no disagreement that the primary consideration must be the elimination of disruptive elements among the immigrants. The issues of controversy were, which elements in fact supplied the agitators? And, would a literacy test that curtailed immigration be economically suicidal? Regarding the former, President Cleveland reasoned in his veto message to Congress in 1897:

> ... Violence and disorder do not originate with illiterate laborers. They are rather the victims of the educated agitator. The ability to read and write as required in this bill, in and of itself, affords, in my opinion, a misleading test of contented industry.... (U.S. Congress, Senate Documents, 1897, p. 3)

Literacy test opponents in Congress argued in 1902:

> Was there ever a menace of harm to the government of the U.S. either in the formation of anarchistic societies or in the development of outbreaks against the authority of law, that did not come from conspirators who were educated men? (*Congressional Record*, 1902, p. 5775)

And: "Frequently and in most instances, you will find anarchy ... under the velvet cover of the so-called educated gentry who come into this country ..." (*Congressional Record*, 1902, p. 5774; see also, *ibid.* 1913b, p. 2601; 1915, pp. 3023, 3029.)

It was frequently argued that illiterates were more desirable than the well-educated. As a New England mill owner put it as early as 1883, "There is such a thing as too much education for working people sometimes.... I have seen cases where young people were spoiled by being educated to a little too much refinement" (quoted in David, 1958, p. 26).

A former commissioner general of immigration testified to the Industrial Commission (U.S. Congress, House Industrial Commission, 1901, Vol. 15; emphasis added):

A young able-bodied man who comes from a foreign land to settle here, with energy and willingness to work, is an acquisition to the country, and while we do not want him to occupy the position which education would enable him to occupy, *we want him to occupy the position where it does not much matter whether he knows his ABC's or anything else.*

Congressmen warned that the literacy test would "tend to exclude a desirable class of immigrants, men who would do the drudgery that this country requires" (*Congressional Record*, 1902, p. 5823). The *Boston Herald*, quoted in the House of Representatives in 1913 (*Congressional Record*, 1913a, p. 2294), warned:

One honest and hard-working illiterate who lives clean and raises a decent family, is worth a hundred of the inefficients our schools turn out annually, who can read and write, but who are too fine to work and who are utterly useless.... We place too high an estimate upon mere literacy.... Envy and discontent ... are the outgrowth of laziness and inefficiency.... I would rather have an illiterate who can steer a plow, wield a sledge, roof a house, lay brick, or dig a good sewer than a dozen half-baked chaps who can write "dog" and read "cat."

In 1915, President Wilson requested a private hearing on the advantages and disadvantages of a literacy test and invited interested parties to confer with him at the White House. Representative Moore of Philadelphia warned Wilson at that meeting, "It would be a great mistake now to place an embargo on willing hands and brawny muscle." Others concurred, "I believe that a calloused hand, a hand calloused by labor, should be a better passport ... than a tongue supple in several languages. I do not think this country needs linguists; I do think it greatly needs laborers" (quoted in *Congressional Record*, 1915, pp. 3027, 3025). Similarly, in hearings before the House Committee on Immigration and Naturalization in 1916, Representative Cochran argued, "The really dangerous man is the one who could meet the literacy test triumphantly" (U.S. Congress, House Committee on Immigration and Naturalization, 1916, p. 15).

The test was also denounced for its potential effect of restricting the immigrant stream that supplied American capital with cheap labor. "I think a test of that kind would be an absolute bar to all further immigration in the U.S.... *We need the leaven of immigration*" (*Congressional Record*, 1902, pp. 5773–5774; see also p. 5828; emphasis added). In 1913, the warning was repeated,

... if this law goes into force you will hear a howl from one end of this broad land to the other against such a bill, because the business interests, conditions in the farming communities, and the necessity in this country for the class of labor you propose to exclude will be such that everybody voting for it will hear as a result of that vote a protest against this class of legislation. (*Congressional Record*, 1913a, p. 2294)

President Taft's 1913 veto included the following message to Congress:

... I cannot make up my mind to sign a bill which in its chief provision violates a principle that ought, in my opinion, to be upheld in dealing with immigration.... For the reasons stated in Secretary [of Labor] Nagel's letter to me, I cannot approve that test. (U.S. Congress, Senate Documents, 1913, pp. 1–4)

The letter from Nagel made it clear that the concern was with the potential effect on the labor market: "So far as the industrial conditions are concerned, I think the question has been superficially considered" (quoted in Fairchild, 1917, p. 457). Fairchild reports of this letter,

Another passage bears the clear implication that if the literacy test could have been supported as a *selective* measure the Secretary might have approved it, but that it could not, and as a *restrictive* measure, it introduced a principle which he could not accept. (Fairchild, 1917, p. 457; emphasis added)

A look at the 20-year debate over the literacy test requirement, then, makes it clear that the concern was with the maintenance of the social, economic, and cultural status quo on one hand, and on the other, the continued need for the cheap labor force that unrestricted immigration provided. Equally clear was the fact that the solution of barring undesirables was considered an ideal solution only if those undesirables constituted a small minority and would not significantly reduce the stream. The irony is that, with regard to public charges, for example, the solution to poverty via the restriction of public charge types is only acceptable as long as it does not interfere with the creation of a surplus labor supply on which the system thrives and which is an underlying cause of poverty. In other words, the solution put forth is only acceptable when it is hopelessly inadequate.

Conclusion

The contradictions and conflicts examined here are critical to an understanding of immigration policy in this period. At the same time, an examination of immigration and immigration policy highlights these contradictions, as they are intensified by the immigration process itself. As immigration at the turn of the century supplied a rapid influx of surplus labor, the dialectic worked itself out in a highly visible way and in fast motion. Poverty, political protest, industrial instability, and the quandary into which state actors were placed followed in rapid succession. But just as immigration intensified and highlighted the dialectical process, so too the immigrants themselves were spotlighted and their personal attributes increasingly designated as its cause, as we will see in the next chapter.

Notes

1. Andrew Carnegie, who fancied himself a prophet of American democracy, referred to the situation at his Homestead Steel Works as war. In a letter to his partner George Lauder, dated July 17, 1892, Carnegie wrote, "Matters at home *bad.* . . . Still we must keep quiet and do all we can to support Frick and those at the seat of war" (quoted in Brody, 1960, p. 59; emphasis in original).

2. An act passed on February 14, 1903, had moved the administration of the immigration laws into the newly created Department of Commerce and Labor, with ultimate administrative power placed in the hands of the secretary of that department.

5 ▪ "Class Unity" in the Face of Conflict: The Immigrant as Villain

Introduction

In the dialectics of law making, the state's attempted resolutions re-create conflict in another guise. The result is an interweaving sequence of contradictions, conflicts, and resolutions that finds no permanent resting place. Immigration in the nineteenth century was a response to capital's labor problems, but this strategy intensified the state's surplus work force-poverty conflict. Furthermore, immigrant workers, increasingly radicalized by the poverty and despair of the underclass, heightened the state's legitimation problems. Much as earlier immigrants had been used as a solution to the labor problem, so immigrants were used now in a unique way to resolve the state's growing problems of ideological control. For, by the beginning of the twentieth century, the new immigrants from Southern and Eastern Europe were singled out as the cause of all industrial capitalism's ills.

"The Corporate Ideal in the Liberal State" (Weinstein, 1968)

As capital-intensive industry came to be based on ever larger and more long-range investments, economic stability and predictability were crucial. The unpredictability of markets and prices was minimized through monopolization, trusts, and pools. The attempt to achieve predictability was further reflected in the rationalization of production processes and managerial calculation. Detailed record keeping for the determination and distribution of labor costs, at the core of Frederick Taylor's efforts in scientific management, was one attempt to minimize and stabilize the costs of production.

If monopolization and scientific management achieved some level of price and cost stability, labor predictability was not so easily attained. The concentration of industry and the deskilling of the work force further polarized the classes and created the poten-

109

tial for a militant labor movement more disruptive than any yet seen. Not only strikes, but workers' self-regulation of the pace and mode of work, were unacceptable in a system dependent on predictability and increasing levels of worker productivity. The final wrenching of control over the production process from the worker in monopoly capitalism was a crucial step in scientific management's stabilization program. As Braverman (1974, p. 90) puts it, "It is not the 'best way' to do work 'in general' that Taylor was seeking, . . . but an answer to the specific problem of how best to control alienated labor."

The answer offered by scientific management was to separate, once and for all, the conceptual and executive functions of labor. This solution accumulated in management all traditional worker skills and knowledge, and dictated exactly in what manner each task was to be executed (see Taylor, 1947, p. 49).

In monopoly capitalism, then, the worker is not only separated from the means of production materially, but intellectually. While control of the product had already been taken out of the hands of those who produced it, this final stage took control from the worker of the production process itself. It thus ensured worker subordination in a way that merely separating the worker from the ownership of the means of production could not. As Marx (1906, p. 397) viewed the beginnings of this process in his own time, workers are "brought face to face with the intellectual potencies of the material process of production, as the property of another, and as a ruling power."

Hand in hand with this attempt to limit the impact of labor resistance, an ideological weapon was fashioned. As monopoly capitalism polarized the classes and scientific management snatched from labor the last vestiges of control over production, progressivism announced an end to class war.

Although many of the social reforms of the progressive period in the United States originated with middle-class reformers, they were compatible with the desire for predictability of the most class-conscious businessmen of the day. Social reforms were seen by these capitalists as a way to minimize both strike activity and, more importantly, the development of class consciousness and alternative political ideologies.

A speech by Chairman Elbert Gary of U.S. Steel to a group of industrialists reflected the new concern with promoting class unity through reform. Brody (1960, p. 153) summarizes Gary's address: "Bitterness between workmen and managers was as deplorable as between business rivals. The solution was the same: to cooperate 'with our men as we have . . . with our competitors.'"

George Perkins of International Harvester, in supporting work-er compensation, urged in 1911 that

> [cooperation] ... is taking and should take the place of
> ruthless competition. ... If this new order of things is
> better for capital ... then in order to succeed perma-
> nently it must demonstrate that it is better for the labor-
> er. (quoted in Karier, 1972, p. 155)

The reformer Herbert Croly pointed out that this "corporate lib-eralism" was "designed to serve as a counterpoise to the threat of working-class revolution" (quoted in Kaplan, 1956, pp. 354–355).

The National Civic Federation (NCF) was a primary instru-ment of this corporate liberalism. It was here that the principle of the tripartite representation of business, labor, and the public originated. An initial aim of the NCF was to mediate in labor dis-putes. Its more general aim, however, was to lend its support to the conservative unionism embodied in the AFL in an effort to neutralize labor's potential for solidarity and class action. Con-servative unions were thus redefined as allies in a war against the more militant and class-conscious factions of the labor movement.

The NCF was founded and dominated by the largest capitalists of the period, and by 1903, it included representatives from almost one-third of the richest corporations in the country. Samuel Gom-pers of the AFL, John Mitchell of the UMW, and presidents of the conservative railway brotherhoods served on the executive com-mittee. As Louis Brandeis, an active member of the NCF, pointed out, it was necessary to represent these unions because "the trade unions ... stand as a strong bulwark against the great wave of socialism" (quoted in Weinstein, 1968, p. 17). NCF official papers pointed out that trade unionism would serve as "an antidote for the socialistic propaganda" (quoted in Weinstein, 1968, p. 17).

In addition to explicit attempts to stabilize the labor move-ment, the NCF itself was held up as a symbol of class unity. This symbolic function became clear early, as its first president boasted at the annual dinner in 1904 that "in no other country in the world could such a gathering be brought about." American democracy, he said, "made possible the comingling in unconscious equality and in conscious cooperation" (Ralph Easley, *National Civic Fed-eration Review*, 1905a).

By no means did all capitalists subscribe to this corporate lib-eralism of the NCF. Although some corporations were internally divided on the issues, by and large it was the smaller capitalists who were opposed to NCF efforts. The National Association of Manufacturers (NAM), comprised primarily of small- and medium-sized firms, was vehemently antilabor and had as primary goals the opposition of the AFL, closed-shop agreements, and protective labor legislation of all kinds (Burch, 1973, p. 109). Between 1906 and 1907, the NAM raised $1.5 million to be used in its war with the AFL (Hillquit, 1965, p. 325). The NAM was among the capitalist anarchists against whom the NCF struggled.

Even those NCF leaders who espoused the unity of class interests and the importance of self-regulation were often ambivalent at the level of day-to-day operating. As Weinstein (1968, p. 1) puts it,

> In the minds of many financial and corporation leaders, there existed a constant tension between their general and particular interests. Many NCF leaders accepted the necessity of conservative unionism as an abstract principle, but opposed unions in their shops.

Their support of progressivism reflected capital's recognition of the need to engineer for order and stability, even if individual capitalists frequently deviated from this ideal. Their pronouncement of class unity despite their individual deviations from that principle can be seen as an attempt to resolve the conflict between the need for legitimation and stability versus the reality of a class-ridden society.

Corporate liberalism enjoyed some limited success. At a time when wealth was more and more polarized and control over production processes was once and for all wrested from the hands of workers, reformist capitalists succeeded in co-opting many of their potential critics. What Gramsci (1971) referred to as *American Fordism* gave a decided boost to capital at a critical time. On one hand, as Reich, Gordon, and Edwards (1973, p. 362) point out, one aim of this welfare capitalism may have been to reduce the labor turnover rate by raising the cost to workers of changing jobs by tying their eligibility for benefits to continued employment. Under Ford's benefit system, for example, "the loss of one's job meant a complete disruption in all aspects of the family's life." Probably the most significant of the successes of "Fordism," however, was its conservatizing influence on the AFL. Already by 1895 the AFL leadership had set forth a policy of focusing exclusively on the organization of skilled labor. The bitter conflicts of the 1890s had pushed skilled labor toward a search for binding agreements with employers that might secure their privileged position. Sympathy strikes were suppressed by union leaders who feared that a broader industrial unionism would defeat their narrow purpose.

With the decline of the Knights of Labor, the AFL was free to pursue their exclusive goals without fear of competition from a union that attempted to promote the interests of all workers.

As monopoly capital advanced and capitalists demonstrated a willingness to make concessions in the interests of stability, the AFL leadership once and for all traded the ideal of industrial unionism for the hope of security for skilled workers. In accepting executive positions with the NCF, Gompers and Mitchell traded a pledge to "not make trouble" in exchange for union recognition (quoted in Foner, 1955, p. 386). Premised on the principle that "there is no necessary hostility between capital and labor" (Mitchell, 1903: ix), collective bargaining was to replace strikes and lockouts. The irony is that, as membership in the AFL grew to two million by 1914, its potential for effective change shrank. Declaring strikes no longer necessary ("Splendid advantages have been obtained by the trade unions without the necessity of strikes or the interruption of industry" [Gompers, quoted in Bimba, 1927, p. 228]), resisting organizing the unskilled, and joining hands with capital against labor militancy, the AFL leadership served as a bastion of capital hegemony.

The conservatism of the AFL leadership was particularly evident in their attitude toward the advantages and disadvantages of organizing the immigrant. Aside from the race antipathy of AFL leaders toward the new immigrant and their reluctance to organize the unskilled in general, AFL leaders hesitated to organize immigrants for fear of their alleged radical tendencies. According to Leiserson (1971,p. 181), the president of a national labor union affiliated with the AFL explained to Leiserson in 1920 that his union had stopped their organizing efforts among immigrants because they found that the IWW reaped the benefits. Another union official advised that the printing of trade union principles in foreign language publications "would only give the agitators among the immigrants better opportunity to make the AFL ridiculous in the eyes of their countrymen" (summarized in Leiserson, 1971, p. 181). One AFL leader from an industrial state declared that he avoided organizing immigrants because they included too many radicals (Leiserson, 1971, p. 182). An executive board member of the United Textile Workers agreed that in his industry "on the whole . . . the foreign elements are Socialists and radical. . . . They do not appreciate the value of negotiation. . . . It is difficult to decide what to do with foreigners" (quoted in Leiserson, 1971, p. 202). Officers of the city central labor body in Lawrence, Massachusetts, complained that the UTW had never tried to organize Lawrence, and that in fact it did not want Lawrence organized, out of fear that immigrant textile workers would be too militant. A Greek doctor in a textile town apparently offered to organize 5000 Greeks in the textile mills, but the union president decided that 2000 of the Greeks were "infected" with "IWW-ism," and that to organize the others would only make trouble (Leiserson, 1971, p. 204). The doctor's offer was rejected. The founders of the IWW aptly referred to the American Federation of Labor as the "American Separation of Labor" (Montgomery, 1974, p. 510).

By the early 1900s, then, skilled labor was led into a bargaining collaboration with capital, while the unorganized, unskilled, largely immigrant work force was excluded from this arrangement. This excluded sector now comprised the primary threat to stability via the IWW and other independent unions. As Montgomery (1974, p. 517) describes it, this new unionism was reflected in "a dozen years of fierce class conflict," as wage strikes and speedup resistance were precipitated from the bottom up. In this struggle, a reversal of roles was apparent, as unorganized immigrants—formerly capital's most effective weapon—supplied the vanguard of the militant labor movement, while American-born skilled workers and their unions comprised the stabilizing element. Of course, new immigrants were still used on occasion as strike breakers, but, in a period in which capital was attempting to stabilize economic relations by offering concessions to trade unions, the militant labor movement was increasingly found on the periphery among the unorganized.

One additional factor influenced this "American Separation of Labor." As Reich, Gordon, and Edwards (1973) argue, political and economic forces within monopoly capitalism encouraged the segmentation of labor markets into primary and secondary sectors, and within the primary sector between subordinate and independent jobs.

The growth in the size of corporations and the deskilling of the work force brought a revamping of authority relations within the firms. In a system in which production is carried out by a massive, deskilled and alienated work force, workers must be rigidly supervised. Hierarchical control or internal segmentation emerged in which job ladders were created and top-down authority was guaranteed. This development was not only functional from a control point of view: the employment of a massive unskilled labor force supervised by a few whose wages are only slightly higher is far cheaper than employing a skilled work force.

Fitch (1911, p. 147) notes that this internal segmentation was executed in the steel industry along ethnic lines.

> ... the labor force has been cleft horizontally into 2 great
> divisions. The upper stratum includes what is known in
> mill parlance as the "English-speaking" men; the lower
> contains the "Hunkies" or "Ginnies." ... the former are
> the "white men," the latter the "foreigners."

Using job ladders that dictated that workers in certain entry-level
jobs have access to only limited promotion opportunities, the ethnic divisions remained intact.

In addition to this internal segmentation, the economy was
divided into primary and secondary labor markets. While the primary sector required stability and predictability, the secondary
sector consisted of small, labor-intensive operations that neither
could afford nor required the stability achieved by incremental
concessions to labor. The demand for secondary sector products
was unstable, labor demand cyclical or seasonal, and employment
unsteady. Again, this sector was almost the exclusive realm of
immigrants, blacks, and women. Noting his countrymen's con-
finement to these lowest paying, insecure jobs, a Ruthenian priest
declared in 1907, "My people do not live in America, they live underneath America" (quoted in Leiserson, 1971, p. 128).

With this segmentation, the "American Separation of Labor"
was complete. Whether these internal and external lines of segmentation were the product of a deliberate strategy to divide and
conquer is open to question. Nonetheless, as Fitch (1911, p. 148)
put it in 1911, "Whatever it was that grouped the labor force as it is
today, the grouping is favorable to continued control on the part of
the employer."

In an economic system fraught with contradictions, however,
even capital rarely gets a free lunch. If trade unions were con-
servatized by capital's conciliatory gestures, and if labor was seg-
mented and divided, it is not surprising that the excluded immigrants developed their own forms of militant resistance.

The Immigrant as Villain

Progressivism and the insistence on class unity was partly a response to the struggle between capital's need for a minimum level
of stability and legitimation versus the reality of class conflict, but
this solution produced its own enigma: how to explain both desti-
tution and the violent protest of a significant element of the working class. In the absence of any real solution to the class conflict,
the pronouncement of class unity merely re-created the dilemma.
One response to this problem was to identify that group most
closely associated with these industrial ills as the troublemakers. If

class interests are harmonious, it is people who are defective. As the chasm between the classes widened as wealth was increasingly concentrated, and as radical political movements and labor militancy advanced, immigrants were blamed for both the poverty and the protest.

Some simply denied the existence of poverty and class conflict: "I defy any man to show that there is pauperism in the U.S." (Andrew Carnegie, quoted in David, 1958, p. 10). "There are no struggles between privileged and unprivileged orders in America, not even that perpetual strife of rich and poor . . ." (Bryce, 1889, p. 647). Henry Clews of Wall Street fame proclaimed rather tautologically,

> Strikes may have been justifiable in other nations but they are not justifiable in our country. The Almighty made this country for the oppressed of other nations, and therefore, this is the land of refuge . . . and the hand of the laboring man should not be raised against it. (1886, p. 601)

It was far more common, however, simply to blame the immigrants for their own poverty and class action. "While we should sympathize with God's poor . . . let us remember there is not a poor person in the U.S. who was not made poor by his own shortcomings" (quoted in Weisberger, 1969, p. 112).

Congressional debates were replete with complaints of the Southern and Eastern European immigrants' inferiority as reflected in their "acceptance" of substandard wages and "un-American" political activity. Scholarly journals echoed the same concern:

> When [the immigrant worker] is out of work . . . he looks about and asks his fellow-citizens, sullenly, if not menacingly, what they are going to do about it. He has brought with him, too, what is called "the labor problem," probably the most un-American of all problems. (Godkin, 1887, p. 173)

It was not only that immigrants were thought to be importers of poverty, radicalism, and "class notions." This stereotype was increasingly intermingled with theories of immigrants' racial inferiority.

Social Darwinism was a central ingredient in anti-immigrant racism. This distortion of the Darwinian theory of evolution and its application to the social world announced that the fittest survived and, therefore, that the polarization of social classes was merely a reflection of inherent abilities. Sumner (1883), in *What Social Classes Owe to Each Other*, and Henderson (1893) conjured up Darwinian notions of biological superiority and survival in a thinly veiled denunciation of the class struggle of the 1880s and 1890s: "Who are these dependents? They are outcast survivals of an imperfect past race, . . . or degenerate offspring of an injured and a defective stock, or examples of an arrested development, *unfit to endure the strain of modern competition* . . ." (Henderson, 1893, p. iii; emphasis added).

The New England social elite of precapitalist America launched the first distinctly racist campaign against European immigrants in the 1890s. This wave of racist xenophobia among the New England elite did not originate with the change of the source of immigration from Northern Europe to Southern and Eastern Europe. It initially consisted of an indictment of foreigners in general and was already evident in the early 1880s, gaining momentum as the class war became more pronounced (Higham, 1955, p. 137). As Higham (1955, p. 87) explains, "The new immigrants had the very bad luck to arrive in America en masse at a time when nativism was already running at full tilt. . . ." Of course, nativism among the working class had been at full tilt for years at mid-century. The bad luck of the new immigrant was that this later nativism originated with an influential group of elites and, as we will see, was soon clutched at by leading capitalists.

By the 1890s, this racist nativism was focused on new immigrants from Southern and Eastern Europe. The change in the source of immigration now bolstered these racist theories, as their proponents could point to a few physiological differences which allegedly reflected racial types. In 1890, Francis Walker, the president of the American Economics Association, warned his audience of scholars against the invasion of races of "the very lowest stage of degradation" (1891, p. 37). It was at this time also that Henry Cabot Lodge, the new immigrants' most influential enemy, voiced his racist fear that immigrants would irreparably pollute America's inherited national character (1891, pp. 27–32). Francis Walker (1896, p. 828) described the immigrants as "beaten men from beaten races, representing the worst failures in the struggle for existence. . . ."

In 1894, the Immigration Restriction League (IRL) was formed in Boston. As Higham (1955, p. 102) describes them,

> The founders were . . . from well-to-do, long-established families. . . . They had all attended Harvard College in the late 1880s. . . . They were determined to mount a

> counteroffensive against the strange invaders who
> seemed so grave a threat to their class, their region, their
> country, and their race.

This organization of elite immigration restrictionists continued for
25 years to demand limitations on new immigration on the basis
that it would irreparably pollute the Anglo-Saxon race.

Had racist nativism been confined to these mutterings of a bitter elite from a passing era, it would probably have amounted to
little more than an historical curiosity, with relatively minor consequences. Two developments, however, pushed anti-immigrant
racism to center stage. Most importantly, these vague notions of
race differences proved useful to leading capitalists.

Capitalists had long explained labor unrest and class cleavages
by insisting that they were imported by foreigners who knew nothing of American ideals (see, for example, *The American Manufacturer and Iron World*, 1885b, 1886a; *The Commercial and Financial Chronicle*, 1887; Swank, 1897, p. 181). Some trade journals
even argued that more selective immigration might defuse militant unionism by barring foreign agitators (*The American Wool
Reporter*, 1894; *Iron Age*, 1887; *Iron Trade Review*, 1896; *Shoe
and Leather Review*, 1886; *Textile World*, 1898). Many industry
journals began to adopt the New England elite's convenient physiological explanation of the immigrant as troublemaker. "Anarchism is a blood disease," reported a leading business magazine
after the Haymarket affair (*The Age of Steel*, quoted in *Public
Opinion*, 1886, p. 355). In 1890, *The Age of Steel* (1890, p. 9)
wrote, "We are absorbing the vicious and diseased of the earth into the national body, and coming face to face with the consequences." *The Commercial and Financial Chronicle* (1892, pp.
162–163) blamed industrial unrest on "race changes" among the
immigrants.

Leading capitalists continued to use this immigrant-as-
inferior explanation of almost all social ills after the turn of the
century. Probably the most notorious anti-immigrant outbursts by
a leading industrialist were those of Henry Ford with the anti-
Semitic campaign on which he spent millions in his weekly *Dear-
born Independent*. As was often the case, Ford's racism was in-
tegrally linked to his fear of social instability. In his mind, the
"International Jewish bankers [made wars] . . . so they can make
money out of them" (quoted in Higham, 1955, 284).

Even when their observations were not explicitly racist, capitalists repeatedly relied on notions of immigrant inferiority to explain class conflict within what they had declared to be a classless

society. The National Association of Wool Manufacturers (NAWM) explained away the IWW: "This baleful organization of European origin" was created by a "foreign invasion of the anarchists and socialists, criminals and outcasts from other nations" (*Bulletin* of the NAWM, 1912, pp. 139–142). The president of the NAM accounted for the anthracite miners' strikes in 1902: "Tens of thousands of the anthracite miners are Poles, Hungarians, Slavs, and other foreigners, who cannot spell a word of English" (Parry, quoted in Wiebe, 1962, p. 191). The American Protective Tariff League rationalized the massive Lawrence textile strike in 1912: All were "Italians and other foreign-born operatives" (quoted in Wiebe, 1962, p. 191).

An investigation into the causes of the Great Steel Strike of 1919 spoke to the widespread belief that the strike had been planned and carried out entirely by foreigners: "A stranger in America reading the newspapers during the strike and talking with steelmasters both in and out of steel communities must have concluded that the strike represented a serious outbreak of Bolshevism red hot from Russia" (Commission of Inquiry, 1920, p. 31). Gary, president of U.S. Steel, declared that the war had "abnormalized" the strikers' minds (quoted in Brody, 1960, p. 247). Besides its function of explaining away injustices by placing the blame on foreigners with abnormal minds, this tactic of attributing militant labor activity to foreigners defined it as un-American. During the steel strike in 1919, a Pennsylvania workman wrote, "Have you heard it—that great piece of rotten trickery that the employer is using? No man can be a loyal American unless he is a scab" (quoted in Brody, 1960, p. 259).

Capitalists, then, seized upon Social Darwinian notions of the immigrant to explain class disunity in the face of their pronouncements of class unity. Rosenblum (1973, p. 177) notes that "it is ironic that the full burden of guilt was laid on the victims of a ruthless exploitation rather than on its American-born perpetrators." It may be ironic, but it is not surprising. This was an ideal solution to capital's dilemma, for it was in fact these recent immigrants who were most often associated with poverty and, increasingly, protest. Welcomed and exploited by capital to resolve its surplus labor problem, immigrants themselves were then used to resolve capital's ensuing legitimation problems.

In addition to this utility to capital, anti-immigrant racism was bolstered by another development. Prior to 1900, "race thinkers" had no general scientific principle upon which to base their claims. By 1900, scientists studying heredity began to demonstrate the way in which certain traits are transmitted across generations. With this study of inheritance, the eugenics movement sprang to the top of the scientific agenda. Sir Francis Galton in England was responsible for studies on inheritance, and by the opening of the twentieth century began preaching the benefits of creating a better breed of humanity through limiting the reproduction of those with "defective genes." As Higham (1955, p. 150ff.) argues, Gabon's eugenics "struck several responsive chords" in the United States. In the first place, the eugenicists' emphasis on the need to "breed out" defective genes coincided well with the New England elite's sense of the imminent danger of race destruction. Secondly, the focus on race improvement and reform through rational, science-based action coincided with the reform mentality of progressivism. Finally, and probably most importantly, it provided a "scientific" rationale for social inequalities, and confirmed what the elite already "knew": they were innately superior. Scientific studies of the transmission of human deficiencies removed the blame for social injustices from the socioeconomic order and placed it unambiguously on defective individuals. In fact, the reductionism of the heredity-eugenics movement went one step further and placed the blame not only on individuals, but on individual genes.

From the beginning of the Spanish-American War in 1898 until the panic of 1907, while the inheritance movement was gaining momentum in scientific circles, it failed to exert influence beyond that small circle. The intense nationalism and optimism accompanying American expansion through imperialism and the momentary relaxation of open class conflict quieted for the moment anti-immigrant racism in spite of the largest immigrant influx yet seen.[1] However, with the panic of 1907 and the accompanying unrest and labor militancy, the inheritance/eugenics movement took off. It did not fuel itself. By 1908, this movement became the pet project of many of America's leading capitalists.

Charles Davenport was the foremost eugenicist in America. Davenport himself was a member of the New England elite, and like them, he frequently complained "that the best of that grand old New England stock is dying out through failure to reproduce" (quoted in Higham, 1955, p. 151). Early in the century, Davenport established a research center at Cold Spring Harbor, Long Island, where he experimented with animal breeding. In 1907, the year of one of America's worst economic breakdowns, he began applying the Mendelian principles he had tested on animals to humans. In 1910, Mary W. (Mrs. E. H.) Harriman initiated her longtime support of Davenport's projects and personally contributed $1.5 million toward the creation of an annex to the Cold Spring Harbor laboratory, in which was to be compiled a racial index of the American population. Andrew Carnegie and John D. Rockefeller also made substantial contributions to Davenport's eugenics laboratory (Hahn, 1977). Hahn (1977) provides a well-documented list of other leading capitalists who, through personal or foundation contributions, supplied a critical boost to the eugenics movement. Felix Adler, W. W. Astor, August Belmont, Cleveland Dodge, Daniel Guggenheim, Mrs. Simon Guggenheim, William Pryor Letchworth, J. P. Morgan, the Rockefellers, Jacob and Mortimer Schiff, and Mr. and Mrs. F. W. Vanderbilt joined Carnegie and Harriman in contributing personal funds. The Carnegie Institute of Washington, the Commonwealth Fund, the New York Foundation, the Laura Spelman Rockefeller Memorial, and the Russell Sage Foundation were among the foundations that provided support for the laboratories, institutes, and journals that were committed to spreading the word of genetic determinism.

While the eugenics movement provided the scientific studies of inheritance required to lend an air of respectability to race thinking, it was ultimately anthropologists and psychologists who supplied the missing pieces for a full-fledged racist nativism. In *The Races of Europe* (1899), William Ripley argued that Europe was composed of three races—the Teutons, the Alpines, and the Mediterraneans—each with distinct physical characteristics. In 1908, as the eugenics movement in biology was gaining momentum, Ripley presented a paper on the perils of crossbreeding, in which he argued that an intermingling of racial types might result in evolutionary throwbacks.

Madison Grant, a longtime member of the New York social elite, carried Ripley's thesis to its logical conclusions, and his work exerted a direct influence on immigration policy, as we will see. In 1916, Grant's *The Passing of the Great Race* was published, the main thesis of which was that the Nordics, as Grant called Ripley's Teutons, represented "the white man par excellence" (1916, p. 150). The influx of new immigrants into North America, Grant warned, threatened a race reversion brought on by a new phenomenon—the "survival of the unfit" (1916, p. 82).

The final component in this evolution of race thinking was the IQ test. The inheritance/eugenics movement had always contained the underlying assumption that the lower classes were characterized by low intelligence, and that it was this low intelligence that was responsible for their allegedly inferior moral character. As Karier (1972, p. 160) notes, there had been since Jefferson a tradition in America that equated talent and virtue. It was therefore natural that these race thinkers associated undesir-

able citizens with low intelligence, or "feeblemindedness" as it
came to be called.

Following Goddard's initial tests with the Binet scale, a flurry
of studies and publications—many from the laboratory at Cold
Spring Harbor and others from the Carnegie Institute in Washington—demonstrated the alleged relationship between moral character and feeblemindedness. Crime, radicalism, unemployment,
and industrial inefficiency—in short, all the ills that plagued industrial capitalism at the time—were explained by reference to low
intelligence, and recommendations were made to place the feebleminded into labor colonies where they could be well regulated
(Goddard, 1920).

Prior to World War I, IQ tests were administered on an individual basis. With the conscription of large numbers of men into
the army, the opportunity was provided to apply these tests on a
mass scale. The president of the American Psychological Association, Robert Yerkes, was assigned the task of testing the intelligence of draftees, and the results were seized upon by eugenicists
and immigration restrictionists. Yerkes concluded that while those
of Northern European origin achieved an intelligence rating equal
to native whites, blacks and those of Southern and Eastern European origin scored significantly lower (Yerkes, 1921).

In 1912, the U.S. Public Health Service employed Goddard to
administer his IQ tests to a sample of immigrants landing at Ellis
Island. Goddard (1913, pp. 105–107) concluded that 83% of Jews,
80% of Hungarians, 79% of Italians, and 87% of Russians were
feebleminded. There was no more doubt. The blame ascribed to
recent immigrants for poverty, unemployment, and labor unrest,
in an otherwise rational and just society, was now "scientifically"
legitimated.

Goddard, addressing a Princeton gathering in 1919, assuaged
any guilt that members in his audience might feel as about their
privileged position (1920, pp. 99–101).

> Here is a man who says "I am wearing $12 shoes, there
> is a laborer who is wearing $3 shoes. . . . It is not right, it
> is unjust." . . . Now the fact is, that workman may have a
> ten year intelligence while you have a twenty.

This rationale for inequality did more than assuage the guilt
feelings of the privileged. For, it now was clear to race thinkers
and worried capitalists what the cause of the labor unrest was that
raged through the country in the postwar years. Goddard urged
social control theorists to apply "the principle of mental levels"

to the "problem that looms up rather large at the present time, namely socialism and especially its extreme form of Bolshevism" (1920, pp. 99, 103). Stoddard (1922, p. 86) identified what he called "Under-Man":

> ... his hatred of superiority knows no bounds ... syndi-
> calism, Anarchism, and Bolshevism ... are essentially
> the product of unsound thinking ... *by unsound
> brains.* ... Bolsheviks are mostly born not made. ...
> How can we expect a man to support a social order ...
> which he is congenitally unable to achieve? (emphasis in
> original)

By 1920, American eugenicists and psychologists—many of whom were themselves New England elites, financed and encouraged by America's leading capitalists and financiers and their newly created foundations—achieved a thoroughly racist explanation for capitalism's irrationalities and inequalities. Ironically for these capitalists, this racism contributed, as we will see, to a substantial restriction on the immigration that supplied them with a golden stream of cheap labor.

Of the role frequently played by culture and ideology in the dialectic, Mollenkopf (1975, p. 255) notes, "Culture cannot successfully be construed as a mere 'superstructure' which mechanically 'reflects' the ideas or the needs of the capitalist class. Instead, it mediates between interest and action, and can shape mass attitudes." And later, "While indeed leading business interests may forge a political ideology like the cold war consensus, they cannot easily control it, and it may subsequently impose difficult requirements on them" (p. 255).

Others have cited the way in which certain ideologies promoted by capital may limit them. Bridges (1974, p. 186) notes, for example, "the promotion of a political ideology of democracy is always open to the challenge that the ideology be realized in fact." Similarly, "the promotion of tax consciousness among citizens may serve as a defense for the State against the financial demands of State workers" (p. 187), but such a tax consciousness could ultimately cripple the state financially. It was in just this way that the ideology of racism, once supported and nourished by capital, boomeranged in the form of immigration restrictions. While the channeling of discontent onto the immigrant served at first to justify the established social order, it ultimately was a critical force in restricting the immigrant supply of cheap labor.

The eugenics movement early came to be associated with the immigration restriction movement of the New England elite. The

Immigration Restriction League (IRL) was quick to relate the eugenicists' work to their cause. Davenport in 1903 had established the American Breeders' Association, which in 1907 became the national forum for eugenicists. A year later, the IRL came to dominate the Association and organized within it a committee on immigration. So completely intermingled did the issues become that the organization apparently considered calling itself the Eugenic Immigration League (Higham, 1955, p. 152).

Just as leading capitalists were not responsible for *initiating* this race thinking but supported it at crucial junctures, so organized labor was receptive to some of its nativist principles but remained in an even more reactive and ambivalent role vis-à-vis the movement. As Higham (1955, p. 72) puts it, "Organized labor moved with the nativist tide in the nineties, but certainly not in advance of it, or with full assurance."

As early as 1895, the IRL sought the support of organized labor for the literacy test requirement, but with only uneven success, at least among the rank and file (Foner, 1955, pp. 362–364). At the AFL convention in 1896, Gompers began his campaign among convention delegates to secure their endorsement of the literacy test. The delegates were immediately hostile to Gompers's proposal. One delegate shouted that it was "not a labor measure, but came from capitalists!" Another angry delegate argued, "The men of wealth [are] more of a detriment than the immigrant." McBride, president of the UMW, said indignantly, "Immigration [is] not the true cause of the industrial difficulty," and he underlined the importance of the new immigrants in strengthening his union (quoted in Foner, 1955, p. 363). Gompers's proposal was soundly defeated that year.

At the 1897 convention, AFL leaders again requested support for the literacy test bill. The debate that ensued was heated, with delegates arguing that the bill violated the AFL principle of the brotherhood of man and others crying out that "the best trade unionists [are] the foreigners" (quoted in Foner, 1955, p. 363). Not surprisingly, just as the New England elite and leading capitalists were beginning to recognize a menace in the immigrant, much of the rank and file of organized labor was beginning to recognize a good unionist. Despite the disagreement among the rank and file, the literacy test requirement, with the help of propaganda literature from the IRL, won the official endorsement of the AFL.

In subsequent years, as the AFL increasingly catered to skilled labor, the leadership contined to support the IRL in its restriction efforts. Arguing that the immigrant lowered wages and broke strikes, the leadership also came to embrace the concept of racial purity. Gompers declared that "the maintenance of the nation de-pend[s] upon the maintenance of racial purity" and that new im-migrants "could not be taught to render the same intelligent service as was supplied by American workers" (quoted in Karson, 1958, p. 137). According to Gompers, the goal of the AFL was "the maintenance of American institutions as they are and only immi-gration restriction could make this possible" (quoted in Leinen-weber, 1968, p. 3).

In addition to their contempt for the new immigrants' stand-ard of living, the AFL leadership argued that immigration re-strictions would bar those who were most likely to be revolu-tionaries (Handlin, 1951, p. 289). The leadership was deeply aware of the hostility many of the new immigrants had toward their ex-clusive union and their conservative labor efforts. While labor since the 1830s had demanded restrictions on the grounds that immigrants were capital's most effective pawn in the class strug-gle, this now took second place to the fear that immigrants might upset that harmony which Gompers, Mitchell, and the NCF were so busy fabricating.

Marx's description of the English-versus-Irish antagonism in nineteenth-century England summarizes well both the origin and role of such hostility in the class conflict:

> Every industrial and commercial centre in England now possesses a working class *divided* into two *hostile* camps, English proletarians and Irish proletarians. The ordinary English worker hates the Irish worker as a competitor who lowers his standard of life. In relation to the Irish worker he feels himself a member of the *ruling* nation and so turns himself into a tool of the aristocrats and capitalists. . . .
>
> This antagonism is kept artificially alive and intensi-fied by the press, the pulpit, the comic papers, in short, by all the means at the disposal of the ruling classes. This *antagonism* is the *secret of the impotence of the English working class*, despite their organization. It is the secret by which the capitalist class maintains its power. And that class is fully aware of it. (Letter from Karl Marx, April 9, 1870, in *On Britain*, by Marx and Engels, 1962, pp. 551–552; emphasis in original)

Not all organized labor was opposed to immigration. Within the Socialist Party, those who were friendly to industrial unionism opposed the racist nativism of New England academics, capital-ists, and the AFL leadership. These internationalists saw as their goal the unification of the working class. As Bill Haywood argued, there were "no foreigners in the working class" (quoted in Leinenweber, 1968, p. 14). In addition, these industrial socialists saw in the immigrant, unskilled worker a powerful contribution to industrial unionism.

By 1910, then, the organized elements of the working class were divided on the issue of immigration restriction, and those who did advocate restrictions followed the lead of other groups. Yet historians frequently attribute the immigration restrictions of the 1920s to universal labor demands (see, for example, Bernard, 1950; Hutchinson, 1953). While some segments of organized labor did oppose unrestricted immigration, it was the New England elite who spearheaded the movement, race-minded eugenicists who provided it with a pseudoscientific basis, and leading capitalists who financed the racist movement that ultimately affected policy. As Tove Stang-Dahl (quoted in Chambliss, 1979, p. 19) notes,

> The presence of a common interest in spite of contradictions is quite common in the field of social control. . . .
> The liberal notion of the State as a neutral safeguard for common interests and values has frequently blurred the actual class conflicts behind the making of social policy.

The Dillingham Commission Report

A forewarning of the influence that the eugenics movement and immigrant scapegoating were to have on immigration policy came in 1912 with the publication of the Dillingham Commission Report. In 1906, an immigration bill with a literacy test amendment had again come before Congress. The bill passed unanimously in the Senate, with Henry Cabot Lodge as major protagonist and influential champion (*Congressional Record*, 1906, p. 7300). The House was less easily won over, and the literacy test amendment was eventually dropped from the bill in the House. In its place, a substitute was inserted, "Section 38: That a commission is hereby created . . . [which] shall make full inquiry, examination, and investigation into the subject of immigration" (*Congressional Record*, 1906, p. 9195). The amendment called on President Roosevelt to appoint a nine-member committee, to be comprised of Senator William P. Dillingham of Vermont (chairman of the Senate Committee on Immigration), Representative John L. Burnett (chair of the House Committee on Immigration and Naturalization), four other senators and representatives, and three industrial experts.

The 42-volume, $900,000 commission report that was produced was a clear indication of the effect that the developing ideology of racism had on this important segment of the state elite. Two conclusions stand out from an examination of the Dillingham Commission Report. In the first place, economic and industrial conditions dominated the 42-volume discussion. The report opened with the declaration that immigration policy should be considered "primarily as an economic problem" (U.S. Congress, Senate Immigration Commission, 1911, Vol. 1, p. 25). No mention was made of America's mission as the "asylum of the oppressed" or her obligation to the "wretched refuse of other lands." Out of 42 volumes, 31 were devoted to the effect of the immigrant on American industry. Each industry in which immigrants were a significant factor was scrutinized as to the immigrant influence on industrial expansion, labor organization, accident rates, labor turnover, and wages.

Second, economic considerations were infused throughout with race thinking. In fact, the issue became the effect of new immigrants of distinct racial characteristics, on industry. From the commission's introductory statement—"The chief basis of the Commission's work was the changed character of the immigration movement to the U.S. during the past twenty-five years" (U.S. Congress, Senate Immigration Commission, 1911, Vol. 1, p. 14)—through the last pages of the 42 volumes, the discussion attempted to demonstrate the inferiority of the new immigrant. Noting that in 1907, 81% of the legal immigration to the United States came from Southern and Eastern Europe, while from 1819 to 1883, 95% came from Northern Europe, the commission declared, *"The new immigration as a class is far less intelligent than the old"* (Vol. 1, p. 14, emphasis in original). And, "Racially, they are for the most part unlike the British, Germans, and other peoples who came during the period prior to 1880" (Vol. 1, p. 14). A "Racial Classification of Immigrants" was the foundation for the inspection of the effect of these races on industrial conditions. Each industry was then examined from the standpoint of what percentage of employees of a given industry were new immigrants and what effect that percentage had on industrial efficiency, wages, labor organization, and unemployment rates. The report concluded that:

1. "These [new] immigrants [have] kept conditions in the semi-skilled and unskilled occupations from advancing" (Vol. 1, pp. 38–39).

2. ". . . a characteristic of the new immigrants is the impossibility of successfully organizing them into labor unions" (Vol. 1, p. 38).

3. Regarding accident rates, "*Here a real race difference is exposed*" [emphasis in original]. Deducing from a sample of 214 accidents in one anthracite coal company and noting that Poles suffered more of these accidents than Lithuanians, the report concludes, "When it is remembered in how many other instances in this report tables have shown *a superiority of the Lithuanian over the Poles*, the conclusion gathers strength that the former show greater skill and carefulness in their work" (Vol. 16, p. 667, emphasis in original).

4. The presence of this "poorer class of immigrant" tended to reduce wages, lengthen the working day, and deteriorate working conditions. "Several elements peculiar to the new immigration contribute to this result" (Vol. 1, p. 38).

5. "There has been created an over-supply of unskilled labor, and in some industries this is reflected in a curtailed number of working days . . ." (Vol. 1, p. 39).

Just as immigrants were demonstrating their potential for militant labor activity, the commission denigrated the new immigrant for his tractability (Vol. 1, p. 540). Conspicuously absent from the 42 volumes is any mention of the contemporary wave of immigrant strikes and the role of immigrant unions such as the IWW.

It was the unanimous recommendation of the commission to implement restrictive measures to limit new immigration. All but one dissenting member favored the literacy test.

Material Conditions

It is important to recognize the role of racism and anti-immigrant ideologies on the commission's report and on later immigration restrictions. It must be emphasized, however, that neither the prevalence of this ideology nor its impact on policy were independent of the material conditions of the period. The commission's report was compiled over a four-year period between 1907 and 1911, which coincided precisely with the unprecedented economic stagnation that Baran and Sweezy (1966, pp. 218ff.) describe as the end of "the big shake-up which began even before the Civil War." Twenty years earlier, in an era of railroad expansion and industrial optimism, the xenophobic tracts produced by the New England elite had fallen on deaf ears.

Cashmore (1978) revealed that it was only after the British Columbian railway link to the rest of Canada was finished in 1885 that the "racial inferiority" of the Chinese became an issue in Canada. As Cashmore puts it (1978, p. 415), "It seems more than a coincidence that this year should also see the first legislation to be passed in respect of [*sic*] non-European immigration" to Canada. In the United States, it was similarly only after the Chinese immigrants' utility in constructing the U.S. western railroad system had waned in the late nineteenth century that Chinese "inferiority" became a concern of the California state elite, and Chinese immigration to the United States was restricted.

Similarly, the racism that fueled the attacks on the new European immigrant was rooted in extant material conditions. In the first place, the full development of the eugenics movement and genetic explanations for unemployment and unrest depended on the financial support of leading capitalists in their search for legitimacy after decades of intense class struggle. Secondly, the movement gained momentum and affected social policy only after high unemployment rates had become a chronic feature of monopoly capitalism, and, as we will see later, revolutionary technologies and alternative sources of cheap labor had made European immigration less indispensable as an industrial reserve. While the development of anti-immigrant ideologies was a major ingredient in the emergence of the restriction mentality expressed, for example, in the Dillingham Commission Report, both the intensity of that ideological development and its later impact on policy were part and parcel of prevailing economic conditions.

The Red Scare

The fear of the immigrant as radical or somehow un-American intensified during World War I. With the United States' entrance into the war, concern about immigrant disloyalty was reflected in the plea for "100% Americanism," which referred to the demand not only for unilateral loyalty, but also for ideological conformity and submission in the workplace. Repressive state and federal laws were enacted to eliminate the alleged influence of German-Americans and other "hyphenates." Strikes were declared "seditious interference in war production" (Preston, 1963, p. 98). The Sedition Act of 1918 made anyone with disloyal opinions subject to a 20-year jail term, and thousands of German-Americans were herded into internment camps.

In Seattle, Washington, arrests of aliens for deportation were initiated by employers. Lumber companies, railroads, and other companies, upon noticing an immigrant troublemaker, would frequently call the immigration bureau and have the suspected radical arrested for deportation. In many cases, the *prima facie* evidence was glaringly inadequate and most of the aliens were eventually released. Coordination between the immigration bureau and employers, however, functioned well in temporarily removing and intimidating the troublemaker (Preston, 1963, p. 166). In his annual report of 1918, U.S. Attorney General Thomas Gregory was proud to announce "that never in its history has this country been so thoroughly policed" (1918, p. 15).

As the war ended, the fear of the "hyphenate" and the fear of immigrant radicalism fused in a concern over a rumored Bolshevik-German plot. As the postwar period unleashed a wave of labor militancy, strikes, and industrial sabotage, attention increasingly focused on the more narrowly defined "Bolshevik infiltration."

Many of American capitalists' worst fears of worker politicization and the role of the immigrant in the labor movement were not entirely unfounded. During the war, labor had made many advances, and as the war closed, even the more conservative unions affiliated with the AFL anticipated continued progress. The generally restrained railroad brotherhoods advocated government ownership of the railroads, and the UMW argued for nationalizing the mines and establishing a labor party. After all, the war propaganda had promised workers a new era. The great wave of strikes that swept the United States in 1919 was labor's response to an unfulfilled promise. Brecher (1972, pp. 104–105) notes that even moderate and conservative union members in Seattle openly supported the Russian Revolution. A moderate union paper, the *Seattle Union Record*, described the situation:

> I believe 95 percent of us agree that the workers should control the industries. Nearly all of us agree on that but very strenuously disagree on the method. Some of us think we can get control through the Cooperative Movement, some of us think through political action, and others think through industrial action. (quoted in Brecher, 1972, p. 105)

Beginning in 1919, the state at all levels hurried to crush the "Reds." Russian immigrant workers were seized by local police for "suspicious appearance." At the federal level, the first of Palmer's Raids was carried out on November 7, 1919, as the new attorney general, A. Mitchell Palmer, authorized raids on the Union of Russian Workers in eleven major cities, arrested hundreds, and marked them for deportation. In January, the Department of Justice, backed up by police in 33 cities, descended on homes and meeting places, seizing 3000 aliens for deportation (Claghorn, 1971; Preston, 1963).

Congress remained supportive of the attorney general's efforts, at least initially. It provided much of the legislation, in the form of immigration and deportation laws, that legitimized the roundups and the involvement of the immigration bureau, as we will see in a moment. When the issue was brought up in Congress as to where the rounded-up "Bolsheviks" should be sent, most seemed to agree with one senator that "I do not care where they go, so long as they get out of here" (*Congressional Record*, 1919, p. 3116, [*sic*]). By 1920, with labor unions put on the defensive by the double blow of a crushing depression and repressive police measures, Congress's anti-radical zeal began to fade. Nonetheless, the suspicion that Southern and Eastern European immigrants might be more trouble than they were worth was firmly implanted.

The Gatekeepers React

The Red Scare, the culmination of decades of anti-immigrant xenophobia and the more specific racist ideologies that rationalized discontent as an individual defect, was accompanied by a series of immigration laws that, while still "selective," suggested a gradual closing of the gate.

The literacy test requirement passed in 1917 after 20 years of debate. The conflict which underlay the 20-year debate continued to be a factor, as the contribution immigrants made as cheap labor was counterposed to their alleged responsibility for the whole repertoire of capitalism's injustices and irrationalities. By 1917, the one most unforgivable sin of recent immigrants was their potential for dual loyalty and industrial disruption. As we will see in the next chapter, Americanization efforts attempted to reform the immigrant stream. The literacy test was to bar at the gates those with allegedly the least potential for reform, i.e., those from Southern and Eastern Europe (*Congressional Record*, 1916a, p. 11792). The *Saturday Evening Post* summed up the attitude of many policy makers: "Why try to make Americans out of those who will always be Americanski?" (*Saturday Evening Post*, 1921, as paraphrased by Higham, 1955, p. 262).

The literacy test enactment marked the first time that an immigration measure passed with the explicit aim of reducing the numbers of immigrants. While the war had almost eliminated immigration, it was warned that the close of the war would bring a flood of "hyphenates" (*Congressional Record*, 1916a, p. 12763; 1916b, p. 316; 1917, pp. 2443, 2456, 2629). In an explicit attempt to reduce that flood while selecting its most desirable elements, the enactment of the literacy test requirement on February 5, 1917, represented a transition between earlier selective policies and the numerical restrictions of 1921 and 1924.

Another act of 1917 (39 U.S. Statutes at Large) established more extensive provisions for the deportation of alien anarchists and other alleged troublemakers. While this act extended the period for expulsion of public charges to 5 years, anarchists and others coming under the "force or violence" clause could be deported under the act without time limitations, and the decision of the secretary of labor to deport was made final.

An act approved on October 16, 1918 (40 U.S. Statutes at Large) and amended in 1920 (41 U.S. Statutes at Large, p. 1008) reflected the heightened concern for the role of the "foreign agitator." Following a strike in the lumber industry in 1917, the Department of Labor had launched a campaign to deport immigrant members of the IWW who were thought to have led the strike. However, the 1917 law provided for deportation only in cases where personal advocacy of anarchism could be documented, not mere membership in an anarchist organization (U.S. Commissioner General of Immigration, 1918). The Department of Labor, in May 1918, sent to Congress a recommendation that the 1917 law be amended to allow for the deportation of IWW members (U.S. Commissioner General of Immigration, 1918). The result was "an Act to exclude and expel from the U.S. aliens who are members of the anarchist and similar classes" (40 U.S. Statutes at Large). The new act provided for the exclusion or deportation of any aliens who "advise," "teach," "publish," or even "believe in" a variety of tactics thought to be associated with anarchism. The act was further broadened in 1920, as the anarchist clause was extended to include advocates of "industrial sabotage."

By the time of the congressional hearings that led to the 1920 amendment, several things were clear. In the first place, it was evident that undesirable political views were not the only concern; rather, the concern was with any contribution to political or economic instability. On the eve of the Great Strike of 1919, the House Committee on Immigration and Naturalization agreed that

> When it is obstructive tactics, the advocacy of that certainly ought to be prohibited. It is bad enough to have it from citizens at this time of the high cost of living, when we ought to be producing more . . . but when it comes to aliens advocating or attempting to destroy our industrial life and our industrial efficiency, and to get this whole country in an uproar, they ought to be deported. (U.S. Congress, House Committee on Immigration and Naturalization, 1919b, p. 19)

Second, the threat of an impending legitimation crisis elicited such alarm that a near consensus was reached in the House Committee that it was better to exclude a few unjustifiably than to risk admitting agitators. "If we open the door ... we may get the fellow in with the bomb in his hand" (U.S. Congress, House Committee on Immigration and Naturalization, 1919b, p. 18).

Third, there was no doubt among members of Congress that it was their right, even their obligation, to exclude whomever they deemed undesirable for whatever reason:

Vaile: If we wanted to be arbitrary about it I suppose we could refuse to admit red-haired men. . . .

Newton: There is absolutely no question of the constitutionality of it. (U.S. Congress, House Committee on Immigration and Naturalization, 1919b, p. 14)

This new mentality provides an interesting contrast to Congress's refusal to consider any immigration regulations in the 1850s, on the grounds that "the barring of any particular class of immigrants" would be unconstitutional (U.S. Congress, House Report, 1856, pp. 1–152).

Finally, both the passage of the literacy test requirement in 1917 and the Red Scare legislation indicate a qualitative change in Congress's willingness to restrict European immigration. Although these selective measures were not yet explicitly numerical restrictions and were still formulated in terms of sifting out undesirable individuals, their potential effect was to limit for the first time the size of the golden stream.

Conclusion

Progressivism and the corporate liberalism espoused by the NCF represented one attempt to grapple with the conflict between the inequalities and irrationalities of a class society and the need in monopoly capitalism for ideological control of the work force. However, with progressivist pronouncements of class unity, it became more urgent than ever to account for the persistent and highly visible class struggle. The ideology of immigrant inferiority fit well into this scenario.

The new xenophobia was not a grass-roots nativism such as workers unleashed in the 1850s. Rather, from its roots in Social Darwinism to its capitalist-financed experiments, its momentum in large part derived from its utility as a legitimating tool in an age of progressive reforms and declarations of class harmony.

It was in one sense an ideal legitimating ideology. The new immigrants *were* poor, their presence *did* allow some industries to reduce wages, and the new immigrants *were* increasingly radicalized. The exploitation of immigrants by employers naturally concentrated the worst industrial ills on them and made it easy to blame the victim. This legitimating ideology, however, was not without its costs, for once established, the ideology of race exerted an independent influence and ultimately became a factor in curtailing capital's cheap labor supply. As Mollenkopf (1975, p. 255) noted, "While . . . leading business interests may forge a political ideology . . . they cannot easily control it."

If the new immigrants were inferior and represented a threat to American institutions, it followed that the immigration that continued to supply industry with cheap labor should be restricted. Congress responded by passing increasingly selective immigration laws. Meanwhile, the Americanization movement was a last-ditch effort to salvage European immigration.

Note

1. Interestingly, it was also in this period that the literacy test had the least appeal in its history. As the Spanish-American War opened, literacy test proponents could not even get the House to consider the bill. In 1903, after an easy defeat in the Senate, one member of Congress reported, "There was no more show of passing that bill with that amendment [the literacy test requirement] on it in the Senate than there would be of passing a temperance proposition in the German wards of Cincinnati" (quoted in Higham, 1955, p. 112).

6 • Last-Ditch Efforts: The Americanization Movement

Introduction

As immigrants were being scapegoated for both poverty and protests against poverty, their employers were far from unanimous on the issue of the benefits versus the costs of continued European immigration. Many had become ensnared by the racism that was so useful as a legitimating ideology. Others sporadically glimpsed the concrete dangers of oversaturating the labor market, as advantageous as that strategy had been to them in the past.

As early as 1883, James Swank, the secretary of the American Iron and Steel Association, warned the business community that jobs must be found not only for "our own helpless classes, but for the shiploads of helpless people who are sent to us by other countries or whom we unwisely bring here" (*American Iron and Steel Association Bulletin*, 1883). The *Shoe and Leather Review* (1885) argued, during a severe economic downturn: "There was a time, years ago, when every laborer who landed on our shores was welcome as an addition to our wealth. But the time has past [*sic*] and the condition has been transposed. He is now regarded as another mouth to feed—another addition to a very poor family. *The American Manufacturer and Iron World* (1885a) put it succinctly: "Our course in squandering the public land and in scheming to increase immigration will (in later years) be looked upon as little less than crime." *The American Manufacturer and Iron World* (1886b) the following year and the *Commercial and Financial Chronicle* (1890) similarly published admonitions that cheap immigrant labor may prove to be expensive.

Capitalists' views of immigration probably varied according to (1) the extent to which their firms relied on immigrant labor and (2) the degree of long-term predictability demanded by their particular enterprise. Beyond this, however, admonitions by capitalists regarding the costs of immigration seemed to ebb and flow with the business cycle. The most urgent warnings went out during economic downturns, the first signs of doubt appearing in the economic crisis of the 1870s. Whether they blamed the immigrants themselves or the overcrowding of the labor market to which the massive influx contributed, many businessmen in the severe depression beginning in 1873 took note of the destabilizing influence of immigration.

In 1877, as he noted with apprehension the unemployed crowding into already congested cities, James Swank urged,

> ... We are fools for attempting to find homes and employment for their [other nations'] poor ... when we cannot employ the labor we have now and are compelled to keep our soldiers under arms to prevent the Molly Maguires they have already sent us from cutting our throats. (*American Iron and Steel Association Bulletin*, 1877, p. 213)

He concluded, "*Let a check be placed upon immigration*" (p. 213; emphasis in original).

When the crisis subsided and labor demand rose, industry journals resumed their defense of the immigrant:

> Every immigrant that lands on our shores adds to the wealth-producing capacity of the nation. More than that, he infuses new life and energy into every branch of business, trade and industry. Both consumption and production are increased by his presence. (*Commercial and Financial Chronicle*, 1882, p. 201)

Railway Age (1883) reminded its readers in 1883 that "while a large number of these newcomers are not desirable citizens, still they must have labor and food, and their coming will increase the development of this new continent." Abram S. Hewitt, a leading iron manufacturer and mayor of New York, defended immigration in the economic upturn of 1887: "Immigration does not mean stagnation; it means progress and prosperity . . ." (The Chamber of Commerce of the State of New York, 1888). *The Age of Steel* (1895, p. 16) in 1895 warned that American industry was "not yet by any means independent" of immigrants.

With the relaxation of industrial conflict for a brief period at the turn of the century and with business optimism generated by the Spanish-American War and American expansion, capitalists once again rose to the defense of the immigrant.

Ralph Easley, the president of the NCF, in "Is There an Immigration Peril?" (National Civic Federation Review, 1905b; see also, 1905c), wrote that the immigration peril was a depiction of "alarmists and was . . . overemphasized." America, he said, was receiving "the best of Europe, not the worst." Just prior to the economic collapse of 1907, the NAM formed a committee to investigate the issue of immigration. It concluded that labor shortages must still be replenished by immigration and argued that an intermingling of races was beneficial (National Association of Manufacturers, 1907).

American Industries (1912) ran an article entitled, "Immigration: Its Value to the Country," in which the industrial contribution of immigration was extolled and readers were reminded of the continued need for unskilled labor. *Iron Age* (1913) lauded immigration as a "floating labor supply."

In addition to offering praise for the cheap labor that immigrants supplied, business periodically defended the immigrant against charges of racial inferiority and radicalism—charges that they themselves frequently resorted to, and even fostered, in times of economic crisis. As early as 1892, for example, *Iron Age* (1892) criticized the racial prejudice against Russian Jewish immigrants.

The periodic defense of immigrants by industry's representatives continued through the first decades of the twentieth century. Even as the industrial scene entered an uneasy calm after the wave of general strikes in 1919, many industrialists rallied to the defense of the immigrant. The Inter-Racial Council (IRC), one of the most active and class-conscious organizations of leading capitalists of the period, argued in 1920 that the common notion that immigrants were responsible for the unrest was not necessarily correct. T. Coleman DuPont, the chair of the IRC, maintained that the American-born had precipitated the strikes and that criticisms of immigration were derived from "sheer Red hysteria, nothing more" (DuPont, 1920). The American Constitutional Association, comprising West Virginia businessmen with interests in coal, agreed, "Bolshevism was conceived in America by Americans" (quoted in Higham, 1955, p. 232; see also Barr, 1920).

Although there was clearly ambivalence towards immigrants expressed among businessmen in this period, their stance on immigration legislation was consistent and unequivocal. In the 1890s some business and trade journals had offered limited endorsement of the literacy test requirement for immigrants. After that time, however, despite periodic reiterations about the inferiority of certain kinds of immigrants and the warning that a massive influx of immigrants might be an economic and political burden, capitalists never stood behind any specific legislative proposals for regulation.

In 1905, the NCF sponsored a national conference on immigration in Madison Square Garden. A heated debate ensued in which the capitalist leaders of the NCF argued in support of unrestricted immigration, while the labor leaders of the NCF warned of the incalculable injury to the organization that open endorsement of an unrestricted immigration policy would provoke (Green, 1956, p. 299). Ultimately, the NCF took a publicly neutral stance on the issue. The Industrial Conference on Immigration 15 years later limited itself to relatively uncontroversial topics.

Those business people who did participate in the legislative debate lobbied against specific regulations. James Emery, a NAM lobbyist in Washington, was present at most congressional committee hearings on immigration and repeatedly warned of the need for immigrant labor. In 1910, a deluge of letters from business enterprises descended on the House Committee on Immigration and Naturalization, warning that the proposed literacy test would dangerously curtail their labor supply. The National Liberal Immigration League, whose members were frequently found at House and Senate committee hearings, argued consistently against restriction on the grounds that it would represent a violation of the asylum role of the United States. The league, comprised of immigrants, business representatives, and progressivist reformers drew substantial financial support from business interests, including U.S. Steel, the Susquehanna Coal Company, and others (*Congressional Record*, 1915, pp. 3027, 3044). The point is that, in spite of capitalists' periodic scapegoating of the immigrant, in spite of their recognition that the continued influx of immigrants at times contributed a critical element of instability, and in spite of their financial support of the heredity-eugenics movement, capitalists opposed all specific restriction proposals.

This apparent inconsistency reflected the dilemma that underlay the issue of immigration in this period, to which leading capitalists were particularly sensitive: if one requirement of capital is a flexible supply of labor, another simultaneous requirement is a minimum level of political and economic stability. Progressivism and the scapegoating of immigrants via the eugenics and IQ movements had been one attempt to resolve this dilemma. However, by pushing immigrants themselves to front stage as the perpetrators of political and economic unrest, this ideological response merely focused and intensified the dilemma over immigration. An anecdote recounted in Roberts (1912, p. 72) depicts this emerging dilemma and the response of one businessman:

After the martyrdom of President McKinley an employer in New England called his general manager and said, "I want you to dismiss all Poles in this Plant." The manager asked, "Why?" The operator said: "I'm afraid. I won't have them around." The subordinate left, looked up the number of Poles in the plant, and the following morning told the operator: "If I dismiss the Poles, it will mean the loss of $75 a day." That settled it—the Poles stayed and the order was toned down to "let no one of them carry a knife."

Facing the dilemma of maximizing profits or preserving economic and political stability, the Americanization response represented an effort to ensure that "no one of them carried a knife." The effort was made all the more urgent by the pervasive ideology of immigrant inferiority to which industrialists and financiers had themselves contributed.

The Americanization Effort

I hear the whistle . . . I must hurry.

(International Harvester's English Lessons for Immigrants, 1915; quoted in Korman, 1965, p. 402)

I am a good American.

(Ford English School, Lesson 1; quoted in Higham, 1955, p. 248)

The extensive state and corporate activities that came under the heading of "Americanization" in the decade preceding the 1921 quota law were varied. What these efforts had in common was that they all "went after the minds of the average and sub-average worker" to prevent them from "becoming class conscious, and . . . organizing trade unions" (quoted in Leiserson, 1971, p. xiv). The Americanization efforts paralleled selective immigration laws in that they, too, represented an attempt to continue to reproduce the work force through immigration without thereby threatening the sociopolitical reproduction of that work force. The difference was that the Americanization solution was an attempt to mold the whole immigrant stream rather than simply sifting out a few undesirable elements.

The Americanization movement gathered momentum in the prewar period, as new immigrants were being declared inferior. It had two main goals: (1) to increase industrial efficiency and (2) to reduce immigrant labor militancy and political radicalism. To achieve these ends, Americanization efforts involved two interrelated strategies. Leiserson (1971), a prominent spokesman for Americanization programs, referred to these strategies as "Americanization through management" and "Americanization through education."

Americanization through management consisted of the application of Progressivist reforms to the immigrant work force. Leiserson (1971, p. 73) noted the changing role of immigrants in the labor movement: "[The] submissive attitude of the immigrant has been changing. . . . In years gone by, when American workers struck, immigrants were brought in to take their places. . . . In recent years, . . . this situation has been reversed." He went on to argue that "employee representation" and "so-called welfare work" were the correct response (1971, p. 76).

By the second decade of the twentieth century, many of the largest corporations, including International Harvester, Standard Oil, Westinghouse, General Electric, and Midvale Steel, had instituted a variety of labor management policies (or "labor control," as a superintendent [quoted in Leiserson, 1971, p. 102] called it), and "industrial representation plans." Cyrus McCormick, manager of International Harvester, explained the rationale behind his company's program of employee representatives on industrial councils: "In the first place, there may be fear of Syndicalism, a fear that if legitimate interests are not recognized in this way . . . they will resort to revolution in order to secure a new state of things in which they shall be on top" (1919, p. 41).

The Massachusetts Bureau of Immigration (1919), which was a pioneer in Americanization efforts, warned employers on the eve of the Red Scare, "unless Americanization work has this basis of just treatment for one and all . . . no propaganda work can have permanent success." One personnel manager even argued,

> "Welfare work" of certain kinds and managed in the right spirit may also be conducive to profits. . . . If the right measures are undertaken, and in the right way, the inevitable result is better business. (quoted in Leiserson, 1971, p. 148)

Industry's attempts to control the labor force were accelerated during World War I. European immigration came to a sudden halt with the outbreak of war, and the effect on the labor market was immediate. *Iron Age* (1915, pp. 1357–1358) lamented that there was no longer the mass of unemployed job hunters "that once crowded the mill gates of Jones and Laughlin," and that the war created "a situation altogether unusual in the labor market."

One response by capital was to redouble efforts at efficiency. The number of establishments with labor management programs, personnel departments, and other scientific systems of labor control doubled in the war period (Leiserson, 1971, p. xi). In 1911, 50 corporation representatives formed the Employment Managers' Association; by 1918, the association had 900 members at its annual convention (Montgomery, 1977, p. 109). In addition to their focus on efficiency, these programs were directed at reducing the labor turnover rate, which, during times of labor demand, rose precipitously. During the war years, the labor turnover rate in some U.S. industries reached 1600–2000% (Marshall, 1918, p. 429). Proponents for the new industrial relations departments stressed their role in reducing these expensive turnover rates (*Iron Age*, 1918; Kellor, 1920; Leiserson, 1971).

Following the war, Frances Kellor (1920, pp. 168, 169), one of the most influential of Americanization advocates, urged employers to use "plant management" to counter "Bolshevism" at the peak of the Red Scare:

> His [Lenin's] propaganda has already followed working men into production. . . .
>
> We should therefore revise our ideas of plant management and our theories of welfare work, if we are to depend on immigrants for a future labor supply and if we are to secure a maximum production. . . .

It was propaganda work or immigration education, as it was called, that formed the crux of Americanization efforts. Education via public schooling had long been viewed as a primary tool of immigrant assimilation, but the offering of separate courses wholly designed to transform recent immigrants into "true Americans" began in the tumult of the 1890s. By 1907, the Daughters of the American Revolution were delivering lectures and printing pamphlets to teach the "spirit of true Americanism" and "obedience to law, which is the groundwork of true citizenship" (quoted in Higham, 1955, p. 237).

The same year, Peter Roberts, through the YMCA industrial department, began organizing classes in English and civics for immigrants. By 1914, 30,000 immigrants were enrolled. Korman (Introduction, in Leiserson, 1971, p. viii) applauded these pioneering efforts and explained that Roberts "wanted to teach citizens how to make the newcomer feel a part of the environment in which he worked so that loyalty to that environment would link him to his employers and to the State." Most large American cities financed their own evening classes for immigrants by 1914. By 1915, 13% of the non-English-speaking population of Chicago was enrolled in English classes (Immigrants' Protective League, 1916).

In 1908, a small group of wealthy New England businessmen formed the North American Civic League for Immigrants, whose ostensible purpose was the presentation of patriotic lectures in foreign languages.[1] Frances Kellor, financed by New York capitalists, opened a New York branch in 1909 devoted to immigrant education. In 1914, this branch became the Committee for Immigrants in America, supported by some of the country's leading capitalists, including Frank Trumbull (railroad president), Felix Warburg (banker), and Mrs. E. H. Harriman (Harriman, it will be remembered, was also at this time contributing personal funds to the blossoming eugenics movement). The same year, at the suggestion of, and with funds from the Committee for Immigrants in America, a division of immigrant education was established in the Bureau of Education. Its purpose was to emphasize the need for immigrant education "to make of all these people one nation" (quoted in Higham, 1955, p. 241).

Immigrant education found its most ardent advocates in the industrial sector. Frederick Taylor (quoted in Roberts, 1912, p. 73) once had advised employers that "the best kind of man to do certain kinds of work should be so stupid and so phlegmatic that he more nearly resembles the ox than any other type—a type to whom you can talk as you would not dare talk to white men." While Taylor assumed that such phlegmatic types would be more submissive and tractable, industries began to recognize that a particular type of education was advantageous. A constant and ever-changing supply of workers through immigration contributed to the biological reproduction of the work force, but it did not necessarily supply industry with the best kind of workers for their purposes. Americanization classes in English, civics, loyalty, and industrial methods—taught in the plant itself, frequently with government funds—were offered as a solution.

The teaching of English was a central element of the immigrant education programs that developed within industry as early as 1906. English classes were initiated with industrial efficiency in mind and were organized accordingly. The president of the Pennsylvania railroad system described the purpose of their English classes: "The original purpose in establishing these courses was to make Italians, who are largely employed in track maintenance gangs, more efficient workmen by teaching them the English language so that they might better understand the orders of their foremen ..." (quoted in Hill, 1919, pp. 634–635). The International Harvester Corporation's English classes, which all non-English-speaking employees were required to attend, epitomized the fusion of English language instruction, job training, and the development of factory discipline:

> I hear the whistle. I must hurry.... It's time to go into the shop. I take my check from the gate board and hang it on the department board.... The starting whistle blows. I eat my lunch. It is forbidden to eat until then.... I work until the whistle blows to quit. I leave my place nice and clean.... (quoted in Korman, 1965, p. 402)

Besides the teaching of English and factory discipline, Americanization from the beginning had another goal—the production of workers loyal to the company and to the country. Management recognized the impossibility of labor control without a common language. One plant manager described the predicament:

> What is one to do with these foreigners? ... Sometimes the Polish workers—usually women—get together in a corner of a room gesticulating and jabbering in their language, and nobody in authority is able to understand a word of it! Then one of them who can make herself understood may come up to the foreman or to me and say, "The workers want so and so." Meanwhile the workers stand around as expressionless and stolid as this radiator beside me.... I might say, "Well, we can meet you half-way." ... Then more gesticulating and more foreign language talking, and set faces, and stubborn resistance. Nothing but all will do—no matter what the mill owners' inconvenience in the matter. (quoted in Leiserson, 1971, p. 100)

In order to realize the psychological control potential of labor management, a common language was essential.

On another level, and increasingly important during the war, English classes focused on the development of patriotism and political conservatism. Ford's English School is widely recognized as a pioneer in Americanization efforts. The first words taught in this school were "I am a good American." Higham (1955, p. 248) describes the later stages of Ford's program:

Later the students acted out a pantomime which admirably symbolized the spirit of the enterprise. In this performance a great melting pot (labeled as such) occupied the middle of the stage. A long column of immigrant students descended into the pot from backstage, clad in outlandish garb and flaunting signs proclaiming their father lands. Simultaneously from either side of the pot another stream of men emerged, each prosperously dressed in identical suits of clothes and each carrying a little American flag.

Most of these factory classes were described by management as voluntary. "Invitations" to attend the Ford English School were disseminated in this way: non-English speaking workers were located by investigators of Ford's "sociological department." These workers were then advised as to the desirability of English classes and extended an invitation to attend.

The following comprised the invitation:

You are expected to attend the Ford English Schools. You must learn to read, write, and speak English. This school was established for your benefit, and you should be glad of this opportunity. You must read your Bulletin and you must be able to read the safety signs placed about the plant. There is no excuse for your remaining away from school. Come to the 3rd floor on the Woodward Avenue side, after you ring out. *COME TODAY.* (Hill, 1919, p. 638, emphasis in original)

Similarly, the Michigan Bolt and Nut Works of Detroit urged in their invitations: "Men attending night school *will be given preference when applying for work with this company. If it should become necessary to reduce our force at any future time, we will endeavor to retain a man with a good night school record in preference to a man not attending night school.* (Signed) MICHIGAN NUT AND BOLT WORKS" (quoted in Hill, 1919, p. 638; emphasis in original).

As America entered the war, the Bureau of Education redoubled its Americanization efforts. In 1917, the National Americanization Committee (NAC) of New York (previously Kellor's Committee for Immigrants in America) turned over its entire New York office to the Bureau of Education for Americanization work. By this time, 32 government agencies were involved in some form of Americanization work (Hill, 1919, p. 625). Kellor and the NAC, once stressing mutual understanding and assimilation, increasingly focused on the maintenance of the economic and political status quo (Higham, 1955, p. 249; Leiserson, 1971, p. viii). One scholar noted,

> She [Kellor] had moved from a position in which the state protected immigrants for their own sake and for the benefit of economic efficiency to one in which employers and the state protected themselves and the republic against the immigrant and his potential radicalism and unionism. (Korman, Introduction to Leiserson, 1971, p. viii)

The National Security League, composed of corporation executives, emerged in 1918 to educate "the great mass, not yet hopeless, of aliens . . . neither speaking nor thinking American . . . and to contradict the lies of agitators to ignorant aliens" (quoted in Higham, 1955, p. 256). In a similar effort, Kellor organized the Inter-Racial Council, which developed out of a New York dinner with 50 of the country's largest employers of immigrant labor. The organization was formed for the explicit purpose of defusing "Bolshevism" and conservatizing labor. T. Coleman DuPont became the first chairman of the council, which quickly enlisted the support of the country's largest industrial corporations. In addition to films and lectures to industrialists on the benefits of Americanization classes for subduing the labor movement and offsetting Bolshevism, the council bought control over the entire foreign language press in their acquisition of the American Association of Foreign Language Newspapers. Kellor was named president and used her control over all the national advertising that went into the press to turn its columns into virtual Americanization classes. Kellor (1920, pp. 124, 127) defended her aims in this way:

> We see it as a fertile field for propaganda. . . .
>
> We see the possibilities of this press to interpret a great country to millions of strangers . . . to further American ideas, trade, and commerce; to improve industrial relations between employers and immigrant workingmen.

In the climate of fear in the postwar period, many states sponsored public English classes for immigrants, and some states enacted compulsory attendance laws. Government responsibility for classes within factories increased from 131 classes in 1919, to 327 in 1920, and to 366 by 1921 (Leiserson, 1971, p. 263). The Massachusetts State Department of Education and the Associated Industries of Massachusetts held a joint conference on Americanization in 1919, and the conclusion of their report summarizes well the goals of these programs in the postwar period: *"The choice is between illiteracy which breeds anarchy, and education which breeds good citizenship"* (quoted in Leiserson, 1971, pp. 262–263; emphasis in original). The NAC, when asked, "What is Americanization?" replied,

> the combatting of anti-American propaganda . . . and the stamping out of sedition. . . . The elimination of causes of disorder, unrest, and disloyalty which make fruitful soil for un-American propagandists and disloyal agitators. . . . The creation of an understanding and love for America. (quoted in Hill, 1919, p. 630)

Secretary of the Interior Franklin Lane replied that Americanization "is not internationalism . . . is not pacifism . . . is not cynicism . . . is not indifference. . . . It is not being carried away with the idea that there is some guiding fate that will lead us in some mysterious way into the happy land" (quoted in Hill, 1919, p. 631).

Samuel Rea, president of the Pennsylvania railroad system, argued that the task of these Americanization programs was that, "First, America must be made to seem to these people a good place . . ." (quoted in Hill, 1919, p. 630). A conference committee on Americanization, involving ten of the country's leading industries, reported,

> The need of Americanization is now recognized as a national problem. Radicalism in the U.S. finds its most fertile field among those of foreign birth who cannot understand the English language. . . . It is our duty . . . to reveal to them the spirit of our institutions. . . . The education of the alien should include: (1) the teaching of English; a common language is first essential; (2) the imparting of knowledge in regard to the U.S., its government, its history and traditions, its institutions, and the advantages of citizenship; (3) instruction in the fundamental economic principles of American industry and the property rights of individuals and corporations. (quoted in Kellor, 1920, p. 149)

The Home Market Club of Boston advocated Americanization *"by tactful measures if possible, but if not by force"* (quoted in Wiebe, 1962, p. 184; emphasis added).

The immigrant's experience in America made these efforts at Americanization both more urgent and more difficult. As the

Ruthenian priest said in 1907, "My people do not live in America, they live underneath America" (quoted in Leiserson, 1971, p. 128). Given this experience of marginality, immigrant devotion to the new land was by no means automatic; Americanization took as its task the instilling of that devotion. The immigrant's experiences as an underclass not only made such efforts critical, but also complicated those efforts, as the ideals taught in Americanization classes frequently contradicted the immigrant's objective experience. This contradiction did not escape the attention of Americanizers. The Delaware Americanization Committee, jointly funded by the state and private corporations, pointed out the need to "*plant* in the hearts of all who live under our flag an understanding love for America," since "for many immigrants *the love they bore the America of their dreams has faded in cruel disillusionment before a grim reality* ..." (quoted in Leiserson, 1971, p. 259; emphasis added). Similarly, the Delaware Bureau of Immigrant Education declared,

> The first experience in the new land is often bitter and discouraging; but this is the faith that has been put into the hearts of the immigrant people of Delaware: *No matter what happens, America cares, America helps, America never willingly neglects her adopted children.* (quoted in Leiserson, 1971, p. 277; emphasis added)

A similar contradiction within the Americanization campaign did not escape the targets of those efforts. The implication of Americanization was that if immigrants could be Americanized, both poverty and social unrest would be reduced. Thus, the immigrant was exhorted to raise his standard of living and not cause trouble at his workplace in the process; in other words, both the immigrant's low standard of living and his demands for an improved standard of living were condemned as un-American.

The immigrant was frequently cynical as to the real meaning of Americanization. An Italian labor organizer, when asked by a group of industrial relations managers, "What is the attitude of your organization toward Americanization?" replied,

> What do you mean by Americanization? ...
>
> I know what some employers mean by Americanization ... and our people resent that kind of Americanization.
>
> Our organization is constantly striving to raise the standards of our people. We try to make them independ-

ent, self-respecting men and women. We want them to earn enough to live as Americans live. . . .

In our industry the workers are not afraid. . . . They walk with their heads erect. . . .

If this is Americanization, then we are strongly for it and we are Americanizing all the time. But because we do this some employers call us foreigners and Bolshevists [*sic*]. As long as we were satisfied with low wages and long hours, as long as we were afraid of losing our jobs, stood for black lists and did not strike, we were all right. We were preferred to American employees. But when we strike . . . then the employer says we are not Americans.

Can you blame us if we resent this? (quoted in Leiserson, 1971, pp. 21–23)

The Americanization movement was the logical consequence of a legitimating ideology that had defined the immigrant as morally inferior during a period of progressive reforms. Not surprisingly, then, the contradictions facing Americanization efforts mirror the inherent contradiction of American Progressivism: in both cases, the stated ideals of democracy and class unity stood counterposed to the workers' objective experiences of exploitation and class struggle.

These were the contradictions that the American state faced by 1920 and that ultimately influenced the restrictive immigration policies of the 1920s. However, both the ideological climate that produced the Americanization movement and the increasingly restrictive immigration policies went hand in hand with, and were made possible by, changing economic conditions and the increasing dispensability of European immigrant labor.

Economic Conditions

The second decade of the twentieth century brought critical changes to the structure and operation of the U.S. economy. These changes, which coincided with the intensification of anti-immigration racism and increasingly restrictive immigration laws, included (1) the development of chronically high unemployment rates, (2) the introduction of mass production technology, the assembly line, and scientific management, and (3) the use of women, blacks, and Mexicans as the major sources of surplus labor during World War I and its aftermath.

The panic of 1907 initiated the end of what Baran and Sweezy (1966, p. 227) called the "big shake-up which began before the

Civil War." Stagnation and unemployment were apparently chronic features of monopoly capitalism, as the troughs of each business cycle were deeper and longer lasting, the peaks spaced farther and farther apart, and unemployment at a relatively high level even during boom periods.

A national conference on unemployment was held in 1914, as official unemployment reached 8% for the first time in the twentieth century. At that conference the secretary of the Chicago Unemployment Commission summarized the unemployment situation, saying that it was not much worse than usual. "That was the tragedy, he continued, unemployment was now chronic and endemic to the economy" (paraphrased in Montgomery, 1974, p. 519). While unemployment for the years 1900–1907 averaged less than 3% annually and never went above 5%, official unemployment averaged 6% in the 8 years between 1914 and 1921, even with European immigration virtually cut off by the war (Montgomery, 1977, p. 232). While the United States's entrance into the war brought some improvement, economic collapse in 1921 pushed unemployment figures into double digits for the first time, at 11.9%.

This upward spiral of unemployment was only partly the consequence of the post-1907 economic stagnation, for a second feature of advancing monopoly capitalism compounded the problem. As the trend toward capital-intensive industry accelerated, the coordination of machine processes revolutionized American industry. Mass production and the assembly line, introduced by Henry Ford between 1908 and 1914, reduced labor costs and increased productivity. The more industry was rationalized in this way, the more working men and women were exposed to the irrationalities of the economic system. As Montgomery (1974, pp. 518–519) describes the period, "Even the frail safeguards of employment stability that union rules and standard rates had represented were swept away, while the urgent need of heavily capitalized corporations to operate only at full capacity made job tenure increasingly spasmodic for many workers."

As the "iron men of machinery" and speedups made many jobs obsolete, Henry Ford enjoyed the benefits of the simultaneous increase of productivity and unemployment rates. In 1914, after his introduction of the $5 wage for an eight-hour day, 10,000 unemployed men rioted for jobs outside his plant.

While the assembly line dictated the ever more rapid pace of work (the pace of Ford's assembly conveyer tripled between 1914 and 1924), unemployment rates, by assuring that resistant workers could be easily replaced, enforced that pace. The unprecedented increase in productivity per worker not only was made possible by high unemployment rates, but itself contributed to the mass of unemployed as fewer and fewer workers were required even for the higher levels of output. This new kind of capital-intensive, scientifically managed industry and the unemployment to which it contributed served functions similar to the unrestricted immigration of the prewar period in terms of both control over the work force and the stabilization of labor costs. Even though wages tended to rise with the outbreak of World War I, labor costs were stable or rose only slightly (Faulkner, 1962). Speaking of his notorious $5-day, Ford wrote that it "was one of the finest cost-cutting moves we ever made" (quoted in Sward, 1948, p. 56).

The stabilization of labor costs and the continued reproduction of a surplus work force, even without European immigration, were not based solely on advancing mechanization and scientific management. With European immigration curtailed by the war, American industries discovered untapped labor reserves closer to home, as women, blacks, and Mexicans were recruited into industry in unprecedented numbers.

Many large corporations hired female laborers for the first time during World War I. Women were employed in large numbers at the Bethlehem Steel Company as operatives and took on other untraditional and highly visible jobs, such as conducting streetcars and subways.

Blacks were actively recruited from southern rural areas where the mechanization of agriculture was leaving them destitute, much as European immigrants had been recruited earlier from the rural areas of Europe. From 1916 to 1918, almost 500,000 Southern blacks migrated to the large industrial centers of the northeast and midwest, in the largest and most long-distance black migration since the forced migration of slavery (Baxandall et al., 1976, p. 132). In 1917, an average of 2800 blacks per month migrated to Chicago alone (Imhoff, 1981, p. 19).

At the Gary Steel Works, the number of black employees increased from 189 in 1915 to 407 in 1916, to 1072 in 1917, and to 1295 by 1918. By 1917, 4000 blacks were employed at the Carnegie plants around Pittsburgh and 1400 worked at Jones and Laughlin (Brody, 1960, p. 186). By the middle of 1917, one observer noted, "Pittsburgh's industrial life is now partly dependent upon the Negro-labor supply" (quoted in Brody, 1960, p. 186). An Iron Age editorial (1917, p. 910) applauded the contribution of the black worker: "The perplexing problem of an adequate supply of common labor . . . has been solved to some degree . . . by the employment of negroes.... Negro labor brought from the South has proved satisfactory in the main. ..."

Steel companies set up recruiting agencies in black areas of the South and in many cases offered to pay the transportation north for willing workers. Railroad companies canvassed the South to replenish their labor gangs, picking up trainloads and carrying them north.

American employers also turned to the "back door" to replenish the surplus labor supply. Mexicans had been recruited into Canada as early as the 1800s with the restriction of Chinese immigration. Now, as the front door was closed with the war, U.S. industries as far north as the Chicago-Calumet region drew labor from the Mexican back door.

So important was this backdoor source of labor that in 1917, after the literacy test had been in force for only a few months, Secretary of Labor William B. Wilson invoked that part of the immigration laws that permitted him "to issue rules and proscribe conditions ... to control and regulate the admission and return of otherwise inadmissible aliens." In one fell swoop, he temporarily exempted Mexican migrants from the literacy test requirement, the head tax, and the contract labor clause (Reisler, 1976, p. 27). For the rest of the war, Wilson continually extended Mexican exemptions, so that Mexican migrants could be obtained for any industry and for the war's duration.

As the war closed, Wilson and Commissioner General of Immigration Anthony Caminetti, under pressure from southwestern sugar beet growers, extended these exemptions through 1920. The influx of Mexican migrant labor was particularly useful to agricultural interests in the Southwest, as it supplied a source of seasonal workers for their still labor-intensive enterprises. W. H. Knox, manager of the Arizona Cotton Growers' Association, reported appreciatively to the Senate Committee on Immigration (U.S. Congress, Senate Committee on Immigration, 1921a, p. 87, emphasis added):

> The industry is dependent entirely upon Mexican labor for its common or hand work, both in the chopping and in the picking. ...
>
> In 1917 we imported about 2500 Mexican laborers, in 1918 we brought in 3500, and in 1919 about 10,000 and this year about 20,000. ... These men are now returning [to Mexico] ... so that *there was no period of unemployment.*

TABLE VI

Production Index Calculated from a Base of 100[a]

Year	Production index
1899	100
1904	122
1909	159
1914	169
1919	214

[a] Source: Day and Woodlief (1928, pp. 32–33).

A sugar beet grower told the same committee (p. 119):

> It takes an immense amount of hand labor to do this work. . . .
>
> If we cannot have access to this surplus labor that we need from the Mexican border to take care of our crops, I don't see how in the world it is going to be possible to take care of the sugar-beet crop of the West.

Legal Mexican immigration increased from 11,000 in 1915 to 51,000 in 1920 (Marshall, 1978, p. 166), helping to fill in the gaps left by the wartime reduction of European immigration. In an interesting reversal of the Americanization emphasis on assimilation, immigration policy makers did what they could to ensure that these Mexican migrants remained socially marginal, constituting a labor reserve only. Mexican workers were allowed to enter the United States for only six months at a time. To enforce this provision, the Department of Labor ordered employers to withhold 20% of Mexican migrants' pay and deposit it with the immigration officials, to be rendered to them on their way back to Mexico.

By the close of the war, it was clear that U.S. industry was not irrevocably tied to massive European immigration. For, despite the curtailed supply of European labor, productive output leaped forward. While production increased only 6% from 1909 to 1914, it rose 26% in the period 1914–1919. Calculated from a base of 100 in 1899, Table VI shows the production index for the first two decades of the century.

Conclusion

At a time when the capital-intensive industries of the turn of the century required predictability, increased monopolization and scientific management provided some stabilization of prices and labor costs. Progressivism comprised an effort to stabilize the political climate by conservatizing the labor movement and preempting the possibility of the full development of socialist political parties. The exclusion of the new immigrant work force from mainstream unions such as the AFL and their concentration in the secondary sector, however, marginalized the immigrant work force and precipitated a reversal of roles such that the immigrant worker was increasingly found at the vanguard of the militant labor movement.

Once again, the solution, in this case Progressivism, merely transformed the dilemma. For once Progressives had announced an end to class conflict, the question now was how to explain the reality of continued class struggle, spearheaded by the marginalized immigrant work force. Racist definitions of the immigrant as genetically or morally inferior placed the blame for the continued symptoms of class conflict on the workers themselves and spawned the Americanization movement to reform the offending immigrants. The Americanization movement, then, can be seen as a last-ditch effort to resolve the tangle of conflicts and resolutions that had their base in the material conditions and related ideological constructs of an advancing capitalist democracy.

The contradictions inherent in the Americanization movement itself, together with the full development of anti-immigrant ideologies rooted in racism, contributed to increasingly selective immigration policies. Neither the racist ideologies nor the restrictive policies to which they contributed were independent of rapidly changing economic conditions. On one hand, after 1907, unemployment rates even in boom periods were higher than pre-1907 levels and were exacerbated by revolutionary mass production technologies. Equally important, as World War I cut off European immigration, U.S. industries discovered more flexible domestic and backdoor reserves, as well as the iron men of machinery. The Mexican backdoor source was considered by some to be superior to the European source of surplus labor, since Mexicans, as temporary or cyclical workers close to home, could be kept socially and politically marginal. In the years following World War I, the suspicion grew among policy makers that unrestricted European immigration might be both too expensive and dispensable.

Note

1. After the 1912 Lawrence Textile Strike, this league became an anti-labor spy agency, specializing in infiltrating immigrant communities for the purpose of gathering information on strike leaders and engaging in anti-strike activity (Higham, 1955, pp. 240–241).

7 · *"The Close of an Epoch"*

(Trevor, 1924, p. 5)

Introduction

Americanization was an attempt to reform the allegedly inferior Southern and Eastern European immigrant without restricting the labor supply, but as race theories became more explicit, such efforts were increasingly regarded as both inadequate and irrelevant. It was furthermore recognized that Americanization—explicitly referred to as *propaganda work*—would prove unsuccessful with immigrants whose objective reality of unemployment, low wages, and poor housing so blatantly contradicted that propaganda.

As both the contradictions that precipitated the Americanization movement and the contradictions within the movement itself stubbornly resisted resolution, rapidly changing economic conditions were transforming the nature of the constraints facing immigration policy makers. The advance of monopoly capitalism through the first two decades of the twentieth century intensified the economic and ideological conflicts associated with the creation of a surplus labor supply while simultaneously freeing U.S. industry from its dependence on European labor. Congressional debates and hearings on the issue of European immigration in the post-World War I period confirm the critical roles played by these persistent contradictions and by the changing economic context of monopoly capitalism in the numerical restriction of European immigration.

In the immediate postwar period, Congress began to consider seriously the possibility of restricting European immigration. At first, a variety of total suspension schemes were discussed, according to which immigration would be halted altogether for a period of from two to five years. The House Committee on Immigration and Naturalization, fearing massive immigration with the close of the war, recommended a temporary suspension plan in 1919. By the end of that year, it became clear that the predicted flood of immigrants was not forthcoming, taking the urgency out of such restrictive measures. Even with the resurgence of immigration by the end of 1920, Congress still considered total suspension too rigid a plan. In its place Senator William P. Dillingham of Vermont, chair of the Dillingham commission of 1907, introduced a plan by which immigration from each European country would be limited to 5% of their numbers in the United States in 1910. This plan simultaneously put a numerical ceiling on immigration and favored immigrants from Northern and Western Europe. A House bill reduced the quota to 3%, limiting quota immigration to a maximum of 350,000 annually. The measure passed easily in both houses and became law in May 1921 (see p. 149).

The words of Albert Johnson, chair of the House Committee on Immigration and Naturalization, in a speech to Congress in 1922 (*Congressional Record*, 1922, p. 12064) were indicative of the understanding that permeated the discussions surrounding the formation and passage of this law: "Gentlemen, the U.S. is paying and will pay a fearful price for the cheap labor already brought in. . . . It has been a great scheme, it helped to make a great country, but it has its limitations." Precisely what those limitations were is clear from a review of the congressional discussions surrounding immigration law making in these postwar years.

The Intensification of Conflicts

The contradictions underlying the construction of a surplus work force had intensified with the development of monopoly capitalism. Both the post-1907 stagnation and the advance of capital-intensive technologies contributed to the upward spiral of unemployment. The advancing unemployment rate compounded both the fiscal strain associated with the material reproduction of labor and the ideological threat presented by a disillusioned work force, at just the time that monopoly capitalism required economic predictability and hegemonic control. These dilemmas were urgently addressed in the congressional debates and became a central concern of immigration policy makers.

The surplus labor versus fiscal strain dilemma

It was repeatedly recognized in these discussions that immigration had been pivotal in the provision of a cheap surplus labor force for U.S. industry. Frank Morrison, secretary of the AFL, testified before the House Committee on Immigration and Naturalization in 1919 that

> It was customary with the packing houses in Chicago that when there were not more than 300 men at the gates to arrange for another shipload to come in. So that

when the men were going to work certain mornings they
would see 500 or 600 people waiting for situations. . . .
They wanted cheap labor, and they brought it in. The
idea was that they wanted an unlimited supply. They also wanted an extra supply to let their workers know that
if they did not want to work under those conditions,
[there were] others to take their places. (U.S. Congress,
House Committee on Immigration and Naturalization,
1919a, p. 62)

The same committee invited John Densmore, the director general
of labor in the U.S. Employment Service, to estimate the effect
that restricting European immigration might have on the labor
supply:

Wilson: With your knowledge of the situation, would
you care to say whether or not we would be able to
take care of the industries of this country by the labor we would have, if we should pass laws barring
immigration, say, for 4 years? (p. 23)

Densmore (p. 12) assured the committee that the proper kind
of restrictions would have no adverse effect on the labor supply,
given the already high rate of unemployment.

Although the immigrant's role in providing a surplus labor
supply was recognized, the attention of these policy makers was
focused on the effect of mass immigration on already high unemployment rates and the consequent burdens on the state. In the
House debates of 1920, economic stagnation and unprecedented
unemployment rates were repeatedly pointed to, as congressmen
denounced those who would continue to seek surplus labor despite the unemployment situation.

Some advocate the unrestricted admission of immigrants because of their desire to obtain a surplus of unskilled workmen. . . . In the past it was the labor of the
immigrant that supplied this need. . . . But the present
and immediate future will not witness a shortage of unskilled laborers. The present surplus in the labor market
from all present indications will remain for some time.
(*Congressional Record*, 1920, p. 187)

Others focused on the concrete dangers of overcrowding the labor
market, despite the success of that strategy in the past.

If we would keep our own raft afloat, we cannot allow it
to be any further crowded. With 2,000,000 unemployed

in this country, with 2,000,000 walking the streets, it is futile to admit any more to become public charges. (*Congressional Record*, 1921, p. 4550)

When we look about us we see in this country to-day no less than 5,000,000 idle men. We see our factories and workshops and farms abandoned. Our production is curtailed to a point that is indeed alarming. And yet it is sought here on the part of some to open the floodgates of this glorious Republic to immigration.... (*Congressional Record*, 1921b, p. 586)

Even in the immediate postwar boom of 1919, the periodic crises of capitalism and the dangers of building up virtually unlimited labor reserves were noted. As Chairman Johnson warned,

We must not presume that such a market will continue year in and year out ... and to permit and continue heavy immigration because we are going to do a big business on the present inflated financial situation with war-broken countries, inevitably we will be left here with the labor of the world on our hands. (U.S. Congress, House Committee on Immigration and Naturalization, 1919a, p. 24)

The surplus labor versus legitimation dilemma

Just as the advancing unemployment rate intensified the surplus labor-material reproduction dilemma associated with immigration, so it exacerbated the poverty-legitimation dilemma. In fact, it was the ideological dimension of the unemployment problem that most concerned members of Congress. Frank Morrison's vivid testimony of the deliberate building-up of labor surpluses at the gates of packing houses in Chicago disturbed and shocked the House Committee on Immigration and Naturalization. Their response to his depiction was a simple question: "That big crowd at the gates of the packing plants is what makes socialists, Bolsheviki [*sic*], and IWW's?" (U.S. Congress, House Committee on Immigration and Naturalization, 1919a, p. 63). John Densmore argued in favor of restrictions, warning the House Committee, "I think everybody agrees just now the way to head off radicalism and IWW-ism and that overworked Bolshevism is to do something to keep employment" (U.S. Congress, House Committee on Immigration and Naturalization, 1919a, p. 12).

The following year, as the House debated the suspension of immigration, again a major concern was the effect of the unemployment rate on social unrest. Representative Knutson (*Congres-*

sional Record, 1920, p. 172) warned, "If we allow a half million, or a million, or a million and a half to come to this country in the next year to aggravate an already bad situation, as far as unemployment is concerned, it is merely going to create more unrest in the country." Speaker after speaker concurred, "Under existing conditions he [the immigrant] will be unable to find employment and with the million or more now without work and the thousands coming daily to our shores, the problem of the unemployed will become constantly more acute.... Unemployment always creates dissatisfaction and unrest ..." (p. 187). Others expressed concern that disillusioned immigrants would provide the leadership for rebellion: "We do not need men and women whose first thought upon learning conditions here is to mount soapboxes and public school rostrums and try to convince those who have been contented with those conditions, that the conditions are all wrong" (p. 185).

W. J. Lauck (1921, pp. 188–189), industrial expert on the Dillingham Immigration Commission and former secretary of the National War Labor Board, in an article cited in the House, warned his readers that oversaturating the labor market through unrestricted immigration would jeopardize the tenuous control of labor that had been so long and diligently worked for through the progressive era:

> ... unrestricted immigration ... holds forth the danger of the destruction of an intelligent, constructive, evolutionary control of the labor movement.... If industrial conditions continue unfavorable, the immigrant workmen who have already either directly or indirectly been brought under the influence of extreme economic doctrines will undoubtedly become receptive to the teachings of revolutionary agitators.... [Some] may hope through the artificial stimulation of immigration and the development of an oversupply of labor, possibly to bring around a temporary reduction in wages and an impairment of existing standards of work. They cannot look forward, however, to a permanent weakening of unionism, for their own activities will either strengthen unionism or entirely destroy unionism, and in bringing about the impairment of organized labor, as it is now controlled and directed, Mr. Gary [of U.S. Steel] and his associates will encompass their own destruction.

Perhaps no congressional speech of this period better reflects the intertwined contradictions among the biological, the material, and the ideological reproduction of a surplus labor force than this speech by Representative Kleczka in 1920: "The admitted aliens, if they fail to find employment, will become sadly disillusioned in their hopes and expectations, and will not only become a burden to the community but will become an easy prey of revolutionary agitators and fomentors of strife" (*Congressional Record*, 1920, p. 187).

There was no confusion in these congressional discussions as to the role played by material conditions in the radicalization of immigrant workers. Interestingly, side by side with this materialist interpretation, and often in the same breath, the personal and/or biological traits of recent immigrants were blamed for that radicalization.

Congress Responds

While congressional attention was focused on the persistent contradictions associated with the immigrant labor supply, earlier resolutions to similar contradictions reappeared to haunt the policy maker. In particular, the depiction of the immigrant as the importer of radicalism and as genetically and morally inferior that had been used to explain away the class struggle now became an important component of the immigration restriction debate.

Immigrant as Radical

Almost without exception, congressional proponents of restrictive measures referred to the danger of importing radicalism along with the immigrant labor force. Starting from the premise that "[p]ractically all the IWW and Bolsheviki are foreigners" (U.S. Congress, House Committee on Immigration and Naturalization, 1919a, p. 270), it was urged that the gates must be closed before the United States was inundated with "Bolsheviki" and anarchists.

> A large percentage of the people we are receiving now are radical in their political opinions.... Something must be done and done at once.... We have more of that kind now than we know what to do with ... (applause). (*Congressional Record*, 1920, p. 172)

> The people who are coming or preparing to come ... have not been trained in the schools of order but have stewed in disorder—the disorder of war, the disorder of persecution, the disorder of revolution, the disorder of anarchy. (p. 173)

The Russian Revolution of 1917 was continually alluded to as members of Congress warned of "Bolshevik expansionism."

> Beyond the seas there are being taught new and strange doctrines. Socialism, Bolshevism, and anarchy are playing unusual parts in the history and welfare of those nations, and are threatening the very foundation of their governments. Bolshevism and anarchy may draw their slimy trail across the map of Europe and write their destructive doctrines into the history of the nations over there, but never with my vote or influence will they make their unholy imprint upon America or American institutions. It is absolutely imperative that this Congress close the door at this time to all immigration except those whose entrance is provided for by the provisions of this bill. . . . [*We must be*] *willing to throw aside any idea of gain or commercialism for the good of America.* (*Congressional Record*, 1920, p. 181; emphasis added)

Similarly,

> We should formulate and . . . enforce a genuine 100% American immigration law. . . . The incoming flood remains dangerously alien. . . . We have a right to say how many shall enter our portals . . . and what sort of material they shall be. . . . *It is our business to see that the flood is barred to our shores.* (*Congressional Record*, 1921a, p. 4550; emphasis added)

Albert Johnson, chair of the House Committee on Immigration and Naturalization, in a speech to Congress in 1922 (*Congressional Record*, 1922, p. 12065) summed up these fears:

> In but a few years these aliens in very despair will be pounding heavily at the very pillars of our government, where those who have come ahead of them a few years back with their socialism, their communism, their Bolshevism, have been merely gnawing like rats at our foundations.

Since immigrants as a class of people were now viewed as politically suspect and morally inferior, since the contribution that immigration made to advancing unemployment and social unrest was clearly recognized, and since—as we will see—Congress was also noting the decreased need for European labor, the whole immigrant stream was now viewed as both a menace and dispensable. A decided shift had occurred since turn-of-the-century exhortations to sift immigrants through selective policies.

The House Committee on Immigration and Naturalization Report in 1919, in advocating suspension, reflected this shift: "It is impossible to keep out revolutionists and Bolsheviki without keeping out substantially everybody" (quoted in *Literary Digest*, 1919b). Frederick A. Wallis, immigration commissioner at the port of New York, was quoted in the House debates (*Congressional Record*, 1920, p. 185):

> If among 1000 aliens seeking entrance to America we suspect that there is even one who is plotting against America, I would rather refuse admittance to the 999 worthy than to take the chance of admitting the unworthy one. So long as I am in charge here my slogan shall be: "When in doubt, deport!"

The "Abnormally Twisted"

Underlying the discussion of the immigrant as radical was the notion that the new immigrants as a class were defective, of unsound mind, and racially inferior. The ideology of race that was spearheaded at critical junctures by leading capitalists as a solution to their legitimation problems now came to prominence as a component of the conflict to be resolved. While a small minority in Congress defended immigration by pointing to the labor contribution that immigrants had always made, the majority now viewed with alarm the so-called racial inferiority of the new immigrant.

Albert Johnson, chair of the House Committee on Immigration and Naturalization, a major spokesman for immigration restriction, and a protagonist of the Red Scare, had direct contacts with both the New England elites and the capitalist-sponsored eugenicists who were supplying the ideology of race with its intellectual trimmings. He had known Prescott Hall of the IRL for years and was kept informed of the League's activities through their lobbyists in the House of Representatives. He communicated frequently with Madison Grant, author of *The Passing of the Great Race* (1916). In 1923, Johnson, a layman with no background in biology, was elected president of the Eugenics Research Association at Cold Spring Harbor.

Both Lothrop Stoddard, author of *Revolt Against Civilization: The Menace of Under-Man* (1922), and Harry Laughlin, noted eugenicist from Cold Spring Harbor, came to testify at the House hearings on immigration restriction in 1920, and the House committee thereafter appointed Laughlin its "expert eugenics agent"

(U.S. Congress, House Committee on Immigration and Naturalization, 1920). In addition, John Trevor, a self-appointed expert on the "biological propensity of Jews toward radicalism," testified to the Senate Committee on Immigration in 1921 (U.S. Congress, Senate Committee on Immigration, 1921, pp. 293–300). After his testimony, Trevor continued to attend all hearings and informal meetings of the House committee, even helping to draft reports.

In the meantime, congressional discussions on immigration continued to reveal strong racist overtones. It was warned by one speaker after another that "We are not getting the class of immigrants that we did 10, 20, 30, or 40 years ago" (*Congressional Record*, 1920, p. 172). Particular disdain was reserved for Jewish immigrants. Johnson had received a report in 1920 from the State Department summarizing comments from consuls overseas on the "pernicious" character of the Jews planning to emigrate. They were, according to the report, "abnormally twisted," "unassimilable," "filthy un-American and often dangerous in their habits." The House committee appended this document to their report in which they recommended immigration suspensions in 1920 (U.S. Congress, House Report, 1920, p. 10). One of the fears registered in the congressional debates of that year was that the forthcoming immigration would contain Jews fleeing Eastern Europe (*Congressional Record*, 1920, p. 172). This group of aspiring immigrants was described in a House report of 1921: "It is only too obvious that they must be subnormal, and their normal state is very low standard" (U.S. Congress, House Report, 1921b, p. 11).

The influence that this racism had on the state elite in formulating immigration restrictions is suggested by Johnson's speech to the House in 1922:

> In concluding I want to commend to all those interested in the racial and political aspects of the question two epoch-making books by Lothrop Stoddard entitled "The Rising Tide of Color" and "The Revolt Against Civilization," an equally important book by Madison Grant entitled "The Passing of the Great Race." . . . (*Congressional Record*, 1922, p. 12065)

The pervasiveness and popularity of such race thinking was rooted in its legitimating utility in the Progressive era and the support that the eugenics movement had secured from leading capitalists and elites; furthermore, as we will see in a moment, its influence was not independent of prevailing economic needs. It is clear, however, that this ideological factor—developed in part as a resolution to the class conflict-legitimation problem—now took its

place as an important element of new dilemmas that policy makers
had to address.

The Failures of Americanization

Two somewhat contradictory concerns emerged, then, from these
congressional discussions. On one hand, the structural conflicts
among the biological, material, and ideological reproduction of the
work force were well-recognized, as the political dangers of main-
taining a destitute and disillusioned army of unemployed were
repeatedly addressed. On the other hand, the alleged inherent
characteristics and personal predispositions of the new immigrants from Southern and Eastern Europe were simultaneously
held responsible for both poverty and radicalism.

Both these concerns contributed to an increasing pessimism
with regard to the efficacy of Americanization. If "Americanism" is
based on genetic traits, then the melting pot is of little use. Thus,
the House committee noted in 1919 that "The far-famed melting
pot has proved to a great degree a delusion and a snare" (quoted
in the *Literary Digest*, 1919b). More importantly, it was noted that
Americanizing propaganda work was difficult in the face of rising
unemployment and an objective reality that was incompatible
with that propaganda. Again, the underlying class conflict-
legitimation contradiction, to which both progressivism and
Americanization efforts had been a response, stubbornly resisted
resolution.

An exchange between Frances Kellor, advocate of Americanization and head of the IRC, and members of the House Committee
on Immigration and Naturalization underlines this concern for the
ideological control of immigrants, given their material conditions:

> Miss Kellor: . . . I think he comes prepared to do
> his share in the new country; that he faces
> great difficulties; . . . and that he tries very
> hard to do his best here.
>
> Representative White: He takes into considera-
> tion that he is ignorant of the language and
> customs and conditions, and expects, there-
> fore, to be subjected to a great many incon-
> veniences that are not the fault of others—or
> of the conditions—but are his own lack of
> knowledge of the situation?
>
> Miss Kellor: I think he does not quite start that
> way. It is more like this: . . . He comes for
> the opportunities of our free educational

system and for the benefits of American institutions. When he arrives, and *begins to
come into contact with actual conditions*,
which he finds difficult, he finds these
things are not obtained so simply as he
thought they would be. (U.S. Congress,
House Committee on Immigration and Naturalization, 1921, p. 16; emphasis added)

By 1919, Congress was seriously reconsidering its traditional
role as the provider of a surplus work force, as the consequent potential for social and political unrest was noted. The following discussion between Moisseiff, an industrialist, and a member of the
House committee in 1919 exemplifies this heightened concern for
long-term stability, as well as short-term profits (U.S. Congress,
House Committee on Immigration and Naturalization, 1919a, p.
264; emphasis added).

> Moisseiff: In order to run an industry you need
> to man it.... No iron clad bill that comes in
> to be repealed in 2 years or 4 years will be
> good; it will cause harm to our indus-
> tries.... Don't let us cripple ourselves.
>
> Representative Baker: Do you think there
> should be any restrictions against the Ger-
> man people?
>
> Moisseiff: I don't like them ... but I think they
> may be efficient working men.
>
> Representative Baker: *Is that all we should
> think about?* Is that the acme of our
> thought, that they are efficient working
> men? ... If a man is a good working man
> and not a good citizen do you think he
> should come here?

Alternative Sources of Labor

The contradictions that had surrounded immigration for at least
40 years, compounded by immigrant-as-enemy race thinking,
were a palpable presence at these congressional hearings and debates. Ominous predictions of the economic and political consequences of continued mass immigration pervaded the discussions.
    The impact of changing economic needs must not be underes-
timated in this development.[1] For one thing, it was clear to these
law makers that the structural conditions of monopoly capitalism

were contributing internally to the surplus labor force on which profit making depended. As Representative Kleczka put it in 1920, "The present surplus in the labor market from all present indications will remain for some time" (*Congressional Record*, 1920, p. 187). Representative Schall concurred, "With 2,000,000 unemployed in this country, with 2,000,000 walking the streets, it is futile to admit any more" (*Congressional Record*, 1921a, p. 4550). Furthermore, it did not escape the attention of immigration policy makers that U.S. industry was far from crippled during World War I when immigration was curtailed.

The advance of industry during the war was not only the result of the internal reproduction of surplus labor through labor management schemes, mechanization, and the recruitment of blacks and women; it also depended on the importation of Mexican and other Western Hemisphere workers to fill gaps in the labor market. Throughout the hearings, interest was shown in the way that wartime exemptions from immigration laws for Mexican labor had worked and whether such a measure effectively increased flexibility without increasing unemployment during periods of depression. It was understood that the advantage of Mexican, Cuban, and Canadian immigration was that, while supplying workers to labor-intensive and seasonal enterprises like agriculture, they returned to their countries—or could be made to return—during recessions or in the off-season.

As early as 1919, John Densmore, director general of labor in the U.S. Employment Service, warned the House Committee on Immigration and Naturalization (U.S. Congress, House Committee on Immigration and Naturalization, 1919a, pp. 24–25):

> Mr. Densmore: If you do anything like that [immigration restriction] you ought to make it flexible enough. . . . If you can make the thing [an "assessment of industrial conditions"] like that from week to week, if you have a shortage of labor opening up, you can open your gate, let enough labor in to fill that shortage and then close it.

> Representative Johnson: Leaving the foreign labor still in when the depression comes?

> . . .

> Mr. Densmore: The department has had a good experience during the war in the importation of Mexican labor, labor from the Baha-

mas, labor that came in notwithstanding
certain parts of the law. . . .

The Chairman: You reserved the right to deport
them when you get too many?

Mr. Densmore: Yes, sir.

Representative Hayes: How did the thing work
out? Were you able to deport them when the
need was passed? . . .

Representative Powers: Are you having any
trouble in getting them out of the country
since bringing them in?

For labor-intensive industry with seasonal demands and for occasional increases in labor demand in the industrial sector, short-
term migrations of workers who would commute with the seasons
and the business cycles constituted an ideal source of labor.

Emergency Quota Legislation

In May 1921, the Emergency Quota Law (42 U.S. Statutes at Large,
p. 5) was enacted, clearing the House with no record vote and
passing in the Senate, 78 to 1. The law provided

> That the number of aliens of any nationality who may
> be admitted under the immigration laws to the U.S. in
> any fiscal year shall be limited to 3 per cent of the num-
> ber of foreign-born persons of such nationality resident
> in the U.S. census of 1910. . . .

Exempt from the act were:

> . . . aliens who have resided continuously for at least five
> years immediately preceding the time of their applica-
> tion for admission to the U.S. in the Dominion of Cana-
> da, Newfoundland, the Republic of Cuba, the Republic of
> Mexico, countries of Central and South America or adja-
> cent islands. (42 U.S. Statutes at Large, p. 5)

The law gave preference to the "wives, brothers, sisters, children under 18 years of age, and fiancees of citizens of the U.S.," as
well as to those who had applied for citizenship and those who had
served in the armed forces; and it provided for a $200 fine plus "a
sum equal to that paid by such alien for his transport" to be imposed on those, primarily steamship lines, who brought in inadmissible aliens.

The legislation, in reverting back to the 1910 census, was expressly devised to discriminate against immigrants from Southern and Eastern Europe, whose numbers relative to those from Northern and Western Europe were far fewer in 1910 than in 1920. There was little disagreement in Congress as to the preferability of old immigrants compared to the new immigrants of Southern and Eastern Europe. As the Senate Committee on Immigration noted in recommending passage of the bill, ". . . the committee does not look upon normal immigration from Northern and Western Europe as in any sense a problem" (U.S. Congress, Senate Report, 1921, p. 6).

A few congressmen objected to such overt discrimination. One member of the House Committee on Immigration and Naturalization responded candidly to such complaints:

> If you can point out any other way whereby we can bring about what you consider the desired result and what I consider the desired result, *without showing such intentional discrimination* . . . why that would be satisfactory. (U.S. Congress, House Committee on Immigration and Naturalization, 1923b, p. 92; emphasis added)

Just as exemptions from the literacy test requirement had been made for Mexicans, this law exempted from the quota most Western Hemisphere nations. As the Minority Report put it:

> An examination of its provisions will show it makes an exception in favor of the people of the States contiguous to the Canadian border in order to provide them with Canadians to be used by them in fisheries, farming, and other industries. It makes another exception in favor of the States of Texas, Utah, Arizona, Colorado, New Mexico, and other border States in order to permit the employment in those States of any unlimited number of Mexicans. It also makes another exception in behalf of the cigar manufacturers of the State of Florida, so that they can have any number of imported help from Cuba and other adjacent islands. (U.S. Congress, 1921b, House Report, p. 18)

The House Committee on Immigration and Naturalization explained these Western Hemisphere exemptions concisely:

> All . . . "nonquota" immigrants are entirely outside of the quota, which is designed entirely as an *immigration bonus* . . . for use *as an escape valve* for the purpose of

preventing absolute rigidity. (U.S. Congress, House Report, 1923, p. 18; emphasis added)

In contrast to the symbolic Anti-Contract Labor Law of 1885 (which so many had criticized for its ambiguities, vague language, and unenforceability) the Emergency Quota Law of 1921 contained few ambiguities, provided strict penalties, and supplied ample machinery for its enforcement. In contrast to almost all previous laws related to European immigration, its effect was immediate and substantial. The total admissible immigration under the quota for the years 1921–1922 was 356,995; the number admitted under the quota was 243,953, and the total number of immigrants—quota and nonquota—was 309,556, compared to 805,228 the previous year. After one year of operation, the principal concern of policy makers was not how to enforce the measure better, as it seemed to be functioning as expected, but rather how to encourage immigration from Northern and Western Europe, which used only 46% of its quota the first year (Garis, 1927, p. 151). By 1924, the law had fulfilled its promise. In 1921, immigration from Northern and Western Europe amounted to 138,551, compared to 525,548 from Southern and Eastern Europe; by 1924, 203,346 immigrants had come from Northern and Western Europe, and 163,346 were from Southern and Eastern Europe.

Capital's Response

An examination of business response to these immigration restrictions makes it clear that a simple instrumentalist view of the "state in capitalist society" is inadequate to account for this substantial change in immigration policy.

The reaction of capital to the issue of immigration restriction in the period immediately preceding the passage of the Emergency Quota Law was varied. Some leading capitalists and their spokespeople appeared ambivalent about restrictions. The *Commercial and Financial Chronicle* (1920), a barometer of medium-sized business opinion for decades, pleaded for "a middle ground that is unassailable." It urged that Congress recognize "the right of protection against the poisonous agents and agencies of anarchy" and the problem of "racial preservation." They offered this parable:

> A husbandman . . . found a frozen snake in the field, and in the goodness of his heart took it home and warmed it to life by his fireside, only to set it free to sting his family to death.

In the same breath, they argued that each country has the "right to control and direct and measure out both emigration and immigration, but not to *prohibit* either" (emphasis in original). Prohibition, they urged, would be yielding to . . . class spirit and interest."

The *Mining and Scientific Press* (quoted in *Literary Digest*, 1921, p. 23) argued that only those who were assimilable should be admitted.

By and large, however, capitalists yearned for a return to "our immigration safety valve" (quoted in Wiebe, 1962, p. 185). The *New York Journal of Commerce* (quoted in *Literary Digest*, 1920, p. 12), in arguing for the repeal of the literacy test requirement, complained,

> The present situation in the United States is characterized by a tremendous shortage of labor. . . . The present immigration laws of the United States are unquestionably antiquated. They neither shut out undesirables nor do they properly provide for the encouragement of the right kind of workers.

Moody's Investment Service (quoted in *Literary Digest*, 1919a, p. 132; emphasis added), similarly pointed to the shortage of labor and reported candidly:

> We look for a heavy immigration with all that this means. For one thing, *it means lower wages*. . . . It also means lower operating costs and better control of operating ratios. It is bound to mean too *some decrease in the present extraordinary power of the labor unions.*

Iron Age complained in an article entitled "Decreased Immigration—Less Production" (1920, p. 1133), presented at the National Conference on Immigration under the auspices of the IRC,

> As a result of this condition [the war], we are to-day about 4,000,000 short in immigrant labor. . . . The result to-day is that the wages of unskilled labor have risen to an abnormal degree. . . . The obvious remedy for this condition is to increase immigration, and in order to accomplish this we face two problems, namely: to get and to hold.

Iron Age urged the "cooperation between industry and the government" in this enterprise of "getting and holding."

Representatives from both large and small businesses were opposed to the restrictions. The IRC headed by Frances Kellor, representing many of the country's largest corporations, advocated the repeal of the literacy test (Kellor, 1920, p. 6), as did the NAM, representing mostly small firms (*American Industries*, 1919). Kellor, the president of the IRC, stated at their national conference on immigration in 1920 that "there is at present a shortage of 4,800,000 unskilled immigrant workers. . . . The Inter-Racial Council believes in the immigrant as a great potential national asset and advocates for him the largest opportunity" (quoted in *Literary Digest*, 1920, p. 12). The National Conference on Immigration concluded by recommending ways to protect immigrants, facilitate their distribution, and coordinate government activities on immigration. As the *Literary Digest* (1920) described the recommendations, "[T]he resolutions tended to encourage immigration in order to keep up production and to keep labor costs from rising."

Kellor (1920, p. 157) did agree with Congress that an oversupply of labor was a potential danger, but "[Immigration policy] should provide for reserves to be called upon when needed and to be taken care of when idle. The very nature of American industry makes such an organization of the labor market an imperative duty. . . ." She was unequivocal that it should be left to business to determine when and how much immigration was necessary:

> The whole subject [of immigration] . . . is first of all a dollar and cents affair. . . .
>
> Much as some of us would like to dwell upon the humanitarian movements which should be part of this period of reconstruction . . . the question is . . . whether future immigration will pay. . . . (p. 131)
>
> Up to the present time immigration has paid better than any other single element in production. This is true because it has cost industry comparatively nothing to secure immigrant workmen; it has cost little per man to maintain their efficiency; and it has cost comparatively little to replace immigrant manpower. This hitherto unfailing source of supply has kept down the cost of production and has increased output, . . . it is production which will be most affected, if the trend of immigration is unfavorable to America. *If, in the future, deposits of men are to be as much a matter of competition to protect and control as are deposits of ore and oil, it is to business that the country must turn for assistance in meeting the new problems of immigration.* (Kellor, 1920, p. 132; emphasis added)

Those business interests that were represented at congressional hearings were unilaterally opposed to the immigration restrictions being considered. James Emery, lobbyist for the NAM, appeared regularly before congressional hearings to testify against restrictive measures. Louis Marshall, representing hundreds of the largest industrial corporations in the country through the IRC, pleaded with the House Committee on Immigration and Naturalization (U.S. Congress, House Committee on Immigration and Naturalization, 1921, pp. 4ff.) for a liberal immigration policy.

If these neglected appeals suggest the inadequacy of a ruling-class influence or instrumentalist account of law creation, the debate that preceded the extension and reduction of the quota in 1924 underscores further the inadequacy of a simple instrumentalist model of law and the state.

The depression that hit in 1920 continued through 1921, and business response to the Emergency Quota Law of that year was relatively quiet. By late 1922, however, capital was once again lamenting the shortage of common labor. *Iron Age* (quoted in *The Nation's Business*, 1922, p. 78) urged the repeal of the Emergency Quota Law:

> The result (of the law) is a premium on common labor here. . . .
>
> Continued wage advances for such labor will keep adding to the cost of manufactured articles. . . .

The Associated Industries of Massachusetts at its annual convention called on Congress to establish a "constructive, national immigration policy" that would take into account "a growing shortage of labor" (quoted in *The Nation's Business*, 1922, p. 78). *The American Contractor* (quoted in *The Nation's Business*, 1922, p. 78) advised builders to "hang on to the labor now employed in the construction industry" and emphatically agreed with the recommendation of the Associated Industries of Massachusetts for a constructive policy.

By 1923, these murmurings against the restrictions became an uproar. The *Commercial and Financial Chronicle* (quoted in *Literary Digest*, 1923, p. 11; emphasis added), complaining of a shortage of both skilled and unskilled labor, concluded, "*There can hardly be too much of either.*" In an earlier issue (1923a), the *Chronicle* called for the abolition of the literacy test, urging, "This country needs more labor." The *Wall Street Journal* agreed, "The U.S. does not need, or desire, the off-scourings of Europe and Asia, but it needs willing labor and a great deal of it" (quoted in the *Literary Digest*, 1923, p. 11). The same year, *American Indus-tries* (cited in *Literary Digest*, 1923, p. 11) conducted a symposi-um on immigration, uniting leaders in finance, business, and industry; there was "almost unanimous agreement that the pre-sent law [the 1921 Emergency Quota Law] should be amended."

William Barr, president of the Lumen Bearing Company and the National Founders Association, in an article in *The Metal In-dustry* (1923, p. 70; emphasis added), urged, as Kellor had, that the immigration problem be left to industry to resolve.

> The fundamental trouble in the immigration problem is the fact that it has been injected into politics [*sic*]. . . . The first restriction imposed was the literacy test which was, and is, utterly unsound. This country has not reached its full development, and there are still neces-sary a tremendous number of workers to do the rough labor. . . . We have, therefore, the literacy test which is utterly stupid, and the 3 percent restrictive limitation which has succeeded in merely steadily decreasing the number of workers available. . . . There can be no real prosperity, no definite industrial expansion unless there is a sufficient supply of unskilled labor. . . . If we are will-ing to concede increased power to the labor unions with which they may further limit the return of prosperity then of course, we are heading for economic disaster. *Why does not Congress therefore open the door?* The existing shortage of labor due to immigration restriction laws will inevitably result in demands for higher wag-es. . . .*Take the immigration problem out of politics, put it in the hands of scientifically trained men and let us have economic laws without the intervention of artifi-cial influences by favored classes who seek their own betterment at the expense of the nation's industries* [*sic*].

Judge Gary, head of U.S. Steel, proclaimed unequivocally at a stockholders' meeting that the Quota Law was "one of the worst things this country has ever done for itself economically," and he argued that "there is a great abundance of labor on the other side of the ocean" (quoted in the *Commercial and Financial Chronicle*, 1923b, p. 1856).

A common recommendation of these capitalists was for a flex-ible quota—one which could be expanded in times of increased labor demand. The Chamber of Commerce of the United States at its 1923 convention urged that if there must be a 3% quota, there should be an additional 2% safety valve for times of economic expansion (*The Nation's Business*, 1923). Others advocated even more flexibility, with powers vested in the secretary of labor to determine biennially the numbers to be admitted, depending on the economic situation (*The Nation*, 1923). The National Association of Manufacturers sent to leading industrialists in 1923 a questionnaire on "What shall we do about our immigration?" In general, the replies were that the literacy test should be abolished and "that on satisfactory evidence of a shortage of labor in any industry the Secretary of Labor should be authorized to take measures for filling it" (quoted in *Commercial and Financial Chronicle*, 1923a, p. 557).

Representatives of capital testifying at hearings before the House and Senate committees spoke without exception of the need for flexibility. The NAM was responsible for the introduction of a bill through Senator Le Baron Colt which would have empowered the secretary of labor to admit desirable immigrants above the quota at times of labor demand. Iron and steel representatives appeared before the House committee for more than a week in January 1923, to emphasize the seriousness of the labor shortage and to urge relaxation of the quota.

> The Secretary of Labor ought to be authorized, upon the presentation to him of satisfactory evidence of a continuing shortage of labor of a particular class or type, to admit otherwise admissible aliens in excess of the quota until in his judgment such condition is improved. (U.S. Congress, House Committee on Immigration and Naturalization, 1923a, p. 336)

Representatives from NAM urged that net immigration should at least be considered, taking into account in the quota the numbers emigrating from the United States. J. M. Larkin of the Bethlehem Steel Corporation similarly complained of the rigidity of the Emergency Quota Law (quoted in *Iron Age*, 1923a, p. 163).

While these representatives of capital rallied in Congress, other representatives were beginning to recognize that industrial expansion had proceeded well without the continual additions to the working population that immigration had supplied. Some warned their colleagues of the dangers of catering to each spurt of the economy:

> Within a year we have gone from a surplus of labor so great that it stirred the national conscience, to an apparent dearth of labor. . . . On the appearance of a shortage there is immediately a demand that the bars be let

down. . . . [But] have we taken effective measures to as-
similate them, so we shall not have again the agitation
over radicalism which disturbed us two and three years
ago? (*The Nation's Business*, 1922, p. 78)

A few capitalists pointed out that the Quota Law had not crippled industry and that through mechanization, new management
technologies, and the tapping of alternative sources of labor, industrial expansion could continue in spite of restricted European
immigration. In an article entitled "Immigration—Or Machinery"
(*American Machinist*, 1923), it was suggested that the "iron men"
of machinery could in the future replace massive immigration.

System: The Magazine of Business (1923) recognized "a shortage of unskilled labor," but noting the "racial inferiority" of Southern and Eastern European immigrants and the dangers of a
flooded labor market in times of economic breakdown, asked, "Are
we using to the best advantage the manpower which we have? Are
we doing anything to abolish the need for unskilled labor?" (p.
590). Their recommendation was to "meet labor shortages with
better management, better equipment, and more modern labor
saving machinery" (p. 590).

Similarly, *Iron Age* (1923c, p. 1573) by 1923 pointed to the
possibility for "developing other sources of supply":

Because the immigration movement is now so restricted,
a great part of the work of getting employees in the iron
and steel industry has been associated with the migration movement of negroes and Mexicans from the South
and Southwest to the North. . . .

While the iron and steel industry is showing deep interest in this new immigration movement beginning
with the fiscal year, July 1, it is evident that it has adjust-
ed itself to the fact that whatever changes may be made
in the immigration laws, they will not be liberalized
greatly. Because of this it is depending upon recruiting
labor from domestic sources from which it has not
drawn largely within the past and also is making earnest
efforts with a great deal of success to overcome the
shortage of labor by improving mechanical efficiency
and by giving added incentives to increase the output
production without increasing the manufacturing costs.
High production figures in a number of lines, among
them pig iron, sheet bars, billets and sheets, are taken to
indicate the fact that the industry has had a great deal of
success in this direction.

The front cover message of *Iron Age* on January 3, 1924, referring in part to the curtailment of the immigrant labor supply,
reiterated the benefits to be reaped from an emphasis on labor
management and mechanization. "American industry learned," it
announced from its cover,

> that it could do a great deal without having all condi-
> tions right. As the year opened, it did not promise pros-
> perity, yet it came nearer to doing that than any year
> since the war. More labor-saving machinery is offered as
> the solution and that will help, but are those not nearer
> right who look more to human engineering to bring the
> answer?

Perhaps the best statement of this rethinking of the immigration issue by a few representatives of capital appeared in *Industrial Management* (1923). Not only the scarcity of labor, they argued,
but the more general labor problem could be solved by increased
mechanization:

> American industry has to decide ultimately whether
> it wants to carry machinery, or imported common labor,
> over the recurring periods of depression. . . .
> The question arises as to whether the best interests of
> American industry will be served by again letting down
> the bars to the unskilled, uneducated hordes of South-
> eastern Europe. Is the solution of this problem not more
> likely to be found in the greater use, and broader appli-
> cation of labor-saving machinery? . . . The important
> thing to be stressed is the fact that the substitution of
> machinery for unskilled labor, of course only as far as
> practicable, is a permanent solution of the problem now
> confronting the American manufacturer. (pp. 248–249)

Thus, while the period 1921–1924 saw many capitalists complaining of labor shortages and those who petitioned Congress and
testified at hearings advocated a more flexible immigration policy,
others recognized that with increased mechanization, labor management, and the use of alternative labor sources, industry could
advance in spite of the quota controls. In fact, 1923—as *Iron Age*
proudly announced from its cover—was one of the best years for
industry since the war (see also *The Metal Industry*, 1923).

The role of the state is to respond to conflicts in such a way as
to maximize profits, while at the same time ensuring the survival
of the political economy as a whole. In filling this role, it may
sometimes interfere with the short-term interests of particular

capitalists, both because dominant economic interests are not always monolithic and because it must often place the very survival of capitalism above the short-term interests of individual capitalists.

The 1921 Emergency Quota Law is a case in point. Despite the outcries of individual capitalists, it was an ideal temporary solution. It put a numerical ceiling on European immigration in an attempt to minimize the social unrest associated with unemployment and cut to a minimum Southern and Eastern European immigration, which had come to be seen as a political and economic menace. However, it allowed virtually unlimited access to temporary migrants of the Western Hemisphere. While emphasis had been placed for a decade on Americanization and assimilation, exemptions were now made for those least likely to Americanize, i.e., temporary workers. Clearly, Western Hemisphere migrants provided a work force par excellence, that is, without the perceived political and economic strains associated with immigrants from the more permanent European source.

The 1924 Extension

As individual capitalists and their representatives were publishing statistics on labor shortages and recommending to their colleagues improved management techniques and mechanization, Congress was debating the extension of the 1921 law.

The race issue continued to be central. Laughlin, the eugenicist from Cold Spring Harbor, presented to Congress his report entitled "An Analysis of America's Melting Pot" (U.S. Congress, House Committee on Immigration and Naturalization, 1923b, p. 1311). In this report, Laughlin used Army IQ tests and data on the "feebleminded" from his Eugenics Record Office to argue that the Southern and Eastern European was hopelessly feebleminded and of inferior racial stock.

The House Committee on Immigration and Naturalization, in reporting their new quota bill to the House (*Congressional Record*, 1924, pp. 5643–5647), attached an introductory statement by Trevor, their non-Congressional eugenics expert. The gist of Trevor's remarks was that the "racial preponderance of the basic strain of our population" must be preserved.

Senator David Reed, sponsor of the new quota bill in the Senate, explained to the press the need for the restrictive measure: "The races of men who have been coming to us in recent years are wholly dissimilar to the native-born Americans" (quoted in *Literary Digest*, 1924, p. 12).

Congress also addressed the issue of labor shortages. Its response to capital's pleas for a more lenient immigration policy was generally threefold. In the first place, it was made clear that while periodic labor shortages may exist in some industries, *as a whole* the supply was adequate. This phase of immigration law making clearly reveals the greater utility of the structuralist, as compared to the instrumentalist model of law creation, and illustrates Marx and Engels' (1955, pp. 11–12; emphasis added) point that the "modern state is a committee for managing the affairs of *the whole bourgeoisie*." When confronted with the iron and steel industry's claim that it had a shortage of 40% in unskilled labor, Commissioner General of Immigration William Husband replied, "Yes, I am also aware of the fact that there is a *surplus* of probably 250,000 workers in the bituminous coal industry" (quoted in *Iron Age*, 1923b, p. 357; emphasis in original).

The House Committee on Immigration and Naturalization (U.S. Congress, House Committee on Immigration and Naturalization, 1923b, pp. 26ff.) concurred with Husband:

> Employers of labor in the U.S. have undertaken to show the Committee that there is a shortage of common labor. . . . The House Committee had before it many witnesses on the labor phase of the immigration problem (Hearings. 67th Congress, 4th session, pp. 227–599) and received letters, telegrams, statements, and arguments from many others. . . . The prosperity of the U.S. does not depend upon additional unskilled immigrants coming to this country. There are 1,500,000 unemployed here now. There are 250,000 coal miners who are unemployed regularly due to over-abundance of workers in that occupation.

Representative John C. Box of Texas, in responding to a lobbyist for large farming interests, expressed well this difference between a policy that responds to the needs of individual capitalists and one whose goal is more "permanent interests" (U.S. Congress, House Committee on Immigration and Naturalization, 1923b, p. 143):

> . . . we feel that those of you who are thinking so much about the profits of a particular business, without disrespect to you, sir, are not fair judges of the permanent interests of your country. . . . I want to know just how you feel, sir, about a proposition that would permit, we will say, the sugar beet growers, the cotton growers from my section, the cane growers from Louisiana, and all of the

farmers of the United States, some of whom want labor of the lowliest kind—lowly black labor literally flooded the south and caused a war, and nearly ruined the nation. If we authorize you to go over there and pick out your bunch, and we authorize Mr. Cotton Farmer to go and pick out his bunch, and we authorize Mr. Gary to go pick out his bunch—we cannot enact class legislation here—and we send each of you, anxious to get labor adapted to his particular needs—one bunch says Italians are the best, another bunch says the Greeks are the best, and another bunch says the Russians are the best, for they are the best garment workers. Another bunch says we want the Germans. Now, we turn over to the great industries of the United States the right to go over there and pick out men to promote their profits. . . . Now, what will be the effect on the United States, if men get limitless numbers of Mexicans—men who need Mexicans—and others get liberal numbers of Italians, and others great numbers of Greeks, and others Russians, and others Spaniards—what will be the effect of the importation of that mass of men who have been very wretched at home; what will be the effect, sir, on our country by a continuation of that policy?

Box summarized his point: "Hadn't we better begin to think of posterity instead of profits?" (p. 144).

As Congress moved to ensure posterity, it moved with the conviction that it would not cripple industry even in the short run. *Iron Age* (1924b) reported that "one prominent member of the Senate, familiar with the iron and steel and related industries, declared that employers constantly are giving more thought to increasing the efficiency of the manpower and mechanical operations and through various wage plans, such as the bonus and piecework, have built up greater production per man." This senator, reported *Iron Age*, advised the Senate that since the passage of the 3% quota law, the iron and steel industry had improved methods of production and had turned increasingly to mechanization and new sources of labor so that "*it had already been prepared to a considerable extent for a still greater cut in the immigration quota*" (*Iron Age*, 1924b, p. 1233; emphasis added).

In the fiscal year ending June 30, 1924, all the quotas were filled before January 1, and many entered after that under exemptions of various kinds. Total legal immigration jumped to 706,896, including 90,000 Mexicans. In his first annual message to Congress on December 6, 1923, President Calvin Coolidge urged,

> New arrivals should be limited to our capacity to absorb
> them into the ranks of good citizens. America must be
> kept American. For this purpose, it is necessary to con-
> tinue a policy of restricting immigration.... I am con-
> vinced that our present economic and social conditions
> warrant a limitation of those to be admitted. (quoted in
> Garis, 1927, pp. 169–170)

The House committee, pointing to the recent increases in immigration under the existing law and reiterating the necessity to
curb immigrants of "undesirable stock," recommended with the
Johnson Bill the reduction of the quota from 3% to 2%. Furthermore, it was proposed that the census of 1890, rather than that of
1910, should be used as a base. This plan would reduce the quota
for Italians from 42,000 to 4000, for Poles from 31,000 to 6000,
and for Greeks from 3000 to 100, since so few of these nationalities resided in the United States as early as 1890 (Garis, 1927, pp.
157, 256–257).

The Johnson-Reed Act passed both houses in 1924 and was
signed by President Coolidge on May 24 (43 U.S. Statutes at
Large). Quota immigration was thereby reduced from 357,803 to
164,667. The law provided for the first time for consular inspection and the granting of visas at the source of immigration. In
addition, the burden of proof of admissibility was placed on the
immigrant.

While the 1924 law substantially reduced quota immigration,
it did not neglect the need for flexibility. Western Hemisphere
immigrants continued to be classified as "non-quota immigrants"
to be used as an "escape valve." Furthermore, the practice of consular inspection was seen as a way to eliminate the lag between
economic breakdown and a drop in immigration. Consuls abroad
were told to utilize the old "likely to become a public charge"
clause during depressions in order to reject applications for visas
(Bernard, 1950, p. 87). In September 1930, the president advised
consular officials to interpret strictly the public charge clause in
order to reduce immigration during the Great Depression. An
immediate and dramatic reduction was secured (Bernard, 1950, p.
87).

With the 1924 quota law, total legal immigration was reduced
from almost 707,000 in 1924 to 294,314 the following year, remaining at essentially that level throughout the rest of the decade.
Only 528,431 entered in the decade 1931–1940, a total lower even
than that of a century earlier (immigration in 1831–1840 numbered 599,125) (see Appendix). Trevor (1924, p. 5) was not exag-

gerating the importance of the bill in which he played such a large role when he said, "The passage of the Immigration Act of 1924 marks the close of an epoch in the history of the United States."

Postscript

Migrating blacks and Mexicans filled temporary labor shortages. By 1926, 35% of Chicago Inland Steel's work force was Mexican (Gutman, 1976, p. 8). Tariff legislation (see Schattschneider, 1935) and a continued decrease in the importance of competition in determining price levels in monopoly capitalism allowed U.S. industry to maintain a stable wage-price ratio despite restricted immigration. At least as important, capital itself was increasingly mobile and, with the help of U.S. foreign policy, was no longer limited to domestic sources of investment, raw materials, or labor.

This is not to suggest that the conflicts that underlay immigration policy were in any real sense resolved in 1924. The developments that solved for capital its potential labor shortage problem in turn produce conflicts of another sort. As capital is exported, unemployment at home and a fiscal crisis rack the American economy. Mexican workers—both documented and undocumented—are simultaneously scapegoated, exploited by capital, and resented by American labor, much like earlier immigrants from across the Atlantic. Black unemployment rates of up to 40% in major urban centers of the north and sporadic black revolt echo the century-old conflict between capital's need for stability and its destabilizing effects.

It is not only that these developments are reminiscent of the earlier dilemmas associated with European immigration. They are driven by the same fundamental contradictions and are linked dialectically to earlier solutions.

Note

1. A short digression will underscore the dependence of the ideological component on compatible material conditions. It also reveals the intellectual and policy contortions that may result when an ideology is at odds with political and economic requirements. The issue arose in the House in 1921 (*Congressional Record*, 1921b, pp. 584ff.) as to whether political refugees should be exempt from the forthcoming quota. On one hand, it was argued, "One of the great principles upon which this government is founded is that we should give asylum to those who are being persecuted because of their religious or political beliefs" (p. 586). On the other hand, it was warned that "Bolshevism

is subversive to our form of government and I do not believe in letting that kind of people in" (p. 586). While some were tempted to act on the ideology of America-as-asylum, it was clearly not only at odds with the need for capital hegemony, but was incompatible with existing immigration law based on those needs. "I do not know about the conditions in Russia or Serbia or other countries in what is known as the Near East, but I do know that there is persecution in certain countries of Europe, and if political offenders had been barred from the U.S. in former days the forebears of a great number of the men present in this House would never have reached America. . . . I believe we should act in justice and in fairness to others as we would like to see justice and fairness done to us" (p. 586).

> Representative Graham: Are Communism and Bolshevism political doctrines? (p. 586)
>
> Representative Fess: And what would be our attitude when a member of the communistic party here of alien subjects may be deported under our present law? We would be admitting an alien under this law who would be deported after he got here. (p. 587)
>
> Representative Jones: We would be admitting people under this rule of the same character and type we are trying to deport, and some of whom would be subject to deportation as soon as they arrived on our shores. (p. 588)

8 ▪ Conclusion

Political discussions of immigration have resurfaced in the 1980s as the "illegal alien" has replaced the immigrant from Southern and Eastern Europe as the source of cheap labor. While undocumented workers are exploited, they are also scapegoated for high unemployment rates, much as the immigrant of earlier in the century was used for economic and political purposes. While this scapegoating does shift attention away from the systemic sources of economic crises and thus serves ideological ends, the focus on undocumented workers as the cause of unemployment precipitates political demands for restriction.

As these biological, material, and political reproduction problems reappear at the top of the political agenda, it is important to examine their roots and place them in historical context. It is important not only because it is timely, but because as immigration issues once again demand political attention, we hear echoes of Albert Johnson's (1927, pp. vii–viii) public interest rendition of past U.S. policies. Johnson, chair of the House Committee on Immigration and Naturalization at the time of the quota restrictions, summarized the immigration experience and the reasons for the restrictions of the 1920s. He began, following the fairy-tale tradition:

> Many years ago ... our people, proud of their institutions, ambitious, hopeful, altruistic, and sympathetic, entertained the thought that their country was destined by an all-wise providence to serve as the world's great harbor of refuge to which the ill-circumstanced of all nations might repair.

He concluded,

> They have come to realize that such a flood ... cannot fail ... to affect the institutions which have made and preserved American liberties. .... Americans everywhere are insisting that their land no longer shall offer free and unrestricted asylum to the rest of the world.

As we have seen, this popular rendition of U.S. immigration history distorts the actual historical record. For more than 25 years, from the early 1830s to the Civil War, American workers

183

demanded protection from competition with immigrant workers; Protestants urged restrictions on the Catholic influence; nativists feared the political influence of the immigrant vote. Together, these forces produced one of the most prolonged and vehement anti-immigrant protest in U.S. history. The nativist agitation was not limited to riots and other forms of personal and collective violence; it spawned nativist journals and newspapers, workingmen's protective organizations, and a broadbased, grass-roots political party. Hundreds of petitions urged Congress at least to regulate immigration, and bill after bill in Congress addressed the issue. Despite the outpouring of demands to restrict immigration over a 25-year period, no bill that aimed at regulating or in any way discouraging immigration even came to a vote. When the Civil War temporarily stemmed the immigrant tide, Congress acted quickly with "An Act to Encourage Immigration."

In addition to Johnson's popular consensus account of immigration policy, a special interest variant often explains past U.S. policies as the result of interest-group pressure. According to this view, immigration legislation is the result of lobbying efforts, threats, or other muscle-flexing by organized groups who perceive that legislation to be in their interest. Again, the historical data belie this explanation of immigration law making. Perhaps the clearest case of organized and united interest group pressure on Congress to regulate immigration involved organized labor's efforts to achieve protection from immigrant strike breakers in the 1880s. Although it is clear from the congressional debates that the Anti-Contract Labor Law was precipitated by labor's demands for protection, it is equally clear that no such protection was to be forthcoming. In addition to the use of vague language and the incorporation of loopholes, no machinery was established nor funds appropriated for the law's enforcement for three years after its passage. Only one employer was convicted under this law, a tiny fraction of immigrants were barred, and the number of immigrant laborers continued to multiply.

Compare this empty gesture to the 1921 and 1924 quota laws, which effectively reduced immigration from Southern and Eastern Europe. The phraseology of these laws was unequivocal; enforcement machinery was efficient and located at the source of immigration; ample funds for enforcement were immediately appropriated; and penalties for violations were strict. The effect was immediate and substantial. One searches in vain, however, for the interest group that was sufficiently organized, united, and disruptive to achieve such impressive results. By 1921, immigrant workers had put to rest their reputation as tractable, as they had demonstrated many times over their capacity for effective solidarity. As a result, the labor movement was no longer united, nor vociferous, on the issue of immigration restrictions. Representatives of capital who lobbied in Congress or appeared before congressional committees were without exception opposed to the restrictions. Trade journals, with a few noted exceptions, warned that the restrictions would constitute economic suicide. Ethnic organizations sent representatives to remind Congress of the economic and cultural contribution of immigrants and to plead for a liberal immigration policy. Of course, immigration restriction was not without advocates. However, in the face of the ambivalence of labor and the opposition of leading capitalists, it is farfetched to assume that such a small but prestigious organization as the Immigration Restriction League—spearheaded by Cold Spring Harbor eugenicists—could single-handedly pressure Congress into such radical action.

The instrumentalist model of law creation cannot account for this history either. It is true that prior to the passage of the literacy test in 1917, immigration law in no case interfered with capitalists' desire for an ever-increasing supply of cheap labor. Even though immigration law favored individual capitalists' interests until 1917, there is no evidence that capitalists—individually or collectively—had direct input on this issue at the legislative level. In fact, American capitalists refused to back any specific legislative proposals on immigration in this period.

More importantly, the 1917–1924 period of immigration law making is inconsistent with this economic elite interpretation. Capitalists who addressed the issue in trade journals and the popular press argued almost without exception that the restrictions would increase wages and jeopardize the competitive edge of American industry. Input at the congressional level by capital's representatives, including spokesmen for some of the largest corporations in the country, was consistently in opposition to the proposed restrictions. Despite this opposition, Congress closed the golden door.

The dialectical-structural model of the state and law more clearly fits the data presented here. The capitalist state must not only promote the capital accumulation process, but it must actively pursue the preservation of the political economy as a whole. Its primary concern lies not in the economic advantage of individual capitalists, but in the perpetuation of capitalists as a class. Given the inherent contradictions within the political economy, the state must resolve a variety of conflicts and dilemmas, often through legislation. It follows not only that particular kinds of conflicts will emerge and demand state action (as suggested by Chambliss, 1979), but also that the state will attempt to resolve them in rather predictable ways. The kinds of conflicts that are likely to emerge will derive from fundamental contradictions within capitalism, and the attempt will be made to resolve those conflicts in a way that interferes as little as possible with capitalist interests without, however, jeopardizing the preservation of the system as a whole.

The dilemmas that recur throughout this history of U.S. immigration are grounded both in the class contradiction and in the more specific contradictions between the need to reproduce a surplus labor supply versus the need to reproduce that labor supply materially and politically. The history of U.S. immigration legislation, then, makes sense as a series of resolutions to such fundamentally irresolvable conflicts. It makes sense that the nativists of the mid-1800s, lacking the leverage of a national labor movement, were responded to with conspicuous inaction. It makes sense that the response to organized labor's demands for protection in the 1880s evoked a symbolic gesture, a "sop to Cerberus." It makes sense, given the continued need of expanding capitalism for cheap immigrant labor at the turn of the century, that the problems of pauperism and anarchism were responded to with individualistic selective policies. It also makes sense, given the fallacious logic of blaming the victim inherent in this solution, that such selective policies resolved nothing. Finally, it makes sense that the first substantial change in U.S. immigration policy occurred in the postwar period. Chronic unemployment and an increasingly radicalized and aggressive labor movement (comprising, to no small extent, immigrant workers) threatened both the legitimation and the smooth functioning of the economy; the racism that had been used to explain class conflict was once and for all "scientifically" validated; and, most important, monopoly capitalism—dependent now more on the iron men of machinery, capital-intensive processes, and domestic labor sources—could do without European labor. It was within this economic and political context that Congress acted to restrict the source of labor that for a hundred years had fueled American capitalist expansion.

At a time when popular myths about past U.S. immigration policies are perpetuated by policy makers, it is important to re-examine the historical record. It is important not only because it provides the background from which to view the contemporary immigration debate, but also because the migration that brought 35 million people to the United States between 1820 and 1924 had a lasting impact on the structure of the U.S. economy, the class struggle, and related ideological developments. A study of the policies that shaped that migration potentially clarifies the critical links among economic structure, ideology, and law making. More generally, it allows us to witness the playing out of some of the most fundamental contradictions in capitalism and to specify the role of the state in that process.

Appendix

Immigration to the United States: 1820–1940[a]

Year	Number of persons	Year	Number of persons
1820	8,385		
1821	9,127	1851	379,466
1822	6,911	1852	371,603
1823	6,354	1853	368,645
1824	7,912	1854	427,833
1825	10,199	1855	200,877
1826	10,837	1856	200,436
1827	18,875	1857	251,306
1828	27,382	1858	123,126
1829	22,520	1859	121,282
1830	<u>23,322</u>	1860	<u>153,640</u>
1821–1830	143,439	1851–1860	2,598,214
1831	22,633	1861	91,918
1832	60,482	1862	91,985
1833	58,640	1863	176,282
1834	65,365	1864	193,418
1835	45,374	1865	248,120
1836	76,242	1866	318,568
1837	79,340	1867	315,722
1838	38,914	1868	138,840
1839	68,069	1869	352,768
1840	<u>84,066</u>	1870	<u>387,203</u>

1831–1840	599,125	1861–1870	2,314,824
1841	80,289	1871	321,350
1842	104,565	1872	404,806
1843	52,496	1873	459,803
1844	78,615	1874	313,339
1845	114,371	1875	227,498
1846	154,416	1876	169,986
1847	234,968	1877	141,857
1848	226,527	1878	138,469
1849	297,024	1879	177,826
1850	<u>369,980</u>	1880	<u>457,257</u>
1841–1850	1,713,251	1871–1880	2,812,191
1881	669,431	1911	878,587
1882	788,992	1912	838,172
1883	603,322	1913	1,197,892
1884	518,592	1914	1,218,480
1885	395,346	1915	326,700
1886	334,203	1916	298,826
1887	490,109	1917	295,403
1888	546,889	1918	110,618
1889	444,427	1919	141,132
1890	<u>455,302</u>	1920	<u>430,001</u>
1881–1890	5,246,613	1911–1920	5,735,811
1891	560,319	1921	805,228
1892	579,663	1922	309,556
1893	439,730	1923	522,919

1894	285,631	1924	706,896
1895	258,536	1925	294,314
1896	343,267	1926	304,488
1897	230,832	1927	335,175
1898	229,299	1928	307,255
1899	311,715	1929	279,678
1900	<u>448,572</u>	1930	<u>241,700</u>
1891–1900	3,687,564	1921–1930	4,107,209
1901	487,918	1931	97,139
1902	648,743	1932	35,576
1903	857,046	1933	23,068
1904	812,870	1934	29,470
1905	1,026,499	1935	34,956
1906	1,100,735	1936	36,329
1907	1,285,349	1937	50,244
1908	782,870	1938	67,895
1909	751,786	1939	82,998
1910	<u>1,041,570</u>	1940	<u>70,756</u>
1901–1910	8,795,386	1931–1940	528,431

[a] United States Department of Justice, Immigration and Naturalization Service.

Bibliography

Abbott, E. (1905). Wages of unskilled labor in the U.S., 1850–1900. *Journal of Political Economics* **13** (June), 321–367.

Abbott, E. (1924). *Immigration: Select Documents and Records.* University of Chicago Press, Chicago, Illinois.

Abbott, E. (1926). *Historical Aspects of the Immigration Problem: Select Documents.* University of Chicago Press, Chicago, Illinois.

Adamic, L. (1963). *Dynamite: The Story of Class Violence in America.* Peter Smith, Gloucester, Massachusetts.

The Age of Steel. (1886a). January 31, pp. 7–8

The Age of Steel. (1886b). May 8, p. 5

The Age of Steel. (1890). August 30, p. 9.

The Age of Steel. (1895). April 6, p. 16.

Alexander, H. (1976). *Finance Politics.* Congressional Quarterly Press, Washington, D.C.

Almy and Brown Papers. (1809). *Records of Almy and Brown Company of Providence, Rhode Island.* Rhode Island Historical Society, Providence.

Althusser, L. (1972). Ideology and ideological state apparatuses. *In Lenin and Philosophy.* Monthly Review Press, New York.

The American. (1882). *The Political Economy of Immigration* **4**, 262–263.

American Industries. (1912). *Immigration: Its Value to the Country* **12**, 30–31.

American Industries. (1919). October, p. 10.

American Iron and Steel Association Bulletin. (1877). August 8, p. 213.

American Iron and Steel Association Bulletin. (1881). August 23.

American Iron and Steel Association Bulletin. (1883). September 12, p. 252.

American Machinist. (1923). March 15, pp. 393–395.

The American Manufacturer and Iron World. (1885a). March 20, p. 10.

The American Manufacturer and Iron World. (1885b). November 27, p. 12.

The American Manufacturer and Iron World. (1886a). January 29, p. 10.

The American Manufacturer and Iron World. (1886b). March 5, p. 10.

The American Manufacturer and Iron World. (1886c). July 16, p. 1.

The American Wool Reporter. (1894). May 31, p. 681.

Anglo-American Times. (1887a). October 28.

Anglo-American Times. (1887b). November 4.

Anglo-American Times. (1889a). August 9, p. 30.

Anglo-American Times. (1889b). November 15.

Anglo-American Times. (1890). May 23.

Axinn, J. and Levin, H. (1975). *Social Welfare: A History of the American Response to Need.* Harper and Row, New York.

Bachrach, P. and Baratz, M. S. (1963). Decisions and nondecisions: An analytical framework. *American Political Science Review* **57** (Sept.), 632–642.

Banker's Magazine. (1875). *The Immigration Movement* **30**, 177.

Baran, P. A. and Sweezy, P. M. (1966). *Monopoly Capital: An Essay on the American Economic and Social Order.* Modem Reader Paperbacks, New York.

Barr, W. H. (1920). Plain facts about immigration. *Blast Furnace and Steel Plant* **8**, 422.

Barth, E. A. and Johnson, S. D. (1959). Community power and a typology of social issues. *Social Forces* **38** (Oct.), 29–32.

Baxandall, R., Gordon, L. and Reverby, S. (1976). *America's Working Women.* Vintage Books, New York.

Bennett, M. T. (1963). *American Immigration Policies.* Public Affairs Press, Washington, D.C.

Bernard, W. S. (1950). *American Immigration Policy—A Reappraisal.* Harper and Brothers, New York.

Berthoff, R. T. (1953). *British Immigrants in Industrial America.* Harvard University Press, Cambridge, Massachusetts.

Billington, R. A. (1938). *The Protestant Crusade 1800–1860: A Study of the Origins of American Nativism.* Macmillan, New York.

Bimba, A. (1927). *The History of the American Working Class.* International Publishers, New York.

Bogart, E. L. and Thompson, C. M. (1920). *The Independent State 1870–1893: The Centennial History of Illinois*, Vol. IV. Illinois Centennial Commission, Springfield.

Boston Pilot. (1852a). July 31.

Boston Pilot. (1852b). September 11.

Bowles, S. and Gintis, H. (1973). I.Q. in the U.S. class structure. *Social Policy* **3** (Jan.–Feb.), 69–96.

Boyer, R. O. and Morais, H. M. (1980). *Labor's Untold Story.* United Electrical, Radio, and Machine Workers of America, New York.

Bradstreet's Magazine. (1886). May 15, p. 369.

Braverman, H. (1974). *Labor and Monopoly Capital: The Degradation of Work in the Twentieth Century.* Monthly Review Press, New York.

Brecher, J. (1972). *Strike!* Straight Arrow Books, San Francisco, California.

Bridge, J. H. (1902). *The Inside Story of the Carnegie Steel Company: A Romance of Millions.* Arno Press, New York.

Bridges, A. B. (1974). Nicos Poulantzas and the Marxist theory of the state. *Politics and Society* **4**(2) (Winter), 161–190.

Brissenden, P. F. (1920). *The I.W.W.: A Study of American Syndicalism.* Columbia University Press, New York.

Brody, D. (1960). *Steelworkers in America in the Non-Union Era.* Harper and Row, New York.

Bromwell, W. J. (1856). *History of Immigration to the U.S.* Redfield, New York.

Bryce, J. (1889). *The American Commonwealth.* Macmillan, New York.

Buhle, P. (1973). Debsian Socialism and the "new immigrant." *In Insights and Parallels: Problems and Issues of American Social History* (W. O'Neill, ed.). Burgess Publishing Co., Minneapolis, Minnesota.

Burch, P. H., Jr. (1973). The National Association of Manufacturers as an interest group. *Politics and Society* **4**(1) (Fall), 97–130.

Burgess, J. (1895). The ideal of the American Commonwealth. *Political Science Quarterly* **10** (Sept.), 407.

Burnham, W. D. (1970). *Critical Elections and the Mainspring of American Politics.* Norton, New York.

Burrows, J. C. (1901). The need of national legislation against anarchism. *North American Review* **173** (Dec.), 727–745.

Busey, S. S. (1856). *Immigration: Its Evils and Consequences.* DeWitt and Davenport, New York.

Bustamante, J. A. (1977). The "wetback" as deviant: An application of labelling theory. *American Journal of Sociology* **77**(4), 706–718.

Calavita, K. (1983). California's "employer sanctions" legislation: Now you see it, now you don't. *Politics and Society* 12(2), 205–230.

Carnegie, A. (1886). *Triumphant Democracy, or Fifty Years' March of the Republic.* Charles Scribner's Sons, New York.

Cashmore, E. (1978). The social organization of Canadian immigration law. *Canadian Journal of Sociology* 3(4), 409–429.

Castels, M. (1975). Immigrant workers and class struggle in advanced capitalism: The western European experience. *Politics and Society* 5(1), 33–66.

Castles, S. and Kosack, G. (1973). *Immigrant Workers and Class Structure in Western Europe.* Oxford University Press, London and New York.

Cavanaugh, F. C. (1928). Immigration restriction at work today. Unpublished Ph.D. Dissertation, Catholic University of America, Washington, D.C.

Chamber of Commerce of the State of New York. (1888). *Annual Report of the Corporations 1887–1888*, p. 46.

Chambliss, W. (1964). A sociological analysis of the law of vagrancy. *Social Problems* 12 (Summer), 67–77.

Chambliss, W. (1978). *On the Take.* Indiana University Press, Bloomington.

Chambliss, W. (1979). Contradictions and conflicts in law creation. *In Annual Review of the Sociology of Law* (S. Spitzer, ed.). Jai-In Press, Greenwich, Connecticut.

Chambliss, W. and Seidman, R. (1971). *Law, Order and Power.* Addison-Wesley Publishing Co., Reading, Massachusetts.

Chickering, J. (1851). Report of the committee to obtain the state census of Boston and also a comparative view of the population of Boston in 1850. *Boston City Documents* No. 60.

Christian Science Monitor. (1978). November 2, p. 7.

Christian Science Monitor. (1979). April 25, p. 7.

Claghorn, K. H. (1904). Immigration in its relation to pauperism. *Annals of the American Academy of Political and Social Science* July, pp. 187–200.

Claghorn, K. H. (1971). *The Immigrant's Day in Court.* Patterson Smith, Montclair, New Jersey.

Clark, V. (1929). *History of Manufacturing in the U.S.*, Vol. I, 1607–1860. McGraw-Hill, New York.

Clews, H. (1886). Shall labor or capital rule? *North American Review* 142 (June), 601.

Commercial and Financial Chronicle. (1865). August 12, pp. 199–200.

Commercial and Financial Chronicle. (1881). December 31, pp. 732–733.

Commercial and Financial Chronicle. (1882). August 18, p. 201.

Commercial and Financial Chronicle. (1887). March 28, p. 669.

Commercial and Financial Chronicle. (1888). August 25, pp. 213–214.

Commercial and Financial Chronicle. (1890). September 13, pp. 317–318.

Commercial and Financial Chronicle. (1892). July 30, pp. 162–163.

Commercial and Financial Chronicle. (1897). December 4, p. 1046.

Commercial and Financial Chronicle. (1920). December 11, p. 2267.

Commercial and Financial Chronicle. (1923a). February 10, pp. 557–558.

Commercial and Financial Chronicle. (1923b). April 28, p. 1856.

Commission of Inquiry. (1920). *The Interchurch World Movement Report on the Steel Strike of 1919.* Harcourt, Brace, and Howe, New York.

Commons, J. R. (1907). *Races and Immigrants in America.* Macmillan, New York.

Commons, J. R. (1918). *History of Labour in the United States.* Macmillan, New York.

Commonwealth of Massachusetts. (1835). *A Bill More Effectively to Suppress Riots,* Legislative Documents No. 37.

Congressional Globe. (1836). 24th Congress, 1st session.

Congressional Globe. (1844a). 28th Congress, 1st session.

Congressional Globe. (1844b). 28th Congress, 2nd session.

Congressional Globe. (1846). 29th Congress, 1st session.

Congressional Globe. (1852). 32nd Congress, 1st session, Appendix.

Congressional Globe. (1854). 33rd Congress, 2nd session.

Congressional Globe. (1855). 33rd Congress, 2nd session.

Congressional Globe. (1856). 34th Congress, 1st session.

Congressional Record. (1882). 47th Congress, 1st session.

Congressional Record. (1884). 48th Congress, 1st session.

Congressional Record. (1885). 48th Congress, 2nd session.

Congressional Record. (1889). 50th Congress, 2nd session.

Congressional Record. (1896). 54th Congress, 1st session.

Congressional Record. (1902). 57th Congress, 1st session.

Congressional Record. (1903). 57th Congress, 2nd session.

Congressional Record. (1905). 59th Congress, 1st session.

Congressional Record. (1906). 59th Congress, 1st session.

Congressional Record. (1913a). 62nd Congress, 3rd session.

Congressional Record. (1913b). 63rd Congress, 2nd session.

Congressional Record. (1915). 63rd Congress, 3rd session.

Congressional Record. (1916a). 64th Congress, 1st session.

Congressional Record. (1916b). 64th Congress, 2nd session.

Congressional Record. (1917). 64th Congress, 2nd session.

Congressional Record. (1919). 65th Congress, 3rd session.

Congressional Record. (1920). 66th Congress, 3rd session.

Congressional Record. (1921a). 66th Congress, 3rd session.

Congressional Record. (1921b). 67th Congress, 1st session.

Congressional Record. (1922). 67th Congress, 2nd session.

Congressional Record. (1923). 67th Congress, 4th session.

Congressional Record. (1924). 68th Congress, 1st session.

Copeland, M. T. (1912). *The Cotton Manufacturing Industry of the United States.* Harvard University Press, Cambridge, Massachusetts.

Creamer, D. (1941). Recruiting contract laborers for the Amoskeag Mills. *Journal of Economic History* I.

Dahl, R. A. (1961). *Who Governs?* Yale University Press, New Haven, Connecticut.

David, H. (1958). *The History of the Haymarket Affair.* Russell & Russell, New York.

Day, E. E. and Woodlief, T. (1928). *The Growth of Manufacturers, 1899–1923.* U.S. Bureau of the Census, Census Monograph VIII, Government Printing Office, Washington, D.C.

Desmond, H. J. (1912). *The A.P.A. Movement* (The American Immigration Collection). New Century Press, Washington, D.C.

Dickson, D. T. (1968). Bureaucracy and morality: An organizational perspective on a moral crusade. *Social Problems* **16** (Fall), 143–156.

Dinnerstein, L., Nichols, R. L. and Reimers, D. M. (1979). *Natives and Strangers: Ethnic Groups and the Building of America.* Oxford University Press, London and New York.

Domhoff, G. W. (1967). *Who Rules America?* Prentice-Hall, Englewood Cliffs, New Jersey.

Domhoff, G. W. (1970). *The Higher Circles.* Vintage Books, New York.

Domhoff, G. W. (1978). *The Powers That Be*. Random House, New York.

DuPont, T. C. (1920). Does America want immigration or emigration? *Current Opinion* **69**, 179.

Earl, H. H. (1877). *A Centennial History of Fall River*. Atlantic Publishing Company, New York.

Edelman, M. (1964). *The Symbolic Uses of Politics*. University of Illinois Press, Chicago.

Edelman, M. (1977). *Political Languages: Words That Succeed and Policies That Fail*. Academic Press, New York.

Edwards, R., Reich, M. and Gordon, D. (1973). *Labor Market Segmentation*. D. C. Heath, Lexington, Kentucky.

Ehrlich, R. L., ed. (1977). *Immigrants in Industrial America*. University Press of Virginia, Charlottesville.

Engels, F. (1942). *The Origins of the Family, Private Properly and the State*. International Publishing Co., New York.

Engels, F. (1950). *The Condition of the Working Class in England in 1844* (translated by F. K. Wischnewetzky). Allen and Unwin, London.

Engineering and Mining Journal. (1880). May 15, p. 335.

Erickson, C. (1952). The recruitment of European immigrant labor for American industry from 1860–1885. Unpublished Ph.D. Dissertation, Cornell University, Ithaca, New York.

Erickson, C. (1957). *American Industry and the European Immigrant, 1860–1885*. Harvard University Press, Cambridge, Massachusetts.

Ernst, R. (1948). Economic nativism in New York City during the 1840s. *New York History* **29**, 170–186.

Fairchild, H. P. (1917). The literacy test and its making. *Quarterly Journal of Economics* **31**, 447–460.

Fall River Mechanic. (1844). May 11.

Fall River Weekly News. (1880). March 25.

Faulkner, H. U. (1962). *The Decline of Laissez-Faire (The Economic History of the United States*, Vol. VII). Holt, Rinehart & Winston, New York.

Fine, S. (1955). Anarchism and the assassination of McKinley. *American Historical Review* **60(4)** (July), 777–799.

Fitch, J. A. (1911). *The Steel Workers*. Charities Publication Committee, New York.

Fite, D. E. (1910). *Social and Industrial Conditions in the North During the Civil War*. Macmillan, New York.

Foner, P. S. (1955). *History of the Labor Movement in the United States*, Vol. II. International Publishers, New York.

Foner, P. S. (1962). *History of the Labor Movement in the United States*, Vol. I. International Publishers, New York.

Foner, P. S. (1964). *History of the Labor Movement in the United States*, Vol. III. International Publishers, New York.

Friedland, R., Piven, F. F. and Alford, R. (1977). Political conflict, urban structure, and the fiscal crisis. *In Comparing Public Policy: New Approaches and Methods* (D. Ashford, ed.). Sage Yearbook in Politics and Public Policy, Sage Publications, Beverly Hills, California.

Friedman, L. (1973). *A History of American Law*. Simon and Schuster, New York.

Friedman, L. (1975). *The Legal System: A Social Science Perspective*. Russell Sage Foundation, New York.

Friedman, L. (1977). *Law and Society: An Introduction*. Prentice-Hall, Englewood Cliffs, New Jersey.

Gambino, R. (1975). *Blood of My Blood: The Dilemma of the Italian-American*. Doubleday, Garden City, New York.

Garis, R. L. (1927). *Immigration Restriction*. Macmillan, New York.

Genovese, E. D. (1967). *The Political Economics of Slavery: Studies in the Economy and Society of the Slave South*. Random House, New York.

Genovese, E. D. (1969). *The World the Slaveholders Made*. Pantheon, New York.

Genovese, E. D. (1974). *Roll, Jordan, Roll: The World the Slaves Made*. Pantheon, New York.

Gibb, G. (1950). *The Saco-Lowell Shops, 1813–1949*. Harvard University Press, Cambridge, Massachusetts.

Gitelman, H. (1967). The Waltham system and the coming of the Irish. *Labor History* **8**(3) (Fall), 227–253.

Goddard, H. H. (1913). The Binet tests in relation to immigration. *Journal of Psycho-Asthenics* **18**, 105–107.

Goddard, H. H. (1920). *Human Efficiency and Levels of Intelligence*. Princeton University Press, Princeton, New Jersey.

Godkin, E. L. (1887). Some political and social aspects of the tariff. *New Princeton Review* **3** (March), 173.

Gold, D., Lo, C. and Olin Wright, E. (1975). Recent developments in Marxist theories of the capitalist state. *Monthly Review* **27** (Oct. and Nov.), 36–51.

Gompers, S. (1925). *Seventy Years of My Life and Labor*. E. P. Dutton, New York.

Gordon, D. (1971). *Problems in Political Economy: An Urban Perspective*. D. C. Heath, Lexington, Kentucky.

Gossett, T. F. (1973). *Race: The History of an Idea in America.* Schocken, New York.

Graham, J. M. (1972). Amphetamine politics on Capitol Hill. *Society* **9**(3) (Jan.), 14–23.

Gramsci, A. (1950). *Il Risorgimento.* Einaudi, Torino.

Gramsci, A. (1971). *Selections from the Prison Notebooks* (Q. Hoare and G. Smith, eds. and translators). Laurence & Wishart, London.

Grant, M. (1916). *The Passing of the Great Race.* Charles Scribner's Sons, New York.

Green, M. (1956). *The NCF and the American Labor Movement, 1900–1925.* Catholic University of America Press, Washington, D.C.

Grossman, J. P. (1945). *William Sylvis, Pioneer of American Labor: A Study of the Labor Movement During the Era of the Civil War.* Columbia University Press, New York.

Gusfield, J. R. (1963). *Symbolic Crusade.* University of Illinois Press, Urbana.

Gutman, H. G. (1976). *Work, Culture, and Society in Industrializing America: Essays in American Working-Class and Social History.* Alfred A. Knopf, New York.

Habakkuk, H. J. (1962). *American and British Technology in the 19th Century: The Search for Labor-Saving Inventions.* Harvard University Press, Cambridge, Massachusetts.

Habermas, J. (1975). *Legitimation Crisis.* Beacon Press, Boston, Massachusetts.

Hacker, A. (1973). Getting used to mugging. *New York Review of Books* April 19.

Hahn, N. (1977). Immigration and the mental deficiency movement: Financing the criminal justice system, 1900–1920. *Paper presented at the annual meeting of the Society for the Study of Social Problems, Chicago.*

Hall, J. (1935). *Theft, Law, and Society.* Bobbs-Merrill, New York.

Hamilton, A. (1791). Report on manufacturing. *American State Papers, Finance* 1 (Dec. 5), 123.

Handlin, O. (1941). *Boston's Immigrants, 1790–1865.* Harvard University Press, Cambridge, Massachusetts.

Handlin, O. (1951). *The Uprooted.* Little, Brown, Boston, Massachusetts.

Hansen, M. (1930). The revolution of 1848 and German emigration. *Journal of Economic and Business History* **2** (Aug.), 630–658.

Hansen, M. (1940a). *The Immigrant in American History.* Harvard University Press, Cambridge, Massachusetts.

Hansen, M. (1940b). *The Atlantic Migration, 1607–1860.* Harvard University Press, Cambridge, Massachusetts.

Hayes, J. L. (1879). *American Textile Machinery.* Cambridge University Press, London and New York.

Haynes, G. E. (1897). Know-nothing legislation. *New England Magazine* **16**, 21–22.

Heald, M. (1953). Business attitudes toward European immigration, 1880–1900. *Journal of Economic History* **13** (Summer), 291–304.

Henderson, C. R. (1893). *An Introduction to the Study of the Dependent, Defective, and Delinquent Classes.* D. C. Heath, Boston, Massachusetts.

Higham, J. (1955). *Strangers in the Land: Patterns of American Nativism, 1860–1925.* Rutgers University Press, New Brunswick, New Jersey.

Hill, H. A. (1875). Immigration and pauperism. *American Social Science Association, Proceedings of Conference of Public Charities*, Detroit.

Hill, H. C. (1919). The Americanization movement. *American Journal of Sociology* **24**(6) (May), 609–642.

Hillquit, M. (1965). *History of Socialism in the United States.* Russell & Russell, New York.

Hofstadter, R. (1963). *The Age of Reform.* Alfred A. Knopf, New York.

Hourwich, I. A. (1912). *Immigration and Labor.* G. P. Putnam and Sons, New York.

Hurd, H. (1884). *History of Norfolk County, Massachusetts.* Philadelphia.

Hurd, H. (1888). *History of Essex County, Massachusetts.* Philadelphia.

Hurd, H. (1890). *History of Middlesex County, Massachusetts.* Philadelphia.

Hutchinson, E. P. (1953). Immigration policy since World War I. *In Immigration: An American Dilemma* (B. M. Ziegler, ed.). D. C. Heath, Boston, Massachusetts.

Imhoff, C. (1981). Stealing away black recruits was risky job. *In These Times* Feb. 4–10, p. 19.

Immigrants' Protective League. (1916). *Annual Report*, 10.

Industrial Management. (1923). April, pp. 247–249.

The Industrial Worker. (1917). February 10.

Iron Age. (1868). October 22, p. 4.

Iron Age. (1868). October 22, p. 4.

Iron Age. (1881a). April 14, p. 26.

Iron Age. (1881b). April 21, p. 24.

Iron Age. (1887). February 3, p. 23.

Iron Age. (1892). April 14, p. 719.

Iron Age. (1893). May 25, pp. 1179–1180.

Iron Age. (1913). December 12, p. 987.

Iron Age. (1915). June 17, pp. 1357–1358.

Iron Age. (1916). November 16, p. 1108.

Iron Age. (1917). April 12, p. 910.

Iron Age. (1918). October 3, pp. 831–832.

Iron Age. (1920). April 15, p. 1133.

Iron Age. (1923a). January 11, pp. 163–164.

Iron Age. (1923b). February 1, p. 357.

Iron Age. (1923c). May 30, p. 1573.

Iron Age. (1924a). January 3, p. 1.

Iron Age. (1924b). April 24, p. 1233.

Iron Molders Journal. (1874). November 10, pp. 104–105.

Iron Trade Review. (1896). April 16, p. 6.

Jefferson, T. (1955). *Notes on the State of Virginia* (W. Peden, ed., with introduction and notes). University of North Carolina Press, Chapel Hill.

Jenks, J. W. (1913). *The Immigration Problem.* Funk & Wagnalls, New York.

Jessop, B. (1977). Recent theories of the capitalist state. *Cambridge Journal of Economics* **1**, 353–373.

Johnson, A. (1927). Foreword. *In Immigration Restriction* (by R. L. Garis). Macmillan, New York.

John Swinton's Paper. (1884a). January 6, p. 1.

John Swinton's Paper. (1884b). August 3, p. 1.

Jones, M. A. (1960). *American Immigration.* University of Chicago Press, Chicago, Illinois.

Kamin, L. (1974). *The Science and Politics of I .Q.* Lawrence Erlbaum Associates, Inc., Potomac, Maryland.

Kansas, S. (1927). *U.S. Immigration, Exclusion, and Deportation.* Washington Publishing Co., Washington, D.C.

Kaplan, S. (1956). Social engineers as saviors: Effects of World War I on some American liberals. *Journal of the History of Ideas* 17 (June), 347–355.

Kapp, F. (1969). *Immigration and the Commissioners of Emigration*. Amo Press, New York.

Karier, C. J. (1972). Testing for order and control in the corporate liberal state. *Educational Theory* **22** (Spring), 154–180.

Karson, M. (1958). *American Labor Unions and Politics*. Southern Illinois University Press, Carbondale.

Kellor, F. (1920). *Immigration and the Future*. George H. Doran Co., New York.

Kellor, F. (1921). Immigration and the future. *Annals of the American Academy* (January), 201–211.

King, W. I. (1915). *The Wealth and Income of the People of the United States*. Macmillan, New York.

Kohler, M. J. (1936). *Immigration and Aliens in the United States*. Bloch Publishing Company, New York.

Kolko, G. (1962). *Wealth and Power in America*. Praeger, New York.

Kolko, G. (1963). *The Triumph of Conservatism*. The Free Press of Glencoe, New York.

Kolko, G. (1965). *Railroads and Regulations*. Princeton University Press, Princeton, New Jersey.

Korman, G. (1965). Americanization at the factory gate. *Industrial and Labor Relations Review* **18**, 402.

Korman, G. (1967). *Industrialization, Immigrants, and Organizers: The View From Milwaukee, 1866–1921*. The State Historical Society of Madison, Wisconsin.

Lathrop, W. G. (1926). *The Brass Industry in the United States*. Amo Press, New York.

Lauck, W. J. (1921). The industrial significance of immigration. *Annals of the American Academy* (Jan.), 188–189.

Lazarus, E. (1886). Inscription on the Statue of Liberty.

Leinenweber, C. (1968). The American Socialist Party and the "new" immigrants. *Science and Society* **32**(1) (Winter), 1–25.

Leiserson, W. M. (1971). *Adjusting Immigrant and Industry*. Paterson Smith, Montclair, New Jersey.

Lipset, S. M. and Raab, E. (1970). *The Politics of Unreason: Right-Wing Extremism in America, 1790–1970*. University of Chicago Press, Chicago, Illinois.

Literary Digest. (1919a). May 24, p. 132.

Literary Digest. (1919b). July 5, p. 28.

Literary Digest. (1920). April 24, p. 12.

Literary Digest. (1921). August 13, p. 23.

Literary Digest. (1923). May 5, p. 11.

Literary Digest. (1924). May 10, p. 12

Lodge, H. C. (1891). The restriction of immigration. *North American Review* **152**, 27–32.

Macaulay, J. (1872). Across *the Ferry.* London.

MacCarthy, J. H. (1917). *Where Garments and Americans are Made.* Writers Publishing Co., New York.

McCormick, C. (1919). *Proceedings of the National Safety Congress, Cleveland* pp. 41–42.

Macdonald, J. S. (1963). Agricultural organization, immigration, and labor militancy in rural Italy. *Economic History Review* **16**(1), 61–75.

McNeill, G. E., ed. (1888). *The Labor Movement. The Problem of Today. Comprising a History of Capital and Labor, and Its Present Status.* M. W. Hozen, New York.

Maltese, F. (1973). Notes for a study of the automobile industry. *In Labor Market Segmentation* (R. Edwards, M. Reich, and D. Gordon, eds.), pp. 85–93. Heath and Co., London.

Manhattan Magazine. (1883). *A National Need and Its Business Supply.* **2**, 60–66.

Marshall, F. R. (1978). Economic factors influencing the international migration of workers. *In Views Across the Border* (S. Ross, ed.). University of New Mexico Press, Albuquerque.

Marshall, L. C. (1918). The war labor program and its administration. *Journal of Political Economy* **26** (May), 429.

Marx, K. (1906). *Capital.* Modern Library, New York.

Marx, K. (1956). Marx-Engels Gesamtausgabe. *In Karl Marx: Selected Writings in Sociology and Social Philosophy* (T. B. Bottomore, ed.). McGraw-Hill, New York.

Marx, K. and Engels, F. (1955). *The Communist Manifesto* (translated by S. Moore; S. H. Beer, ed.). Appleton-Century-Crofts, New York.

Marx, K. and Engels, F. (1962). *On Britain.* Foreign Language Publishing House, Moscow.

Marx, K. and Engels, F. (1965). *The German Ideology.* Laurence and Wishart, London.

Marx, K. and Engels, F. (1968). *Theories of Surplus Value,* Vol. II. Progress Publishers, Moscow.

Massachusetts Bureau of Immigration. (1919). *First Annual Report,* p. 21.

Massachusetts Labor Bulletin. (1905). No. 37 (Sept.), p. 186.

Mayer, M. and Fay, M. (1977). The formation of the American nation-state. *Kapitalistate* **6** (Fall), 39–90.

Meltzer, M. (1976). *Taking Root: Jewish Immigrants in America.* Dell, New York.

The Metal Industry. (1923). February, p. 70.

Miliband, R. (1969). *The State in Capitalist Society.* Basic Books, New York.

Miliband, R. (1977). *Marxism and Politics.* Oxford University Press, London and New York.

Miliband, R. (1983). State power and class interests. *New Left Review* **138** (March-April), 57–68.

Mills, C. W. (1956). *The Power Elite.* Oxford University Press, London and New York.

Miner's Journal. (1829). July 4.

Mitchell, J. (1903). *Organized Labor: Its Problems, Purposes, and Ideals.* American Book and Bible House, Philadelphia, Pennsylvania.

Mollenkopf, J. (1975). Theories of the state and power structure research. *Insurgent Sociologist* **5**(111), 245–264.

Montgomery, D. (1972). The shuttle and the cross: Weavers and artisans in the Kensington riots of 1844. *Journal of Social History* **5**(4) (Summer), 411–446.

Montgomery, D. (1974). The new unionism and the transformation of workers' consciousness in America, 1909–22. *Journal of Social History* **7**(4) (Summer), 509–529.

Montgomery, D. (1977). Immigrant workers and managerial reform. *In Immigrants in Industrial America, 1850–1920* (R. Ehrlich, ed.). University Press of Virginia, Charlottesville.

Morse, S. (1841). *Foreign Conspiracy Against the Liberties of the United States.* H. A. Chapin, New York.

Mulkern, J. R. (1963). The Know-Nothing Party in Massachusetts. Ph.D. Dissertation, Boston University, Boston, Massachusetts.

The Nation. (1919). October 25, p. 540.

The Nation. (1923). May 23, p. 598.

National Association of Manufacturers. (1907). *Proceedings of the 12th Annual Convention of the National Association of Manufacturers* pp. 24–25, 198.

National Association of Wool Manufacturers. (1870). *Bulletin* II.

National Association of Wool Manufacturers. (1878). *Bulletin* VIII.

National Association of Wool Manufacturers. (1881). *Bulletin* XI, p. 127.

National Association of Wool Manufacturers. (1912). *Bulletin* 42, p. 139–142.

National Civic Federation Review. (1905a). I (January), p. 1.

National Civic Federation Review. (1905b). II (June), pp. 1ff.

National Civic Federation Review. (1905c). III (September-October), p. 17.

National Labor Tribune. (1875). August 17, p. 2.

The Nation's Business. (1922). December 29, p. 78.

The Nation's Business. (1923). June 5, p. 42.

Native American. (1884a). July 16.

Native American. (1884b). November 29.

Native Eagle. (1845). December 1.

Native Eagle. (1846a). February 16.

Native Eagle. (1846b). March 2.

Nelson, M. N. (1922). *Open Price Associations*. University of Illinois Press, Urbana.

Nevins, A., ed. (1937). *Selected Writings of Abram S. Hewitt*. Columbia University Press, New York.

New Jersey Bureau of Industry and Labor. (1884). *7th Annual Report*, p. 295.

New Jersey Bureau of Statistics of Labor and Industries. (1887). *Tenth Annual Report*.

New York Bureau of Labor Statistics. (1885). *Third Annual Report*.

New York Herald. (1878). May 20.

New York Journal of Commerce. (1892). December 13, p. 2.

New York Times. (1915). February 1, p. 8.

North, D. C. (1966). *The Economic Growth of the United States, 1790–1860*. W. W. Norton, New York.

O'Connor, J. (1973). *The Fiscal Crisis of the State*. St. Martin's Press, New York.

O'Donnell, P. (1977). Industrial capitalism and the rise of modern American cities. *Kapitalistate* **6**, 91–128.

Offe, C. (1972). Political authority and class structure: An analysis of late capitalist societies. *International Journal of Social Sciences* **2** (Spring), 73–108.

Offe, C. (1974). Structural problems of the capitalist state, class rule and the political system on the selectiveness of political institutions. *In German Political Studies* (K. von Beyme, ed.), Vol. 1, pp. 31–57. Sage Publications, London.

Page, A. C. (1976). State intervention in the inter-war period: The Special Areas Acts, 1934–37. *British Journal of Law and Society* **3**, 175–203.

Parnet, R. D. (1966). The Know-Nothings in Connecticut. Ph.D. Dissertation, Columbia University, New York.

Parsons, T. (1937). *The Structure of Social Action*. The Free Press of Glencoe, New York.

Parsons, T. (1951). *The Social System*. The Free Press, New York.

Pearce, F. (1976). *Crimes of the Powerful*. Pluto Press, London.

Pennsylvania Bureau of Labor Statistics. (1873). *First Annual Report*.

Philadelphia Times. (1882). June 18, p. 1.

Piven, F. F. and Cloward, R. (1977). *Poor People's Movements: Why They Succeed, How They Fail*. Pantheon, New York.

Polsby, N. W. (1960). How to study Community power: The pluralist alternative. *Journal of Politics* **22** (Aug.), 474–484.

Poulantzas, N. (1969). The problem of the capitalist state. *New Left Review* **58** (Nov.-Dec.), 67–68.

Poulantzas, N. (1973).*Political Power and Social Classes*. New Left Books, London.

Preston, W., Jr. (1963). *Aliens and Dissenters: Federal Suppression of Radicals, 1903–1933*. Harvard University Press, Cambridge, Massachusetts.

Proper, E. E. (1967). *Colonial Immigration Laws*. AMS Press, New York.

Public Opinion. (1886). Vol. I, p. 355.

Qualey, C. C. (1938). *Norwegian Settlement in the United States*. Norwegian-American Historical Association, Northfield, Minnesota.

Quinney, R. (1974). *Critique of Legal Order*. Little, Brown, Boston, Massachusetts.

Railway Age. (1881). April 28.

Railway Age. (1883). May 31, p. 301.

Reich, M., Gordon, D. M. and Edwards, R. (1973). Dual labor markets: A theory of labor market segmentation. *American Economic Review* **63**(2) (May), 359–365.

Reisler, M. (1976). *By the Sweat of Their Brow: Mexican Immigrant Labor in the United States, 1900–40*. Greenwood Press, Westport, Connecticut.

Ripley, W. (1899). *The Races of Europe*. D. Appleton & Co., New York.

Roberts, P. (1912). *The New Immigration*. Macmillan, New York.

Robertson, R. M. (1964). *History of the American Economy*. Harcourt, Brace & World, New York.

Rosenblum, G. (1973). *Immigrant Workers: Their Impact on American Labor Radicalism*. Basic Books, New York.

Roy, A. (1970). *A History of the Coal Miners of the United States*. Greenwood Press, Westport, Connecticut.

Rusche, G. and Kirchheimer, O. (1939). *Punishment and Social Structure*. Columbia University Press, New York.

Sargent, F. P. (1904). Problems of immigration. *Annals of the American Academy* **24** (July-Dec.), 153–158.

San Francisco Evening Bulletin. (1863). November 6.

Saturday Evening Post. (1921). May 14, p. 20.

Saxton, A. (1971). *The Indispensable Enemy: Labor and the Anti-Chinese Movement in California*. University of California Press, Berkeley.

Scharf, J. T. (1881). *A History of Baltimore City and County from the Earliest Period to the Present Day*. L. H. Everts, Philadelphia, Pennsylvania.

Schattschneider, E. E. (1935). *Politics, Pressures, and the Tariff: A Study of Free Private Enterprise in Pressure Politics, as Shown in the 1929–1930 Revision of the Tariff*. Prentice-Hall, Englewood Cliffs, New Jersey.

Scott, F. D. (1968). *World Migration in Modem Times*. Prentice-Hall, Englewood Cliffs, New Jersey.

Shaughnessey, G. (1925). *Has the Immigrant Kept the Faith? A Study of Immigration and Catholic Growth in the United States, 1790–1920*. Macmillan, New York.

Shaw, D. V. (1976). *The Making of an Immigrant City: Ethnic and Cultural Conflict in Jersey City, N.J., 1850–77*. Arno Press, New York.

Shoe and Leather Review. (1885). May 7, p. 607.

Shoe and Leather Review. (1886). May 6, p. 780.

Smith, T. R. (1944). *The Cotton Textile Industry of Fall River, Mass*. King's Crown Press, New York.

Solomon, B. M. (1956). *Ancestors and Immigrants*. Harvard University Press, Cambridge, Massachusetts.

Soule, L. C. (1960). The Know-Nothing Party in New Orleans: A reappraisal. Ph.D. Dissertation, Tulane University, New Orleans, Louisiana.

Springfield Republican. (1863). March 26.

Stearns, L. R. (1979). Fact and fiction of a model enforcement bureaucracy: The labor inspectorate of Sweden. *British Journal of Law and Society* **6** (Summer), 1–23.

Stephenson, G. M. (1917). *Political History of the Public Lands, 1840–1862*. Russell & Russell, New York.

Stephenson, G. M. (1926). *A History of American Immigration, 1820–1924*. Ginn and Company, Boston, Massachusetts.

Stoddard, T. L. (1922). *The Revolt Against Civilization: The Menace of the Under-Man*. Charles Scribner's Sons, New York.

Strong, J. (1885). *Our Country: Its Possible Future and Its Present Crisis*. American Home Missionary Society, New York.

Sumner, W. G. (1883). *What Social Classes Owe to Each Other*. Harper and Brothers, New York.

Sumner, W. G. (1886). Industrial War. *Forum* **2** (Sept.), 3.

Sutherland, E. H. (1924). *Criminology*. Lippincott, Philadelphia, Pennsylvania.

Sutherland, E. H. (1949). *White Collar Crime*. Holt, Rinehart and Winston, New York.

Swank, J. M. (1897). *Notes and Comments on Industrial, Economic, Political and Historical Subjects*. The American Iron and Steel Association, Philadelphia, Pennsylvania.

Sward, K. (1948). *The Legend of Henry Ford*. Rinehart Publishing Co., New York.

Swinton, J. (1894). *Striking for Life*. New York.

System: The Magazine of Business. (1923). May, pp. 587–590.

Taeuber, C. and Taeuber, I. B. (1958). *The Changing Population of the United States*. Wiley, New York.

Taylor, F. W. (1911). *The Principles of Scientific Management*. Harper and Brothers, New York.

Taylor, F. W. (1947). *Taylor's Testimony Before the Special House Committee. Scientific Management*, New York.

Textile World. (1898). **14** (January), 36.

Thomas, B. (1954). *Migration and Economic Growth*. Cambridge University Press, London and New York.

Thompson, F. V. *Schooling of the Immigrant*. Carnegie Corporation, Boston, Massachusetts.

Trevor, J. B. (1924). An analysis of the American Immigration Act of 1924. *International Conciliation* **202** (Sept.).

U.S. Attorney General. (1918). *Annual Report of the Attorney General*, p. 15.

U.S. Bureau of the Census. (1960). *Historical Statistics of the United States, Colonial Times to 1957*. U.S. Government Printing Office, Washington, D.C.

U.S. Bureau of Statistics of Labor. (1872). *Third Annual Report*, pp. 517–520.

U.S. Commissioner General of Immigration. (1904). *Annual Report*, p. 38.

U.S. Commissioner General of Immigration. (1909). *Annual Report*, p. 133.

U.S. Commissioner General of Immigration. (1910). *Annual Report*, p. 122.

U.S. Commissioner General of Immigration. (1918). *Annual Report*, p. 40, 41.

U.S. Congress, House Committee on Foreign Affairs. (1868). Report of the Committee, 40th Congress, 2nd session, H. Rept. 76, pp. 1–4.

U.S. Congress, House Committee on Immigration and Naturalization. (1916). Hearings: Restriction of Immigration, 64th Congress, 1st session.

U.S. Congress, House Committee on Immigration and Naturalization. (1919a). Hearings: Prohibition of Immigration and the Problem of Immigration, 65th Congress, 3rd session.

U.S. Congress, House Committee on Immigration and Naturalization. (1919b). Hearings: Deportation of Aliens for Disloyalty, etc., 66th Congress, 1st session.

U.S. Congress, House Committee on Immigration and Naturalization. (1920). Hearings: Biological Aspects of Immigration, 66th Congress, 2nd session.

U.S. Congress, House Committee on Immigration and Naturalization. (1921). Hearings: Immigration; Proposed Restriction of Immigration, 67th Congress, 2nd session.

U.S. Congress, House Committee on Immigration and Naturalization. (1923a). Hearings: Immigration and Labor, 67th Congress, 4th session.

U.S. Congress, House Committee on Immigration and Naturalization. (1923b). Hearings: Restriction of Immigration; Europe as an Emigration-Exporting Continent and the U.S. as an Immigration-Receiving Nation, 68th Congress, 1st session (December 1923, January 1924).

U.S. Congress, House Executive Documents. (1836). 24th Congress, 1st session, H. Exec. Doc. 219.

U.S. Congress, House Industrial Commission. (1901). Reports of the Industrial Commission, 57th Congress, 1st session, H. Doc. 184, Volumes 14, 15.

U.S. Congress, House Miscellaneous Documents. (1855). 34th Congress, 1st session, H. Misc. Doc. 40.

U.S. Congress, House Miscellaneous Documents. (1888). Ford Committee Report, Volume 15, 50th Congress, 1st session.

U.S. Congress, House Report. (1838). 25th Congress, 2nd session, H. Rept. 1040, pp. 2–3.

U.S. Congress, House Report. (1856). 34th Congress, 1st session. H. Rept. 359, pp. 6–10.

U.S. Congress, House Report. (1884). 48th Congress, 1st session, H. Rept. 444, Vol. II, p. 12.

U.S. Congress, House Report. (1891). 51st Congress, 2nd session. H. Rept. 3472.

U.S. Congress, House Report. (1920). 66th Congress, 3rd session, H. Rept. 1109.

U.S. Congress, House Report. (1921). 67th Congress, 1st session, H. Rept. 4.

U.S. Congress, House Report. (1923). 67th Congress, 4th session, H. Rept. 1621.

U.S. Congress. Reports of Congressional Committees. (1856). 34th Congress, 1st session. Reports of Congressional Committees 359, pp. 1–152.

U.S. Congress. Senate Committee on Education and Labor. (1885). Report on Relations Between Capital and Labor, Vols. I–III.

U.S. Congress. Senate Committee on Immigration. (1921). Hearings: Emergency Immigration Legislation, 66th Congress, 3rd session.

U.S. Congress. Senate Dillingham Commission. (1911). *See* U.S. Congress, Senate Immigration Commission.

U.S. Congress. Senate Documents. (1836a). 24th Congress, 1st session, S. Doc. 342.

U.S. Congress. Senate Documents. (1836b). 24th Congress, 2nd session, S. Doc. 5.

U.S. Congress. Senate Documents. (1845). 28th Congress, 2nd session, S. Doc. 173, pp. 198–202.

U.S. Congress. Senate Documents. (1897). 54th Congress, 2nd session, S. Doc. 185, p. 3.

U.S. Congress. Senate Documents. (1908). 60th Congress, 1st session, S. Doc. 426.

U.S. Congress. Senate Documents. (1913). 62nd Congress, 3rd session, S. Doc. 1087, pp. 1–4.

U.S. Congress, Senate Immigration Commission. (1911). Immigration Commission Report, 61st Congress, 3rd session, S. Doc. 747.

U.S. Congress, Senate Miscellaneous Documents. (1855). 33rd Congress, 2nd session, S. Misc. Doc. 19.

U.S. Congress, Senate Report. (1864). 38th Congress, 1st session, S. Rept. 15.

U.S. Congress, Senate Report. (1921). 67th Congress, 1st session, S. Rept. 18.

U.S. Secretary of the Treasury Report. (1892). *Causes Inciting Immigration, Report of the Secretary of the Treasury*, Vol. I.

U.S. Statutes at Large. 13 U.S. Stat. at Large, pp. 385–387.

U.S. Statutes at Large. 22 U.S. Stat. at Large, p. 214.

U.S. Statutes at Large. 26 U.S. Stat. at Large, p. 1084.

U.S. Statutes at Large. 27 U.S. Stat. at Large, p. 569.

U.S. Statutes at Large. 28 U.S. Stat. at Large, p. 390.

U.S. Statutes at Large. 32 U.S. Stat. at Large, p. 1213.

U.S. Statutes at Large. 34 U.S. Stat. at Large, p. 898.

U.S. Statutes at Large. 39 U.S. Stat. at Large, p. 874.

U.S. Statutes at Large. 40 U.S. Stat. at Large, p. 1912.

U.S. Statutes at Large. 41 U.S. Stat. at Large, p. 593.

U.S. Statutes at Large. 41 U.S. Stat. at Large, p. 1008.

U.S. Statutes at Large. 42 U.S. Stat. at Large, p. 5.

U.S. Statutes at Large. 42 U.S. Stat. at Large, p. 540.

U.S. Statutes at Large. 43 U.S. Stat. at Large, p. 153.

U.S. Supreme Court. (1875). *Henderson et al. v. Mayor of New York et al.*, 92 U.S. 259.

U.S. Supreme Court. (1915). *Gegiow v. Uhl*, 239 U.S. 3.

Van Vleck, W. C. (1932). *The Administrative Control of Aliens: A Study in Administrative Law and Procedure*. The Commonwealth Fund, New York.

Voice of Industry. (1846). September 18.

von Beyme, K., ed. (1974). *German Political Studies*, Vol. I. Sage Publications, London.

Walker, F. A. (1891). The tide of economic thought. *Publications of the American Economic Association* **6** (Jan.-March), 37.

Walker, F. A. (1896). Restriction of immigration. *Atlantic Monthly* 77 (June), 828.

Walker, F. A. (1899). *Discussions in Economics and Statistics*. D. Dewey, New York.

Walker, J. (1973). Labor-management relations at Hopewell Village. *Labor History* **14**(1) (Winter), 3–18.

Ware, C. (1931). *Early New England Cotton Manufacture*. Houghton Mifflin, New York.

Ware, N. (1929). *The Labor Movement in the U.S., 1860–1885*. D. Appleton & Co., New York.

Warne, F. J. (1905). *The Coal-Mine Workers*. Longmans, Green, New York.

Weinstein, J. (1968). *The Corporate Ideal in the Liberal State, 1900–1918*. Beacon Press, Boston, Massachusetts.

Weisberger, B. A. (1969). *The New Industrial Society.* Wiley, New York.

Whitt, J. A. (1979). Toward a class-dialectical model of power. *American Sociological Review* **44** (Feb.), 81–99.

Wiebe, R. H. (1962). *Businessmen and Reform: A Study of the Progressive Movement.* Harvard University Press, Cambridge, Massachusetts.

Williams, E. (1961). *Capitalism and Slavery.* Russell & Russell, New York.

Wittgenstein, K. (1898). *The Causes of the Development of Independence in America.* R. Spies & Co., Vienna.

Wittke, C. (1953). Immigration policy prior to World War I. *In Immigration: An American Dilemma* (B. M. Ziegler, ed.). D. C. Heath, Boston, Massachusetts.

Wolfe, A. (1974). New directions in the Marxist theory of politics. *Politics and Society* 4(2) (Winter), 131–159.

Wolfe, A. (1977). *The Limits of Legitimacy.* The Free Press, New York.

Wolman, L. (1915). The extent of labor organization. *Quarterly Journal of Economics* **30**, 486–518; 601–624.

Workingman's Advocate. (1867). September 28.

Workingman's Advocate. (1869a). February 27.

Workingman's Advocate. (1869b). December 25, p. 2.

Workingman's Advocate. (1873). November 29, p. 1.

Yerkes, R. M., ed. (1921). *Physiological Examining in the U.S. Army.* U.S. Government Printing Office, Washington, D.C.

Young, E. (1872). *Special Report on Immigration.* U.S. Treasury Department, Bureau of Statistics, Washington, D.C.

Young, T. M. (1903). *The American Cotton Industry.* Charles Scribner and Sons, New York.

Ziegler, B. M., ed. (1953). *Immigration: An American Dilemma.* D. C. Heath, Boston, Massachusetts.

Zolberg, A. R. (1978). The main gate and the back door: The politics of American immigration policy, 1950–1976. *Paper presented at Council on Foreign Relations, Washington, D.C., April 12.*

Index

215

Inter-Racial Council (IRC),
137, 145, 164, 170-171

IQ test, 121-122, 138, 177

Iron Age, 53, 135, 140-141,
150-151, 170, 172, 175-
176, 179

Isolation of immigrant workers, 51-52, 86-87

J

Johnson, Albert, 104-105,
156, 158, 161-163, 183-
184

Johnson-Reed Act, *see* Quota Law of 1924

K

Karier, Clarence J., 121

Kellor, Frances, 141-142,
144-145, 164-165, 170-
171

Kensington weavers strikes,
26, 29, 32-33, 41

Knights of Labor, 46-47, 51,
55-56, 84, 87, 113

Know-Nothings, iii, 29-33

Kolko, Gabriel, 11, 95

L

Labor detective agencies,
79, 154

Labor shortages, 24-25, 36-
37, 106-107, 150-153,
165-181

Labor surpluses, 37-38, 52-
53, 74-77, 83, 96-102,
108-109, 119, 148-153,
156-160, 165-166, 175-
179

Labor turnover, 112, 141

Lauck, W. J., 159

Laughlin, Harry, 162-163,
177

Lawrence textile strikes, 89-
90, 119, 154

Legitimation, 8, 12-16, 75-76,
100-101, 109, 112, 115-
116, 132-133, 135, 148,
158-160, 162-164, 184

Leiserson, William, 91, 113-
114, 139-148

Lincoln, Abraham, 39

Literacy test, 103-107 124-
124, 131-134, 137-138,
151, 169-171, 173-174

Lodge, Henry Cabot, 104,
117, 126

M

Marx, Karl, 4-7, 11, 23-24,
110, 125
    and Engels, 6, 9, 125,
    178

McKinley assassination, 104,
139

Mechanization
    immigration laws and,
    148-150, 153, 166,
    175-176, 179
    strikes and, 37-38, 43-
    45
    unskilled labor and, 24-
    26, 43-45, 54, 60-
    61, 75, 94

Mexican immigration, iii, 148-
153, 165-169, 175, 181

Miliband, Ralph, 4, 6, 11, 19-
20

Mitchell, John, 111, 113, 125

Mode of production and immigration, 3-5

Mollenkopf, John, 7-8, 10,
123, 134

Monopoly capitalism, 19, 83,
92-96, 100, 109-115,
129, 148-150, 153-156,
165-167, 181

Montgomery, David, 32-33,
41-42, 114, 149

Morgan, J. P., 94, 121

Morrison, Frank, 156-158

Morse, Samuel, 29

About the Author

KITTY CALAVITA is Chancellor's Professor Emerita of Criminology, Law and Society at the University of California, Irvine. Much of her work examines the interplay of political, ideological, and economic factors in the implementation of immigration law, the treatment of white-collar crime, and, most recently, prisoners' rights. In all of these cases, she explores what they can tell us about relations of power and state processes.

Her books include *Inside the State: The Bracero Program, Immigration, and the INS* (1992; reprinted with new foreword, 2010); *Big Money Crime: Fraud and Politics in the Savings and Loan Industry* (1997); *Immigrants at the Margins: Law, Race, and Exclusion in Southern Europe* (2005); *Invitation to Law & Society: An Introduction to the Study of Real Law* (2010; second edition, 2016); and *Appealing to Justice: Prisoner Grievances, Rights, and Carceral Logic* (2015).

ALSO IN THE *CLASSICS OF LAW & SOCIETY* SERIES

Lawrence M. Friedman, *Contract Law in America* (new foreword by Stewart Macaulay)

Mortimer Kadish & Sanford Kadish, *Discretion to Disobey: A Study of Lawful Departures from Legal Rules* (new introductory note by Steven Alan Childress)

Martin Shapiro, *Freedom of Speech: The Supreme Court and Judicial Review*

Kitty Calavita, *Inside the State: The Bracero Program, Immigration, and the INS* (new preface by the author)

Jerome H. Skolnick, *Justice Without Trial: Law Enforcement in Democratic Society* (new foreword by Candace McCoy)

Joel F. Handler, *Law and the Search for Community* (new foreword by Frank Munger)

Jerome E. Carlin, *Lawyers on Their Own: The Solo Practitioner in an Urban Environment* (new foreword by William T. Gallagher)

David Garland, *Punishment and Welfare* (new preface by the author)

Stuart Scheingold, *The Law in Political Integration* (new foreword by Jörg Fedtke)

Stuart Scheingold, *The Politics of Law and Order: Street Crime and Public Policy* (new foreword by Malcolm M. Feeley)

Cynthia Fuchs Epstein, *Women in Law* (new foreword by Deborah Rhode)

Sheldon Messinger, *Strategies of Control* (new contributions by Howard Becker and Jonathan Simon)

qp

Visit us at *www.quidprobooks.com*.

www.ingramcontent.com/pod-product-compliance
Lightning Source LLC
Chambersburg PA
CBHW050349270326
41926CB00016B/3669